RALPH WALDO EMERSON

RALPH WALDO EMERSON

The Infinitude of the Private Man

A Biography by
MAURICE YORK ◆ RICK SPAULDING

WRIGHTWOOD PRESS

CHICAGO • RALEIGH

"Every age has its objects & symbol, & every man. Why not then every epoch of our life its own; & a man should journey through his own zodiack of signs."

—RWE, 1845

CONTENTS

Acknowledgements

A WORK THAT CALCULATES THE TIMELINE OF ITS DEVELOPMENT IN TERMS OF a decade, that counts its readers and advisors off by the dozen, and that numbers its sources in piles and pounds as well as bits and bytes must necessarily accumulate a lengthy list of debts, both direct and incidental. First of note are the faculty at Bard College, who provided patient guidance and assistance through the early phases of research and writing—in particular Liz Frank, Ben La Farge, Terry Dewsnap, and Robert Kelly. We owe a special thanks to Kay and Graham Evans for providing a place of quiet sanctuary and fellowship where key phases of writing and revision took form. This book would not have been possible in the least without the generations of Emerson editors who have devoted uncounted years to the task of bringing his journals, letters, notebooks, and lectures into print, as well as those biographers and scholars who have bent themselves to the task of elucidating his life and work. We owe special thanks to the many readers and supporters of the manuscript through its seemingly countless revisions, including Christy and Henry Barnes, Jennifer Greene, and many others too numerous to list here. Emory University and North Carolina State University provided key institutional support during the final phases of revision. Above all, we owe our deepest thanks to Dasa and Alice, who now know Emerson better than they wished and met mild obsession with good humor and tolerance throughout the hours, weeks, and years that have finally culminated in the publication of this volume.

—MY, October 2007

PREFACE

CRITICS AND SCHOLARS OF AMERICAN HISTORY AND LITERATURE GENERALLY agree that Ralph Waldo Emerson was the father and founder of the literature and culture of the United States. Not only have the major writers and thinkers of this country been influenced by his thought, whether by adoption or rejection of his leading ideas, but the very fabric of American popular and literate culture has so completely absorbed his aphorisms and apothegms that they flow from the pens or keyboards of writers in virtually every medium to universal recognition. The decades since his death have been witness to the tireless efforts of dozens of editors who have worked to bring thousands of pages from his journals, letters, lectures, and sermons to the public, and those manuscripts in turn have provided the source material for generations of biographers and critics, adherents and opponents, to revise and re-assess Emerson's achievements as a writer, an American, and a human being. A century and a quarter after his death, we can say that we are still coming to know him; the last volume of his lectures was published only within the last ten years, and the modern edition of his *Complete Works* remains a work in progress.

Despite this great body of literary evidence and production, Emerson continues to be an enigmatic figure, often quoted but little understood. He is not conflicted or tortured enough to be a popular subject of study in colleges, and his primary significance in high school is most often to serve as a stepping stone or gateway to some other writer or to a literary movement. Emerson does not, in fact, seem to have any masterwork—no *Scarlet Letter* or *Moby Dick*, no *Huckleberry Finn*, no *Walden* or *Leaves of Grass*—to point to as his greatest achievement and the quintessential expression of what he had to say and contribute as an author. While the most popular of his essays and poems are continually anthologized and read, there is no single work that contains the vital essence or most complete expression of Emerson's thought. Commentators who attempt to assemble an Emerson "philosophy" by stringing together concepts from his most important essays are often stymied by his tendency to adopt points of view that disagree with or flatly contradict what he has said elsewhere. He seems at times the protean victim of his most famous line, that "a foolish consistency is the hobgoblin of little minds." Call him a transcendentalist, call him a polytheist, call him a deist or rabid individualist, at some point he will check the claim and prove himself immune to affiliation with any party or system. His sentences become glittering motes of gold dust in the afternoon sun, his paragraphs weighty ingots of precious bullion for his readers to steal away in the apparent absence of a greater treasure. This seeming difficulty with Emerson's published works has perhaps fueled the drive to make his voluminous private papers available so that the development of his thoughts can gain some measure of clarity or insight by being placed in the context of his biography.

There are many biographies of Emerson, the range of them naturally reflecting the many possible and necessary types of biography. The life of a human being represents such a complex interweaving of perceptions, passions, desires, friendships, enmities, alliances, and a host of other threads that no one story could hope to gather them into one tapestry, try though some might. The critical biography, the intellectual biography, the hagiographic tome, the personal reminiscence, the memoir—each may follow any one of these threads or attempt them all, and every one will choose the primary influences to use as warp and weave, whether they be books, experience, society, politics, culture, family, friends, or some other. Emerson himself took interest in character above all else when looking at a life—what he called the law of a person's being. Character to him was the constant through the shifting moods and illusions of life, an acrostic that reads the same forwards or backwards. Yet character is composed of virtues and vices that express themselves in our actions and thoughts, in every attempt of the Self to act on the world around it, and these are changeable. A virtue may be developed or a vice emerge and capsize virtue. The story of the advance or retrograde of an individual through virtue and vice is the biography of character.

An immediate obstacle presents itself in the path of any biographer who wishes to describe the growth of character. It is the problem of trying to distinguish character from personality, of trying to sort out the likes and dislikes, the desires and inclinations, from the true core, the constant that runs beneath. There is the World and the Individual, and the interplay between the two is so rich and complex that the most basic question must be, what is the real self? Is it the one that sits in company with friends and family, the one that is seen in public and reported in the newspapers? Or is it the one that emerges in the solitary retreat of a study or forest path and is known only to itself through its own thoughts? The tools for a biography of character are the same as for any other. There are the reports of contemporaries—their letters, diaries, memories, records of conversation—but these have their own bias, their own inconsistencies of perception. Then there is the report of the individual, which admits even thornier questions of circumstance and condition that cloud our confidence in the veracity of his own thought—what audience, what pressure, what mood, what weather? Is he acting out of freedom, or is he being influenced—even by his own emotions, rationalizations, and unconscious desires? That single ideal held so long in the heart, when it finally finds outward expression, can be denounced by all the world as profane and blasphemous, leaving to history a hundred judgments of who was in the right or wrong. Every step, every breath may be opposed by someone or some thing, or the least unworthy accomplishment praised out of all proportion.

The struggle of the individual emerging into the world, that contest of the Self as it meets Fate, is the story of self-development, of the advance or retrograde of character. Emerson's belief was that a god slumbers within the breast of every mechanic, farmer, poet, engineer, teacher—every human being. The process of awakening occurs first in thought as the Self becomes conscious of its own thinking and then seeks expression by shaping its surroundings according to its thoughts. As the Self interacts with the world, it naturally encounters the obstacles of Fate in the form of trials it must pass through; these trials are the markers along the path of self-development. Emerson was given some advantages by birth, but he faced a great many trials, particularly the deaths of those most beloved by him as he watched a virtual slaughter of family and friends, from the passing of two siblings and his father before he was eight to the deaths of his first wife and two brothers in the prime of their youths, the death of his first-born son at age five, and of his best of friends, Henry Thoreau and Margaret Fuller, long before their time. His family's poverty and the infirmities and mortal diseases of his own body piled pain upon grief.

Given the circumstances of his life, his story could have come out much differently, for Emerson was quite unremarkable as a child and in his early adulthood. Keenly aware of his disadvantages in talent and resources, Emerson was yet determined to become a productive "citizen of the world." What he wanted was some guide or signpost to stake out the reliable path for him to follow. His models of greatness and success were many and fine— the poets and thinkers from ancient Greece and Rome to modern Europe, his luminous ancestors, his brothers, his wise Aunt Mary—but he was deeply doubtful whether he could summon enough strength from within himself simply to overcome the conditions of Fate and breathe the free air, much less rise to significance. The old dualism took hold, the sense that the course of human life must be guided towards success or failure by the whim or intervention of powers greater than himself. The bashful boy left no stone unturned, no spirit undisturbed in his search for that enkindling fire. Gods, angels, elementals, giants and mythical beings, the very spirits of the dead— all were invoked or supplicated for whatever power or aid they could lend. Protestant Christianity, the tradition into which Emerson was born, offered an even more potent force to provide such strength and guidance. Emerson's ultimate effort to structure his self-development in service to a higher power was to dedicate himself as an instrument of God's will through the institution of the ministry.

That path turned out to be a constraint, an ill-fitting garment, as fruitless as his earlier search for the classical Muse. It was a flaw of character, he determined, that made it so. His thoughts and actions continually wandered from the strict discipline he felt was necessary to become a champion of God's church in a materialistic and fallen age. It was perhaps the path that was imperfect, more likely his own ability to follow it, and he was determined to find the root cause. In trying to reconcile the expression of the Self with obedience to something other than the Self, he turned deeply inward to the only measurable source that could not betray or deceive him—his own thoughts, recorded in his Journal every day. What he found there startled him—not a collection of nouns, verbs, syllables, phrases that yielded their secrets to idle scrutiny, but a flowing, leaping, surging world governed by rules and forces that were only dimly understandable—a world of raw, unmediated spirit. True thoughts, Emerson saw, were spiritual realities quite apart from the objects perceived by the physical senses. Clearly what was needed were new senses to discern new realities, spiritual faculties of perception for the signs and signals of the world of thought. The strangeness and unmitigated power of that world brought Emerson to a new concept of the path of self-development: the effort of the Self, through the improvement of character, to develop faculties of perception that allow it to move with greater ease in its native home of thought and spirit.

Emerson found that if he was to make any progress he needed a method of correlating the thoughts once he had them captured on the page. He could make no sense of them scattered as they were among days and weeks and years. His tools for discovering the relation between different thoughts set down at different times, for pairing concepts and drawing out correspondences, were honed and refined in the Journal. Emerson's Journal in this sense is one of his greatest achievements, the faithful record—not haphazardly, but consciously—of the inspiration working through him. It is a tour through the growth of his thought, like watching from an armchair as a magnificently complex plant unfolds its leaves into the world. The thoughts themselves came from elsewhere, he was sure; he described himself as an observer who simply ordered and reported on them. "I can no more manage these thoughts that come into my head than thunderbolts," he wrote; "But once get them written down, I come & look at them every day, & get wonted to their faces, & by & by, am so far used to them, that I see their family likeness, & if I once see where they belong, & join them in that order they will stay so." He described his experience of thought in terms of watching a "flowing river, which, out of regions I see not, pours for a season its streams in to me," and himself standing by, "not a cause but a surprised spectator of this ethereal water." He saw this mystic stream flowing out into the world, embodying itself in nations, buildings, trees, people, manifesting itself in everything down to the last farthing. In the Journal Emerson became the observer of thought, simply a reporter who brought news and descriptions of what he saw coming from this higher world.

But how to describe the spirit in an age when it is hidden from sight, how to outline the activity of thought itself in words? Emerson was convinced that describing new perceptions required a new language, yet he lectured in Lyceums and popular halls to common people. His language had to be compatible with the everyday experience of the man and woman sitting in the gallery. One of Emerson's early insights was that this new language should be as close to nature as possible, for in fact every law of nature, he perceived, is also a law of the mind, as well as the expression of a cosmic or spiritual principle. He seized upon the observations of science for their power of analogy and combined them with anecdotes from history and literature to illustrate his meaning. By creating pictorial language that placed familiar words in new contexts, he discovered that he could construct vessels of speech that were robust enough to carry what he had to report. Emerson's listeners heard him speaking in words that were familiar to their ears, but imbued with an entirely new sense. Self, intellect, head, hands, star, stream, gravity, all took on an altered significance. When placed next to each other in sentences and paragraphs, they created an entirely new matrix of language, one that yet sounded conversant with experience. Emerson was experimenting not only with a new mode of language, but new forms and vehicles to convey the thought—a new art of the lecture. His goal was to create a home or temple from which the inspiration itself could speak.

The Journal has great value as the unbroken tablet for Emerson's observation of thought, but as the continuous record of his works and days it also serves to reveal the growth of his character as it developed over the course of his life. The Journals show Emerson in the mode of perpetual exploration and discovery, show him building up hypotheses and testing them, setting out upon a path only to find it leads nowhere and coming back to try the footing on a different trail. His successes in mastering his emotions, his shortcomings in yielding to close-mindedness or anger, his choices to commit himself wholeheartedly to a just cause or withdraw to his study and lamp are laid bare, providing a developing picture of a human being in each stage of his life. A chronicle of 10,000 days can be overwhelming viewed close up, an endless diversion of peaks, valleys, canyons, gulleys, rivers, and plateaus that even a master mapmaker could not etch out in fine enough detail. Step back a little, however, or take a higher vantage point, and character, like the curve of the horizon, smoothes the differences and irregularities, revealing the inviolable law that under-girds them—as Himalaya cannot break free of the globe. There lies Emerson's path of self-development, the journey of that irrepressible inner force that sought to supercede the day and confront the many trials brought against it by the hand of Fate, that essential kernel that absorbed the relentless pain, took it down deep to work upon it and transform it, till by turns it became a source of new strength—a power of character, a virtue. As Emerson's character grew, so too the events that rose to meet it, till the gathering years became an age, and every age an epoch.

One of Emerson's earliest insights on the path of self-development was that as the Self gains strength it yearns to express the fundamental rule or principle of its own being, to shape the very air, if need be, in order to teach the world that one law. "A man is a method," he wrote, "a progressive arrangement; a selecting principle, gathering his like to him wherever he goes." One would expect to find in Emerson's daily writing the remarkable story of the progress of such an irresistible force and its culminating feat in a deed as transformative and powerful as founding American culture. Yet the Journal surrenders the unexpected discovery of a dark undercurrent—a yawning void, something missing or simply absent in the midst of the conventional fame and success, the many friends, the loving family that crowded around him. Always just under the surface, often suppressed but never dismissed or forgotten, was a feeling of unhappiness and dissatisfaction, a persistent sense that he should be doing something greater. A second glance, a questioning look, picks up another well-hidden thread woven into Emerson's life and work, a project that he identified as the chief task of his life, but which has never seen the printed page in any form other than his preliminary efforts. It was a project he started in 1838 with an imperative written to himself in the Journal, "Write the natural history of Reason," and not completed until thirty-three years later in a cycle of lectures delivered at Harvard University. What is important for the biographer is not so much that last moment of expression as the fact that Emerson pursued this task—largely in the background of his other work, largely unnoticed—for his entire career. The reality of that one thought, that one thread through over three decades, helps to answer the question of what it was that Emerson truly hungered for, what motivated him, what could frustrate him and push him so far towards the brink of despair that one day far-advanced in his career he simply gave up and stopped writing—and what could bring him back from that precipice.

Stepping back from Emerson's life to follow the thread of this project,—which he sometimes called the "New Metaphysics," but most often the "Natural History of the Intellect,"—reveals a new pattern in the weave that changes the appearance of his life's tapestry. Just as the trials of character are way-stations on the path of self-development, Emerson's more famous and celebrated works become only scattered leaves or footsteps along the path of developing this greater task. As the observer of thought, Emerson came to the conclusion that great ideas rule and roll through history, ideas that are greater than any individual, but which may anoint one or another person as the chief exponent of it for a time, as Dante the ideal of heavenly beauty, Newton the mechanics of the Cosmos, Napoleon the power of the democratic middle class, or Franklin and Jefferson the ideal of freedom from tyranny. These ideas are the source of all culture, religion, politics, and economics. They are the tides of that mystic stream of spirit that pushes all before it, makes its own banks, and, Emerson suspected, makes the observer too.

The Natural History of the Intellect was the most complete response Emerson formed to the imperative he gave himself in 1838 and the last cycle of lectures he ever gave. Emerson considered this project to be the capstone of his career, the chief task of his life. These lectures—delivered in 1871—represent his last effort to bring together the best thoughts of his life on the topic most dear to his heart. The lectures have remained unpublished until now, and not without reason. The manuscript of the lectures—the many manuscripts, in fact, stored in twenty folders at Harvard's Houghton Library—are quite difficult because of the poor, hurried handwriting and the seemingly chaotic lack of organization among the pages themselves. Accomplished editors dating back to Emerson's first biographer, James Eliot Cabot, have looked at the same manuscript and concluded either that there was little new in it, or that it was too fragmentary to salvage. The former assertion is partially correct if one looks only at the words on paper. Over the course of thirty-three years, Emerson, according to his accustomed mode of work, re-used sentences and ideas in many different contexts after he first recorded them in the Journal; yet if we take him at his word, it could take him weeks, months, even decades to place them in their right relation to one another, in their correct and natural order according to the inspiration that gave them. Well over half of the text contains writing that is new and was never published in any context by Emerson or Cabot, and as a complete work unto itself the *Natural History* is unrepresented in any of Emerson's writings that have been published since, though an essay composed by Cabot contains some fragments and the valuable, recent edition of Emerson's *Later Lectures* (edited by Bosco and Myerson) brings to light two of Emerson's early versions of the project. To the assessment of the fragmentary nature of the lectures, the complete cycle is forthcoming from this press (*The Natural History of the Intellect: Emerson's Unpublished Last Lecture Cycle*) so that readers can judge of their worth for themselves; the detailed history of the manuscript at Harvard—its provenance, its complications and complexities, our editorial process and the decisions we made—appears in the critical edition of the lectures (*The Natural History of the Intellect: Emerson's Cambridge Course of 1871, a Critical Edition*).

The present biography characterizes the major trials of Emerson's path of self-development and along the way picks up an additional thread, this hidden thread of the life's task, in order to describe it, not necessarily in the best or most complete way, but in an indicative way. The resulting effort to outline the development of Emerson's character and thought through sixty years of journals and thirty-three years of lectures, essays and poems seeks to explore what happens when a human being is truly inspired,—what results when a pure stream of thought, an inspiration, manifests at last through an individual who has spent a lifetime pursuing the betterment of his character for just such a moment. Emerson's deepest desire was to trace the greater tides of thought and spirit that flow through history, and especially those that have come forth in rivulets and streams in America. He sought to wake his fellow citizens to their own nobility and divinity, their origins in spirit—that spirit manifest also in Nature as the looking glass of their own being—so that they might experience the beatitude of the Intellect for themselves. For his adult career Emerson believed this awakening could happen in many ways, and he was always waiting and watching for the moment so that he could report and describe it. He finally realized that the moment of waking to the Intellect would not happen as the result of some cataclysmic event for the entire country, not even the Civil War, but rather would reveal itself as a hard-won prize to each individual who put forth the effort to reach it. Emerson at last recognized that he himself had to fulfill the unique task laid before him and step forward as a guide to show the path to the spirit through self-development and the higher faculties of Imagination and Inspiration. Of his contemporaries he was in the opportune position to take on this duty. He had traveled the path himself.

PROLOGUE:
THE SAGE OF CONCORD

On a balmy day in mid-September, 1881, Walt Whitman laid aside his work on a new edition of *Leaves of Grass* and boarded a train in Boston for the forty-minute ride to Concord. It was his first time visiting the little town, whose residents he had come to know so well. Bred on the streets of Brooklyn, accustomed to crowds and bustle, industry, commerce, and the crush of humanity, the aged poet enjoyed the soothing refreshment of the languid Concord river, the gentle roll of hills and meadows, the long afternoon shadows cast by the sun as it retreated from the expansive and peaceful sky. In the evening he joined a large gathering of friends at F.B. Sanborn's house, where Louisa May Alcott, her father Bronson Alcott, and many others had come together to reminisce about Henry Thoreau and read from his letters. Emerson, Whitman's old mentor, arrived late, greeted several people in the room, and then settled into a chair, content in the twilight of his years to listen quietly to the fine conversation around him. Whitman had not seen his friend in many years; his presence captivated the poet at once. Emerson's eyes were clear and sharp. He wore an expression of perfect sweetness and serenity, emanating peace and sympathy. His demeanor bespoke a character that gave gentle proof of an immortal world just beyond the threshold of the one that met his gaze. Whitman himself simply withdrew from the conversation, content to sit in silent reverie for the better part of two hours with the man who had launched his career by hailing his first book of poems when all others had disdained it.

The next day, Sunday, Whitman made a tour of the historic town and paid his respects to its sacred places: the Old Manse, ancestral home of the Emerson family and once the residence of Hawthorne; the battle ground, proud memorial to the Revolution with its "Minute Man" statue; Sleepy Hollow Cemetery, resting place of Thoreau and Hawthorne; and Walden Pond, site of Thoreau's famous experiment in pure living. Pausing at the latter, he tossed a stone on the cairn that had grown up on the site of Thoreau's cabin. That evening he was welcomed into the Emerson home for the first time. He spent several hours there in conversation with the Emerson family and the Sanborns and stayed on for dinner. Emerson himself spoke little, a word or a phrase in just the right place, always with a gentle smile—a noted contrast to the dynamic and sometimes heated discussions that the two men had during their first evening together twenty-five years earlier. Yet, as on the night before, it was the simple fact of being in Emerson's sight that made the occasion exceptional. Whitman left Concord cherishing the precious hours spent with Emerson and considering what good fortune had been his to have spent such a blessed weekend with the beloved essayist and lecturer, the man who had served as teacher and guide not only to the gray poet from Brooklyn, but to so many thousands of his countrymen through his tireless revelation of the unrealized infinitude of the Individual and the measured development of the Self necessary to bring the human being into right relation with the great tides of Spirit that roll through history, culture, society, and nature.

It had not been Emerson's habit to endear himself to his audiences; his persistent intent was to disturb, exhort, inflame, and inspire those who came to hear him, rather than to provide the gallery with a pleasant diversion for the evening. Responses to his presence at the lectern could range anywhere from perfect silence to angry hollering that forced him off the stage. Written over the course of an active career that lasted some forty-five years, Emerson's seven volumes of essays and two books of poetry, in addition to hundreds of lectures delivered to thousands upon thousands of people from Maine to California, had made him one of the most well-known and influential literary figures of his time. His life had spanned the crucial decades of the emergence of the American nation, and, while he had often held himself aloof from events as a scholar and commentator, he had also descended into the thickest issues of the day as an outspoken citizen and advocate. He had acted as figurehead of the Transcendental rebellion against Harvard and the Unitarian establishment; witnessed the Paris revolution of 1848; spoken out for women's suffrage and against the institution of slavery; and lectured in support of the Union cause during the darkest and most uncertain hours of the Civil War. While his words had often been called controversial or simply mystifying, in these last years of his life his fellow citizens had come to regard him as Whitman experienced him that evening: the Sage of Concord.

I.

ANCESTRAL VOICE

On May 25, 1803, Ralph Waldo Emerson was born, the fourth child of the Reverend William Emerson, Unitarian pastor of the First Church in Boston. Ralph was the third son in the seventh generation of a family that traced its heritage back through a virtually unbroken line of ministers to the Great Migration of the Puritans from England to America in 1635. Six generations of Emerson men had tended to the needs of the faithful in the rough wilderness of the new country; six generations of ministers had guided their congregations through fat and famine, through birth and death, through peace and revolution. The call to the ministry, the impetus to dedicate one's life to shepherding the souls of a community of believers in the name of the Gospels, lived in the Emerson family with singular vitality. From his earliest days, Ralph Waldo was shaped by this powerful ancestral voice in chorus with the other influences of his early circumstance: the ebullient strivings of the young nation he had been born into; the intense sorrow of his family's life; the care and tutelage of his father's sister, Aunt Mary; and the unfailing support of his brothers.

In 1803, the fledgling experiment of the people of the United States of America was, by count from the inauguration of the first President, only fourteen years old. Even the name of the country was still in some dispute; there were those who lobbied to have it christened Columbia after the guiding spirit of the Revolution, the Goddess of the golden hair and mighty sword who was first announced as the patroness of General Washington by the slave poetess, Philis Wheatley. Washington himself, hero of the war, mighty Hercules of his people, was four years in his grave. For such a young people, the Americans built their mythology quickly, idealizing their first President, the Father of their country, and immortalizing him in song, poetry, painting, and sculpture, memorializing his death even years later in sweeping paeans and lamentations. Washington was among the most popular native subjects for the arts in the thirteen states, second only to Columbia herself, who stood in glory with her shield and banner, accompanied by the great Eagle; or sat in state with the Liberty cap on her staff, an olive branch in her right hand. The Revolution had its heroes and villains, the Founding had its high ideals and introduced a new thought into the world: that a People could govern itself. Through fervent depiction of battles and generals, of Columbia and her consorts, the arts were alive in America, yet it was a derivative art. Sculpture, architecture, and painting were all defined by the tropes and conventions of European neoclassicism, and the poetry often limped along in the shackles of heroic couplets.

America showed her real strength in the economic sphere, not the cultural, and 1803 was a watershed year. President Jefferson purchased the Louisiana Territory from the French for a modest sum, doubling the size of the country in a single negotiation, and a population of five million souls began to look westward for opportunity. The country unfurled along with the new flag, open, vast, and promising. Lewis and Clark started down the Ohio River to begin their expedition to explore the vast new territory, and Robert Fulton succeeded in propelling a boat up the Hudson River against the current by harnessing the power of steam. The industrial brawn needed to turn the new land's verdant potential into badly needed revenue had its first triumphs over nature. Industry, Agriculture, and Commerce rallied to the side of Columbia in the verses of the poets. In Europe, Britain, none the weaker for her defeat on the wild colonial shore, declared war on France as Napoleon swept through Switzerland and marched into Italy. On the sidelines of the war, Denmark became the first country to ban the slave trade, a deed that was echoed an ocean away in the New World when Haiti declared its freedom from France, becoming the first free black republic. In the United States, the dark hypocrisy of human bondage only deepened as some 75,000 more souls were sold into slavery and carted to plantations, cities, and estates from New York to Georgia that same year. The industry and agriculture needed to launch the ship of freedom was being built on the bloodied backs of millions of chained Africans.

Ralph Waldo was born in one of the bustling cultural and industrial centers of the nation, the seaport town of Boston, which was just at the beginning of the population boom that would make it a major city in the first third of the new century. The life of the Emerson children was relatively quiet, however, for their mother, Ruth, mistrusted the neighborhood children and did not like for her own boys to play in the street. Ruth, a studious and prayerful woman, was thirty-five when Ralph Waldo—or simply Ralph to his family—was born. Her growing family had already been touched by sorrow. Her first-born, Phebe, had died at the age of two just three years before. Ralph joined a family of two other boys, John Clarke, then four, and William, who was two. Ruth bore a fourth son, Edward, in 1805 and was pregnant with a fifth in 1807. That year John Clarke, whom she had come to love deeply, died suddenly at the age of eight. Ruth was shaken badly and lapsed into a depression that lasted for months. What should have been a happy moment at the birth of her fifth son only brought further hardship: Robert Bulkeley was mentally retarded and required constant care and supervision. The next year brought a ray of hope, the birth of the beautiful and energetic Charles, her sixth boy. Ruth enjoyed another three years with her husband and five surviving sons. The last addition to the family—a daughter, Mary Caroline—was born in 1811.

The Reverend William Emerson died on May 12, shortly after Mary Caroline's birth and two weeks before little Ralph's eighth birthday, leaving his wife with six children under the age of ten. His death left the family almost destitute, and the situation of the Emersons was initially so bad that Ralph and Edward, his younger brother, had to share a coat in the winter. Ruth received five hundred dollars a month from her late husband's congregation as well as the use of the old parsonage to live in for a year. Though she began to take on boarders to augment their income, poverty haunted the Emersons relentlessly. Ruth put forth a tremendous effort to manage the family affairs, but the strength that she needed to manage the increasingly complex finances of such a large family was drawn off disproportionately by the string of tragedies that had begun even before her husband's death. Ruth kept house and children and boarders going for month upon weary month, but the final, unsettling blow finally came with the death of Mary Caroline.

The last child of William and Ruth lived only three years. The First Church had already extended the time that Ruth could stay in the parsonage two years beyond the original term, but they could not allow her to remain there indefinitely. After Mary Caroline's death in 1814, the Emersons began the first of the six moves that they would make over the course of the next three years.

In the fall of 1814, after two years of pleading from Ruth, William's sister, Mary Moody Emerson, agreed to abandon her cherished solitude and live with the family in order to care for the youngest children—Ralph Waldo, Edward, and Charles. The eldest brother, William, had already enrolled at Harvard. Mary Moody was thought by her acquaintances to be a great eccentric; her more distinctive habits included sleeping in a coffin and wearing a shroud. Throughout her life she rarely stayed under one roof for more than a year or two at a time. At four-foot three inches tall, she was a sharp-tongued, piercingly intelligent woman with a fire in her belly, fiercely independent and possessed of relentless energy and unassailable piety. Later in life Emerson wrote, "My aunt had an eye that went through & through you like a needle. 'She was endowed,' she said, 'with the *fatal* gift of penetration.' She disgusted everybody because she knew them too well."[1]

In her capacity as tutor for the children, Mary Moody encouraged the brothers and molded their development until they were old enough to enter the Latin School and, finally, Harvard, the intellectual and religious center of Massachusetts society. The importance that she placed on attending Harvard was rooted in the long history of the family and the service of the Emerson men to the ministry—every one of them had attended Harvard College before taking up the cloth. Emerson would later write that "the depth of the religious sentiment which I knew in my Aunt Mary, imbuing all her genius and derived to her from such hoarded family traditions, from so many godly deaths of sainted kindred at Concord, Malden, York, was itself a culture, and education."[2] Peter Bulkeley, founder of the town of Concord, Massachusetts in 1635, stood at the head of this line of "sainted kindred," and the details of his life of piety are recorded in the masterpiece of one of the great leaders of the early Puritan community in America, Cotton Mather's *Magnalia Christi Americana*. Bulkeley's son, the Reverend Edward Bulkeley, succeeded to his father's pulpit and had a daughter Elizabeth, who joined the Bulkeley family with another of the preeminent pastoral families in Massachusetts by marrying the Reverend Joseph Emerson.[†] Joseph Emerson was the son of the Reverend Thomas Emerson, a minister who had come to America in the same year as Peter Bulkeley, 1635. Joseph's son, Edward, a member of the third generation of Emersons in America, was the only break in the ministerial line, though he was a deacon. Edward Emerson's lasting contribution to the family legacy was his marriage to Rebecca Waldo, daughter of Cornelius and Rebecca (Adams) Waldo, the first in America of the Waldo name. On Rebecca Waldo's gravestone were inscribed these verses:

> Prudent and Pious, meek and kind,
> Virtue and Grace Adorned her Mind.
> This stone may crumble into Dust;
> But her Dear Name continue must.

Two children born to the next generation of Emersons were given the Waldo name, but the first died in infancy and the second lived only to the age of 39. The prophecy inscribed on Rebecca's headstone would only

---

† See the chart of Emerson's genealogy in the appendix.

be fulfilled by her great-great-grandson. Names in the Emerson family were hereditary much as the profession and familial characteristics, and, indeed, seemed to reaffirm the strong ties that bound each generation to the one before. Thus was Edward Emerson's eldest son named Joseph after his grandfather; he was himself a minister, as was his brother John. Joseph united the Emerson family with yet another family of Massachusetts worthies when he wed Mary Moody, daughter of Reverend Samuel and Hannah Moody and the namesake of Emerson's eccentric Aunt Mary. Three of Joseph and Mary's twelve children took the mantle of the ministry. One of these three was William, who was grandfather of Ralph Waldo and, at the outbreak of the War for Independence, minister of the church that his ancestor Peter Bulkeley had founded at Concord over 130 years before. William's fourth child, also named William, became the eleventh minister with the Emerson name and the sixteenth in the broader family tree since the Great Migration of the 1630's. It was Mary Moody's hope that Ralph Waldo, a seventh generation Emerson, would be counted in this noble line as well. In a very real sense Aunt Mary became the voice of the past, the mouthpiece of the ancestral call to the ministry and the means by which the weight of the family vocation came to rest upon her nephew.

That all of her nephews should go to Harvard was beyond question. Mary Moody took it as her duty to prepare them for that undertaking, though more for the sake of her beloved nephews and the family name than that of Harvard. The kind of liberal Unitarianism that had taken control of the college, the same that the boys' father had professed, had made her so angry with her brother that she could not even grieve for him when he died. Two years after his death, she still wrote to Ruth of her departed brother's defects, which she was sure stemmed from his "corrupted views of the gospel." Nevertheless, she gave up her habitually solitary lifestyle to stay with the Emersons and moved with them for the next several years. She was a staunch Calvinist in her passions and intellectual habits, though publicly she denounced the religion itself. Emerson said of her that "she wished everyone to be a Calvinist but herself," and she had no compunction about setting others on the right path. Self-educated and well-read, she took upon herself the education of all of the Emerson boys, acting as both mentor and adviser throughout their lives. Though she loved all of the boys tremendously and doted on each of them to the point that she feared she was giving them too high of an opinion of themselves, she could take no interest in the profession of the law to which Edward and Charles would dedicate themselves. Ralph arrested her fullest attention; in him she saw hope. "If your exertions do not swell the literature of the age," she wrote him when he was sixteen, "a dearer part you may act—As minister of the blessed religion of Jesus, Angels may echo your name and saints greet you where time & death are no more."[3] For his own part, in his letters to his aunt, Ralph encouraged her to take on the role of his spiritual teacher and guide.

Though her influence on Ralph Waldo's belief in the family calling would eventually fade, Aunt Mary's powerful role as a mentor of character, indeed as a prophet of character, would remain with him throughout his life. Her letters and spiritual diaries, with their torrent of thoughts that struck so forcefully she often had no time to waste on complete sentences and correct spelling, proved to be an important influence on the development of Emerson's own Journals. Never willing to let him rest easy in a theory or speculation, Aunt Mary continually forced him to make his thinking active and find the real connections between his expressions of spiritual insight and their grounding in the practical world. Of her writing Emerson would later say, "[her] style is that of letters,—an immense advantage—admits of all the force of colloquial domestic words, & breaks, & parenthesis, & petulance—has the luck & inspiration of that,—has humor, affection, & a range from the rapture of prayer down to details of farm & barn & *help*." Even thinking of her prose imparted a sympathetic, restless cadence to his own writing. It is primarily this agitated, living, fluid language that opened Emerson to a realm of thinking outside of books, thinking that jumped from idea to idea, drawing the most unlikely connections from life, reading, and religion and weaving them together by means of the strength of the thought alone. Her letters could be shockingly blunt, though hardly ever transparent, and she delivered her opinion and observation with a tone of authority that was rarely conciliatory. When William, the eldest Emerson brother, was only twelve, she wrote him:

> Without offense let me sayy that however lofty the pinicle of fame on which you are mounted, however vast the multitude of your admirers, and magnificent your power, if you have not an open ingenuous temper, & humble, pious heart, your memory, after a few uncertain days, will perish, or your name be mentioned with contempt. Riches are but the dust of the earth; honor, which cometh from the breath of man, empty as air, & learning but the collection of other men's property. Would you be great, throw aside your pomp, descend into the tomb—behold there that the worm is thy sister, and corruption thy appointment. Pass the few days in which it carries thee on it's surface in purifying thyself for the society of all the truly great and good in the universe.[4]

She was in some ways a monotone, urging the boys ever to turn their faces from materialism, honor, glory, and the honeyed words of cheap admiration, and to embrace humility, virtue, and piety through a life of service to God and humanity.

The "fame" that Aunt Mary would have her nephews achieve was not a first rank among men for accomplishments particularly unusual or out-standing, but rather a memory that was venerable because "in the most delightfull spot, you could point to your grandchildren that within a few miles reposed the ashes of your pious ancestors—who preached the gospel—and that the very place w'h gave you birth & contains your fathers should witness your last aspirations after the sovereign God."[5] Such was not the fame that Charles sought, that Edward pursued, that Ralph Waldo dreamed of, that William wished he could have. Ambition was a family char-acteristic. Here was this wild new country, vast and industrious, brimming with possibility and striving, yet largely untamed by the arts and poor in its poets. In their closely-knit group, the brothers fostered far greater dreams, privately and openly, and they relied on each other for help in achieving them. The strength of their ambition is best illustrated by the frequency of Aunt Mary's admonitions about the hollow and fleeting nature of honor and renown among men. The only ones who understood their shared ambitions and fears, the brothers became each others' greatest supporters and sternest critics. The pathetic picture of Ralph and Edward having only a single coat between them captures the spirit of sharing and mutual support that became the heart of the family, a family that could not have survived materially with-out the willingness of each member to step aside for the sake of one of the others. His brothers considered William to have made the greatest sacrifices, for, being the eldest and the first through college, it became his responsibility to begin teaching in order to support the younger three. The names that his brothers conferred on him express both the esteem in which he was held and the magnitude of the burden that he was asked to shoulder: he was "the Mogul," "His Deaconship," "the Majesty of Tartary."

The family considered Ralph Waldo to be the least promising of his brothers, slow-witted and silly. Under his aunt's tutelage, however, he became a quick study, as if the death of his father had moved him out of childhood, as out of a dream, and placed him in the hands of one who could nurture his intellectual development properly. Emerson experienced the expectations of his aunt as the voice of the generations, a voice calling to him with the authority and weight of ancient tradition, urging him to take up the ministry. In this way the family calling, the sacred undertaking to serve the people as their minister and to guide them according to Christian duty and the word of the Gospel, settled around his shoulders as if it were the very robes of his father.

II.

ORDEALS OF SOUL

The Hollowness of Academia

Harvard College was founded in 1636 in a colony that, only a few years earlier, had been barely capable of sustaining a stable population, much less an institution of education that aspired to the stature and viability of its models in England. The core subjects in Harvard's original curriculum were theology and the mediaeval Trivium. Schooling lasted for three years and focused on three academic exercises: the recitation, which gave the student the responsibility to "demonstrate systematic thought;" the declamation, which was essentially a forum for the students to display classical allusions and learn to "systemize coherently;" and the disputation, which took place in the presence of a moderator and encouraged the students to learn to "contend expertly."[1] About one hundred years later, Harvard's curriculum shifted towards the Enlightenment thinkers. The College adopted Locke's view of human understanding in the mid-1740s, and the thinking of both Locke and Newton permeated the curriculum by the last quarter of the century. The sciences, which in the 1640's had been confined to the natural history of plants, grew to be one of the main occupations of the institution, along with divinity and law. The College acquired apparatus for demonstrations in physics and chemistry, and the livelier method of lecturing replaced teaching by recitation. In the decade before the 1820's, Harvard was focused on expansion. Innovative equipment was purchased for the instructors to demonstrate scientific principles. Money was raised for a new observatory, several buildings were erected on the campus, and the contents of the library were catalogued and appraised for the first time. Twelve new professorships were created, including the first permanent position for Latin in 1811. Edward Everett, who came to teach at Harvard in 1819, brought with him the most recent deconstructionist scholarship of Wolf, who theorized that the *Iliad* and *Odyssey* had been written at different times by several different authors, and J.G. Eichorn, who introduced the German "higher criticism" of the Bible.[2] A new level of competition was introduced with awards for essay writing and oratory, and, in the spirit of renewed academic competition with the continent, the Phi Beta Kappa society established "the American Scholar" as the traditional topic for lectures at its annual dinner.

For Ralph Emerson, called "Emerson fourth" to distinguish him from the other Emersons at the school, the opportunities that Harvard College offered seemed to lie in a somewhat different direction than the regular course of study. Given free access to a library, the boy virtually devoured every printed page in sight, poring over volume after volume of various authors and subjects with little or no regard for system or direction. He started numerous notebooks—not true journals, but simply records of his reading—which he filled with quotations and ideas taken from writers as diverse as Sir Walter Scott and Plutarch. His thoughts often focused on a core of favorite writers, and thus he saw himself standing on the shoulders of Plato, Shakespeare, and Milton. He took up the study of the old masters with youthful enthusiasm and set about educating himself in his own way, taking long walks through the forests and over the hills around Cambridge and spending even longer hours in the college library, his notebook near at hand.

Much was expected of Ralph as an Emerson. When he was a freshman, his older brother graduated from Harvard and his two younger brothers, both promising brilliance, were coming up behind him. Yet Ralph plugged along near the middle of the class, winning few awards and being named class poet only after six others turned down the honor. The only subject that seemed to inspire him was oratory, and he often praised professors Everett and Channing for their eloquence. The other professors he thought to be stodgy and uninteresting, and he found himself reading miscellaneous books from the library rather than his course books.[3] His poor skill at mathematics embarrassed him, and chemistry and physics were simply "hateful." Though he learned his Latin and Greek, as did everyone else, he always preferred translations. Emerson's efforts to win the Bowdoin prize for essay writing showed the extent to which Harvard had failed to stimulate or develop his writing talent. His first attempt at the prize, an essay on Socrates, was flat and uninspired, and he failed to develop his thesis with any clarity. He tried again with an essay on "The Present State of Ethical Philosophy." This time he sent the essay to Aunt Mary, and in no less than three surviving letters she responded with her criticisms and suggestions on the topic.

Perhaps because his thesis showed the arc of the development of ethical philosophy from the Greeks to Dr. Price, the author of his textbook, he tied for second prize. A further sign of his disenchantment with Harvard's brand of education was his involvement in founding an unnamed literary club, a group with a charter and elected officials that met regularly in various students' dorm rooms in order to debate given topics and discuss literature and poetry. Their reading list included everything that Harvard would not teach: the novels of Scott, the new Romantic poetry, and the most recent literature from the *Edinburgh Review* and the *North American Review*.

The ambition for fame drove the Emerson brothers to seek success at Harvard, but for Ralph the atmosphere of rigorous academics led to deep-seated feelings of inferiority. The intense competition with his peers, especially in debates, turned the learning process into a great intellectual game in which he always felt himself a step behind, and, consequently, the thoughts he had gathered from books lost their liveliness and interest as they became ammunition in a losing battle. In October of 1820, three years into his matriculation, he observed despairingly that he found himself "often idle, vagrant, stupid and hollow. This is somewhat appalling and, if I do not discipline myself with diligent care, I shall suffer severely from remorse and the sense of inferiority hereafter. All around me are industrious and will be great, I am indolent and shall be insignificant."[4] The feeling had only worsened by December when, trying to find what compensation he could, he wrote of his fellow students, "My more fortunate neighbors exult in the display of mathematical study, while I, after feeling the humiliating sense of dependence and inferiority, which, like the goading, soul-sickening sense of extreme poverty, palsies effort, esteem myself abundantly compensated if, with my pen, I can marshal whole catalogues of nouns and verbs, to express to the life the imbecility I felt."[5] In addition to this feeling of inferiority, Emerson was beset by the imperative to become a minister, which was constantly repeated to him by his aunt, who wished that he might "draw a golden lot in the urn of love & honor or be led by the 'precious Jewel of adversity' to a high character in religion."[6] On the very walls of his college room hung portraits of several of the signal lights of the ministry to which he aspired. Mary Moody presented Ralph with high ideals, but talk of sainthood and perfection of character could become simply overwhelming at times, and he came to take her injunction to enter the ministry almost too literally. He even chastised himself for neglecting his destiny while still enjoying good health, writing, "I must prepare myself for the great profession I have purposed to undertake. I am to give my soul to God and withdraw from sin and the world the idle or viscious [sic] time and thoughts I have sacrificed to them."[7]

The feeling of being "idle, stupid, vagrant and hollow" that Emerson described in the Journal passage of October, 1820, is especially important to clarify. The hollowness in particular provides a key to what was happening to him at Harvard. His professors could not even foster the one talent that he possessed innately, one that would become world famous. If they could do nothing for his writing ability, how much less could they provide him with inspiration? Neither was he indifferent to success, as his journals indicate. Rather, he seemed to have been incapacitated, as if something vital had been taken away from him. He felt the need to apply "discipline" to his studies if he were ever to hope to match his colleagues' achievements. He attempted to work within the academic regimen, and he dutifully received the correct thoughts from his professors and gave them back again in essays. He was aware that his efforts did not meet the academic standard, yet his short-coming was not owing to any lack of effort or an absence of desire on his part to stand as an equal among his peers. He was caught in a perpetual cycle that removed the life and vitality from his intellectual exploration: his habits were not suited to the academic model, but his desire to succeed there made him apply himself even more assiduously in conforming to that model, which led to further disappointment. Emerson was not actually mediocre, but what he described as hollowness produced mediocrity.

In opposition to the hollow thoughts of academia stood a warm, buoyant enthusiasm that he felt toward fantasy and poetry. Even as he pushed himself to become a minister, he was irresistibly drawn to the immortal fame of a poet. Two different professions battled for his heart, and the choice between them was never certain in his mind while he was still in school. His own description of himself as a scholar/poet aptly represented the two very different influences that worked on him in his college years. His notebooks gave much space to drafts of poetry and fantastic stories, often in the ornamental and verbose style popular among the Southern boys, who had a strong presence at Harvard. His tendency towards the world of imagination and myth appeared most clearly in the dedicatory passages of his various "Wide World" journals, in which he invoked fairies, witches, the elemental spirits of Earth, Air, Fire, and Water, and the giant Califo. In many ways this world of fantasy served as his escape from the more negative influences of Harvard, but the enthusiasm that characterized this aspect of his inner life at times boiled over into his studies, particularly where Everett was concerned. Everett's oratory was so inspiring, his presence so overwhelming, that he became Emerson's idol. The ebullient passages that Emerson wrote in his Journal after hearing Everett speak reveal that this professor had fired the boy's dreams of becoming an orator and poet. At this point in his life Emerson was not fully dedicated to the ministry, had not yet fully embraced it as his own, but rather considered it as the natural, given course that he would fall into according to the family's expectations. To be a poet, to achieve the sublime heights of oratory and expression, to draw out the circumference of the universe with his pen, was his true inner desire. As much as his duty told him to take up the calling of his forefathers, his fancy told him that he was to take his place among the great poets of history and occupy an immortal throne as a crafter of words.

I Love My Wide Worlds

In February of 1820, when Emerson was sixteen years old and in his third year at Harvard, he opened a blank notebook, entitled it "The Wide World No. 1," and gave it this commission: "These pages are intended at their commencement to contain a record of new thoughts (when they occur); for a receptacle of all the old ideas that partial but peculiar peepings at antiquity can furnish or furbish; for tablet to save the wear and tear of weak Memory, and, in short [to act generally as a] *Common Place Book*." The Journal became a tool to dig into, turn over, and examine the tradition of the ministry. Whereas the influence of his family heritage directed his gaze outward and into the past, the Journal brought his perception inward, towards himself, so that he began to establish a center and a periphery. Thus did Emerson take up a call from his inner being, a call answering the one that came from the familial tradition through the authority of his father's voice, as if to say, "I cannot simply follow this authority blindly, but I must make my own way." The Journal did not so much give him the wherewithal to *resist* the tradition as to make it a subject for objective contemplation and examination, along with, or perhaps chief among, the many subjects that he found himself drawn to. The Journal also served to nurse Emerson's poetic strivings, the part of him that sought to take flight in worlds that were home to poets and philosophers, gods and spirits. Always these two aspects maintained a healthy balance in the early journals, and though the first seemed sometimes to predominate, the boy's serious and studious side never got the better of his sense of humor and of the fantastic.

The idea of the "Common Place Book" had its origins in the earliest curriculum of Harvard, in the practice of declamation. In order to be appropriately equipped with a full arsenal of quotes to have at hand during this highly intellectual exercise, the students began to gather material into notebooks and arrange it under topical headings such as "War," "Peace," "Government," and "Ethics." Emerson's early journals were ostensibly based on a system of journalizing developed by Locke, in which the writer placed a pre-conceived list of categories on a grid at the front of his blank volume. As the journalist made his way through his reading, he would pull out certain passages and copy them into his notebook. The journalist would then assign each entry to one of the pre-devised categories of the index, dutifully recording the page number where it fell in the journal onto the grid in the front. Every time that a quotation fell under a new category, a new page was started, always on the left-hand side so that two different categories never faced each other. This method isolated each thought from every other in an attempt to approach the idea itself by collecting small pieces of it and later assembling these pieces together. Functionally, this system expanded ever outward, attempting to include enough facts and ideas to describe every field of knowledge and existence until the whole of the limitless macrocosm were somehow comprehended, its boundaries defined. Emerson's early journals were dutifully titled "the Wide World" and "the Universe."

As Emerson's journals matured, the formal Lockean model merged with the Puritan journal of self-examination, a distinctly American form of the journal that focused on introspection and the maintenance of an accurate daily record of the events of one's life in order to observe the working of the hand of God. Aunt Mary, who kept just such a journal for her entire life, influenced her nephew in this direction. The two sent their journals back and forth, reading them and commenting upon them. Emerson copied hundreds of pages of her letters and writings into his journals and notebooks throughout his life, even taking her journals with him to study as he would Plutarch or Plotinus, and in his later life he thought of her as one of the best writers in New England, though she was never published in her lifetime. In one letter the nomadic Mary, sounding almost frantic, asked for her nephew to send back her journals immediately, for they were the only treasure and token that she had of her life. Mary also provided a model of restless, energetic thinking, a living and active thought process apparent in her letters, in which she often became so enraptured that she would leave out whole words and skip "illogically from one thought to the next within the same sentence." The Journals in their final form could not emerge while Emerson was still under the influence of the old tradition. When they finally did, the indices were at the back and the categories were formed only after the volume was complete, when Emerson would comb over the entries and, according to his favorite definition of classification, added similarity to similarity, fact to fact, and coordinate the topics organically according to the order inherent within. Whereas the Lockean categories had been rigidly independent of each other, the Emersonian ones were fluid and organic, and the same passage could reappear under three or four different headings, to be recombined and re-used in new contexts and new relations.[8]

So it was that the journals became Emerson's great experiment, a realm in which he was free to express his innermost thoughts, to record his observations and convictions, and, most importantly, to play. He was unafraid to adopt the styles and even the very words of the writers and ora-tors whom he most admired, borrowing the thoughts and expressions of such men as Chateaubriand, Everett, and Barrow quite openly, and even put-ting their sentences into his own words to improve upon them and make them "uniquely and wholly Mr. Emerson's." This youthful game developed into the ability to completely absorb and digest the material that he had read and to turn it out again as his own pure thought. Words flowed into him sounding as Shakespeare, de Stael, Coleridge, but they flowed out Emerson, Emerson, Emerson. It is particularly significant that at the same time he started the journals in 1820, he asked his family to call him Waldo from then on, a name that he felt closer to than Ralph. Writing in the Journal became a daily task that he set for himself every evening, a meditative act by which he built for himself a spiritual haven of peaceful reflection. The name change that accompanied the initial creation of this haven signaled his discovery that there was within him another aspect somewhat greater than Ralph Emer-son, son of ministers. It was the beginning of his exploration of Self.

The Selfishness that Chills

When Waldo graduated from Harvard in the summer of 1821, the financial situation of the Emerson household was deteriorating. He had to abandon both his dreams and his calling and take up his duty to his family by becoming an apprentice at William's finishing school for young ladies, which was run out of their mother's home in Boston. He had great difficulty settling into the routine and became frustrated at his awkwardness in front of the class, owing in part to the shyness and inexperience of "a bashful boy, unused to girls." The new profession, forced on him by circumstance, seemed tedious, distasteful, and endless. He was "a hopeless school master, just entering upon years of trade to which no distinct limit is placed; toiling through this miserable employment even without the poor satisfaction of discharging it well, for the good suspect me, and the geese dislike me." He felt himself wasting away at the school and could not see how the position helped him to his goal of the ministry, considering it rather a block and delay. He answered the assertion that it would make him more fit for the office whereto he aspired by writing, "but if I come out a dispirited, mature, broken-hearted miscreant—how will man or myself be bettered?"[9] Only days away from the age of nineteen, he felt the river of time flowing ever faster past him, whilst he remained stagnant, stock-still, unable to find refreshment or even purchase in its waters. The grand dreams and hopes that he had built for himself in his "days of innocence and energy," when he had envisioned himself rising up to take his place among the greatest men of society, he now saw floating away like "castles in the air." He endured the "goading sense of wasted capacity" and played the fallen fool, "idolatrous of glory," feeling himself trapped in "a child's place, [which if I hold] longer, I may as well quite resume the bauble and rattle, grow old with a baby's red jockey on my grey head and a picture book in my hand, instead of Plato and Newton."[10]

Emerson's isolation, his retreat into what he likened to a tortoise's shell, made communication with his students awkward. He felt himself the clumsy master of a flock of gabbling geese. He considered himself to be a "cold being," even "frigid," lacking all warmth towards others. Though the gender of his students certainly contributed to and heightened his sense of discomfort, the source of his emotional coldness itself lay much deeper than the uncertainties of a boy becoming a man. Emerson became obsessed with his fallen state and relentlessly attacked himself on all grounds: "Look next from the history of my intellect to the history of my heart," he wrote; "A blank my lord. I have not the kind affections of a pigeon. Ungenerous and selfish, cautious and cold, I yet wish to be romantic . . . There is not in the whole universe of God . . . one being to whom I am attached with warmth and entire devotion."[11] The coldness he felt signified the new progress of the negative force that had begun to work upon him while at Harvard. The hollowness he had experienced there had resulted in a certain intellectualism and distance, and now a cold antipathy cut him off from the most basic empathy with his students and his fellow human beings. Emerson experienced a great trial in the realm of feeling or emotion as the desert of academia became a frozen wasteland of the heart.

During these long months, Emerson retreated often to his study and filled his Journal with page upon page of rambling thoughts. In the Journal of his first year at William's finishing school, he looked outside of himself to such subjects as faith, prayer, and church doctrine that probably came to his attention through the contemporary arguments being waged among Trinitarians, Arminians, and Unitarians—arguments in which the Divinity School at Harvard itself was very much involved. The disagreements surging back and forth between those sects stoked Emerson's natural tendency to question the old traditions and assumptions of the Church, especially the idea of "the benevolence of God" and the doctrine of the inherent sin of the human soul. When he attempted to engage Aunt Mary with such weighty issues, her contribution to the discussion often took the form of strict criticism of her nephew's fumbling theories and adopted allegiances. She thought Harvard "a garnished sepulchre where may be found some relics of the body of Jesus" and saw these intellectual engagements as mere distractions that led her nephew away from the true character of religion. All of these doubts, arguments, and theories he recorded in the pages of the Journal, including his Aunt's letters. In November of 1822, after months of exhaustive review of the issues from every side, he concluded: "My adventurous and superficial pen has not hesitated to advance thus far upon these old but sublime foundations of our faith; and thus, without adding a straw to the weight of evidence or making the smallest discovery, it has still served to elevate somewhat my own notions by bringing me within the prospect of the labours of the sages."[12]

Whereas he turned to the world around him to spur his thoughts about the ministry, he addressed the strong inner desire to be a poet quite differently. Almost all of the early "Wide World" journals began with a dedication in the form equivalent to the age-old convention of invoking a Muse, to inspire the thoughts to be recorded in that particular Journal. The inspirations he sought invariably failed him, and, recognizing this, he would invoke a new mythological or natural force to inspire him. This restless

search for a Muse was prompted at least in part by Mary Moody, who frequently wrote about inspiration and often inquired after the health of her
nephew's own Muse. These periodic and unsuccessful efforts to uncover the
well-springs of inspiration led Emerson to identify an ebb and flow to his
"thinking seasons." When the easy fluidity of thought and eloquence abandoned him, he grew despondent and plaintive. The regularity of these
somewhat mechanical and awkward attempts to find a Muse became almost
humorous. His intent in making an invocation was that he would write about
his chosen spirit as often as possible. After lapsing into thoughts about various other topics, he would come to the end of the journal and, realizing that
he had written hardly at all about his "Muse," more often than not would
conclude that the chosen spirit had abandoned him, or had taken no notice
of him at all. Though it was a positive impulse to try to find inspiration from
a higher being, Aunt Mary saw his efforts as a caricature and attributed his
failure to a flaw in his character. "Oh would that Muse forever leave you,"
she wrote in a letter dating from the summer of 1822, "till you had prepared
for her a celestial abode. . . . Yet with this gift [of poetry] you flag—your
Muse is *mean* because the breath of fashion has not puffed her. You are not
inspired, in heart, with a gift for immortality, because you are the Nursling of
surrounding circumstances— You become yourself a part of the events
which make up ordinary life—even that part of the economy of living which
relates in the order of things *necessarily* to private & social affections, rather
than publick & disinterested."[13]

Nevertheless, Emerson continued his dedications, his search for
inspiration. On July 11, 1822, less than two weeks after he received Mary's
letter, Emerson started a new journal, "The Wide World No. 7," with a ded-

ication to what he called the Spirit of America, a folk spirit that he addressed
as "a living soul, which doth exist somewhere beyond the Fancy, to whom
the Divinity hath assigned the care of this bright corner of the Universe." As
with the other muses to which he wrote dedications, the Spirit of America
was not Emerson's invention. Though he did not call her by name, this being
was none other than Columbia, once the war-like Goddess of the Revolution, now taking her place as the patroness of the young Republic. Columbia,
graceful protectress of Liberty and Peace, figured powerfully in the imagination of the nation's poets, and now Emerson sought her out himself.
Unlike his intricate and sometimes tortured investigations of the tenets of
faith and the nature of God, his consideration of the Spirit of America was
refreshingly direct and even bold. The invocation stood out from the rest in
that he pursued his subject at some length. He came "to the shrine, which
distant generations shall load with sacrifice, and distant ages shall admire
afar off" and hailed "the Genius, who yet counts the tardy years of childhood,
but who is increasing unawares in the twilight, and swelling into strength,"
wanting to take a portion of her task for his own.[14] Of special concern to him
was the vast untamed force of will in America and the need for poets and a
literature in order to educate and pacify it. He envisioned the future progress
of the nation, under the guidance of this Spirit, as a boon arising out of the
decaying states of Europe to lay "deep and solid foundations for the greatness of the New World." Here in America, he wrote, the titanic struggles of
human ambition and striving would repeat themselves in the heroic effort
to establish this bold new endeavor, for "new Romes are growing, and the
Genius of man is brooding over the wide boundaries of infant empires,
where yet are to be drunk the intoxicating draughts of honor and renown...."

Other Cleopatras shall seduce, Alexanders fight, and Caesars die." The young nation was building "pillars of social strength, which we occupy ourselves in founding thus firmly to endure to future ages as the monuments of the wisdom" of the bold experiment in democracy. He predicted that in the coming struggle these pillars would "be shaken on their foundations with convulsions proportioned to their adamantine strength;" the hour, he wrote, was near at hand.[15] Emerson's desire to approach the inspiring Spirit who stood behind this unfolding panorama lived very strongly within him as the dream of becoming a poet, a champion of her cause. That he recognized the Spirit of America, and that he wished to bring her consciously into his writing, indicates something of the scope of the growing divergence between his youthful ideals of minister and poet. Yet the weary months at the girls' school continued to drag by.

There was one central question that Emerson wrestled with: what is the nature of greatness, what does it mean to be a great man? In the spring of 1823, he began to consolidate and clarify the ideas and experiences of the last several years in an attempt to define the means by which one might gain the path to true knowledge. He determined that the perfection of a man's nature consisted in a fixed equilibrium of body and mind, for "the masters of the moral world . . . have not gained that rare fortune by any extraordinary manners of life, or any unseemly defiance of the elements, or of death," but rather they "conformed to the fashions of the times in which they fell, without effort or contempt." By taking in "a mightier vision of the state of man than their fellows had done, [they] did not see *differently* from them, but *saw beyond* the common limit." These masters of the moral world did not know different things from their fellow men, from their fathers; they knew the

NERVOUSNESS IS PRECISELY THE
UNFULFILLED POTENTIAL OF HUMAN
ATTENTION IS THE ESSENCE OF HUMAN
ORDEALS OF SOUL → 33   SPIRIT.
"OVERCOMING NERVOUSNESS"
— R. STEINER

same things in a different way: God in an apple seed, angels in the colors of

sunset. To know that man was other than flesh, that a higher state existed

above that of the physical world, did not require some occult vocabulary or

obscure idea, mere words to replace words. It wanted only a deeper percep-

tion. The "common limit" of seeing was that which perceived only the sense

world, the world of sight, sound, and touch. The "mightier vision of the state

of man" encompassed man as a moral being, a spiritual being whose perfec-

tion lay not in the satisfaction of his animal desires, but in the ordering of his

life according to higher laws. Thus these great minds "quietly founded a king-

dom of their own, which should long outlast the ruins of the transient

dynasty in which it grew . . . Men of God they were,—children of a clearer

day."[16] There were yet vacant seats at the Table of the Gods, waiting for

those who would answer the call to greatness. In spite of the disillusionment,

the embarrassment and tedium, the coldness that threatened to chill his very

heart while he was at the girls' school, here was his chance to raise himself

beyond his circumstance. Here was his reminder to himself that it was not

heroic deeds that determined greatness, but the perfection of character.

The dramatic struggle between his warmer, buoyant, poetic tendency

and his grounded, traditional, ministerial tendency seemed to come to a

head as he grappled with the question of his present vocation as an educa-

tor. Quite certain that the mechanical, rationalized universe of Newton and

Locke taught in colleges was not the path to true education, he was at a loss

for what should replace it. Emerson was sure that the seat at the Table of the

Gods could be filled by the scholar/poet, but he was perplexed by what he

needed to study in order to prepare himself. Turning the problem over night

after night and coming no closer to a solution of how best to organize his studies, he moaned in his Journal that "unknown troubles perplex the lot of the scholar whose inexpressible unhappiness it is to be born in this day." The various religions, systems of education, philosophies, politics, morals, sciences, and literatures all clamored for his attention, and for the scholar "a chaos of doubts besets him from the outset;" he is almost drowned by the intellectual sea that surrounds him. "Shall he read, or shall he think? . . . Shall he nourish his faculties in solitude or in an active life? . . . Must he read History and neglect Morals; or learn what *ought to be*, in ignorance of *what has been*."[17] All of these musings were just so many words in the end. There were no events, no actions, no signs to fuel the poetic dream, and Emerson began to move away from his earlier efforts to find a source of inspiration in the spirits of earth and sky and the gods of legend. He abandoned even Columbia and turned increasingly to the God of his family's religion to provide the needed inspiration.

In his frustrating search for a source of inspiration, unable to predict or even preserve his "thinking seasons," he finally lighted on a model, a man who had discovered how to yoke inspiration. Taking Milton's example, he tried to bind the ebb and flow of productive thought to a time of year, the weather, and even the position of the stars.[18] Milton became his type for the poet, an example of the "sublimest of all . . . continually summoned and inspired by a Spirit within him," a man whose labor was "not a work to be finished in the heat of youth or the vapors of wine but by devout prayer to that eternal Spirit who giveth knowledge." Emerson began to edge away from the confounding perplexities of Reason in favor of the pure simplicity of Faith. Faith asked no convoluted questions, required no laborious addition of thought to thought in pursuit of some unknown result. It simply wanted devotion and offered immortal beauty of the soul in return. In February of 1824 he wrote, "Material beauty perishes or palls. Intellectual beauty limits admiration to seasons and ages; hath its ebbs and flows of delight. . . . But moral beauty is lovely, imperishable, perfect. . . . None that can understand Milton's *Comus* can read it without warming to the holy emotions it panegyrizes."[19] A month later he was lamenting, "what has reason done since Plato's day but rend and tear his gorgeous fabric. And how are we the wiser? . . . we are now reduced to a little circle of definitions and logic round which we humbly run. And how has Faith fared? Why, the Reformer's axe has hewed down idol after idol, and corruption and imperfection, until Faith is bare and very cold. . . . From Eden to America the apples of the tree of knowledge are but bitter fruit in the end."[20] The question of poet or minister took a sudden sharp turn. The path of knowledge was no longer a means of approaching the spiritual world, was not even one among several options for comprehending a moral life, but was the very enemy of Faith and the Church, almost the embodiment of the error of original sin.

In the fall of 1823, William, who had worked selflessly since the age of seventeen to provide money for the family while his brothers made their way through school, had received an opportunity to go to Germany to study towards his PhD in theology with some of the foremost biblical scholars in the world. With Waldo graduated from Harvard and able to carry the girls' school while Edward and Charles completed their college education, William was finally free to pursue his professional education. William departed for Europe in December of 1823, leaving the girls' school entirely in his younger brother's care. Already feeling suffocated by the duties of being a teacher and the necessity of earning money for the family, there could be little more disheartening for Emerson than being left as the sole caretaker of this unlooked-for responsibility. As the poetic dream became more impractical by the month, the profession of religion rose in his estimation. Pursuit of a divinity degree might even be, as William had shown, a door that would allow an exit from the drudgery of the classroom. Stymied by his attempts to connect with specific spiritual influences and beings, Emerson now accepted a large idea of God as the source of inspiration. He fell victim to the great danger of his favorite poet's religion and flirted with hypocrisy. How cold is it for a failed teacher to stand in front of a class and see his students as a flock of soulless birds, only to return to his desk at night and seek to discover the true path for his own education? The seed of hope that he had planted in the Journal had grown into a thorn bush.

III.

TRIUMPH OF THE GOD OF FIRE

The Dupe of Hope

The Unitarians did not differ from their fellow Congregationalists on any points of theology that would engender open conflict or create a rift between them and their brethren. At least, such was the public position that they clung to with a kind of quiet ferocity, firmly claiming their right within the historic order of Congregationalism. In keeping with this position, they called themselves not Unitarian, the name of a certain group of dissenters in England with whom they wanted no association, but "liberal Christians." The subtle drift towards Liberalism, which had at its heart the rejection of the doctrines of the Trinity and of innate depravity and of all creed-making in general, took place surreptitiously. Jonathan Mayhew, the first in New England to openly oppose the doctrine of the Trinity, led the West Church in Boston for nineteen years, from 1747-1766. His colleague in promoting Liberalism, Charles Chauncy, pastored the First Church in Boston for sixty years until his death in 1787, when the Reverend

John Clarke accepted the care of his flock. When Clarke died in 1798, the congregation turned to William Emerson to fulfill the pulpit; William paid tribute to his predecessors by naming a son after each of them. The only discernable public step taken in affirmation of the new theology during this period was a vote by King's Chapel in Boston, on June 19, 1785, to expunge from the order of service all teachings and implications of the Trinity, yet by the turn of the century nine out of ten congregational churches in Boston had abandoned the Trinity for a Unitary God. The success of the Liberal theology was confirmed in 1805 when Harvard, the "nursery of Puritan theology," appointed the liberal Henry Ware as Hollis Professor of Divinity, openly breaking the uneasy balance that had thus far prevailed between the liberal and conservative wings. The latter, who wished to see at least a moderate Calvinist appointed to the position, adamantly opposed the action. After five more appointments in the next two years confirmed the dominance of the Liberals at Harvard, the conservatives broke with the College entirely.

The leader of the conservative Evangelicals, Jedediah Morse, united the Old Calvinists and the Hopskinsians against the Liberals and led the movement to found the strictly orthodox Andover Seminary in 1808. The Liberals, still firmly maintaining their rightful claim to the Congregational tradition, refused to acknowledge any break in the church or to be drawn into open controversy, preferring instead to maintain a cerebral discussion in the realm of scholarship. Morse, however, wished to draw his opponents into open conflict and expose their heresy, which he finally succeeded in doing in 1815 with an article that alleged extensive ties between the liberals and the Unitarians in England. Denying these allegations, but forced to accept the name, the American Unitarians finally took an aggressive stance and rallied behind William Ellery Channing's "choice between rational Christianity and infidelity." Channing, a fellow of Harvard and minister at the Federal Street Church in Boston, further solidified the Unitarians with his "Baltimore Discourse" in 1819, in which he enumerated for the first time the specific points of belief on which the Unitarians differed from their opponents.[1] In 1825 the rift in Congregationalism became final with the formation of the American Unitarian Association. The Unitarians counted among their number the foremost theologians, educators, and writers in Boston and claimed the lion share of the old moneyed families of New England. The Association counted one hundred twenty-five member churches, all but twenty-five in Massachusetts, with the weight of its influence resting primarily in a radius of thirty-five miles from its center in Boston. Harvard, which claimed every one of the Unitarian leaders as alumni, had become the "headquarters of intellectual and religious liberalism" in America.[2]

On April 18, 1824, one month before turning twenty-one and becoming "legally a man," at the height of the churning controversy between the Liberals and the Evangelicals, Ralph Waldo Emerson dedicated himself to the Church and planned to take up the professional studies at Harvard that would lead him down the path to the ministry. With this act he abandoned forever, he thought, his dream of becoming a scholar/poet. The journal entry declaring his intention to become a minister was lengthy and almost painfully introspective. Starting from the observation that "my abilities are below my ambition," he took stock of his strengths and weaknesses and enumerated all of the reasons that the ministry was his only choice of profession. He already had a "strong imagination" and a consequent love of poetry, but noted that "my reasoning faculty is proportionably weak." The ministry was then the best choice because "the highest species of reasoning upon divine subjects is rather the fruit of a sort of moral imagination." Though he felt equal to preaching in the manner "most in vogue," comparisons of himself with his classmates convinced him "that there exists a signal defect of character which neutralizes in great part the just influence my talents ought to have," though he did not know what this defect was. A lack of talent disqualified him for other professions: he did not have the "logical mode of thinking and speaking" required by the law, nor the "seducing mannerism" demanded by medicine. The quality he *did* have that was promising for the profession of Divinity he claimed through heritage, for "I inherit from my sire a formality of manner and speech, but I derive from him, or his patriotic parent, a passionate love for the strains of eloquence." All being in order as far as talent, he was encouraged to expect success in the first responsibility of the clergyman's office, that of public preaching. He anticipated that his "defect of character" might hamper his ability to accomplish the second duty, that of "private influence," or actually *ministering* to people. This fact did not discourage his commitment, however, for "I judge that if I devote my nights and days *in form*, to the service of God and the War against Sin, I shall soon be prepared to do the same in *substance*."[3]

On January 4, 1825, less than a year later, Emerson closed the girls' school in order to take his room in Divinity Hall and officially begin his studies. Such an action had been made possible in part by Edward's graduation from his brilliant years at Harvard the previous summer. Valedictorian of his class by a wide margin, he had given a triumphant commencement oration at which the Revolutionary War hero Lafayette had been present. Carried by his ambition to hold the first rank among his contemporaries, he went immediately to study law in the office of Daniel Webster, teaching as well in order to earn money. Even as Edward disappointed Aunt Mary's hopes by pursuing the profession of the law, Emerson himself did not seem conscious of taking up the ministry as the family calling. "It is my own humor to despise pedigree," he wrote. "I was educated to prize it. The kind Aunt whose cares instructed my youth . . . told me oft of the virtues of her and mine ancestors. . . . But the dead sleep in their moonless night; my business is with the living."[4] Through the medium of the journals, he had attempted to take up the task of understanding the tradition of the ministry not merely as an inheritance requiring his acquiescence, but as a vocation that had meaning to him as a free individual. He wanted to dedicate himself to the profession with clear thinking, out of his own free will. He wholeheartedly withdrew to the solitude of his books and his lamp, ready to make the tradition of his fathers his own. "I have nothing to do with society," he wrote, and at the bidding of a "solemn voice [that] commands me to retire," he withdrew into himself. The choice itself, however, had been determined for him long before, even before he was born. It was no choice at all. His attempt to cast the acceptance of his fate in the language of choice and freedom showed not true free will, but a rationalizing process arising out of the same unconscious forces that had started to work in him in his early college days. Even if he could despise pedigree, he certainly could not escape it, and the ministry was no more his than the coat he had shared with Edward in the winters as a little boy. [5]

An air of fatality shrouded his mind as he confronted the reality of his actions, and his thoughts became dark and brooding. "I thought of the passage of my years," he wrote upon closing the school, "of their even and eventless tenor, and of the crisis which is but a little way before, when a month will determine the dark or bright dye they must assume forever."[6] The demands of the call that he had accepted burdened him greatly, and he became increasingly obsessed with the future, which loomed as a dark cloud over his soul. He imagined that a few weeks would irrevocably determine whether he rose to brightness and immortal success or sank to ignominy and abject defeat. The fear that his decision engendered seemed to cloud his judgment and sense of reality; yet it drove him to persevere in the task he had chosen. The unconscious force at work within Emerson moved beyond internal hollowness and coldness and began to have an outward effect on his life. He took up his studies as a mechanical labor and pushed himself relentlessly. The extent to which this kind of mechanical thinking and behavior overtook Emerson in the month before he entered Divinity Hall became manifest in a Journal passage that is so un-Emersonian it almost seems to belong to someone else's journal. Throughout his life, Emerson's habit of study was to plunge into a book with intense energy, mine the contents of a few pages for the best sentences, and move on as quickly to the next book. The thought of the moment guided his choice of reading material. But this winter the golden realm of books seemed to become little more than impending drudgery. On December 1, 1824, he wrote, "I may digress . . . to utter a wish not altogether fruitless, that there might be an order introduced into the mass of reading that occupies or impends over me."[7] He then proceeded to lay out an intellectual plan for exactly what he would study and at what time of day he would study it. The idea that reading could "occupy or impend" over one such as Emerson indicated that something had gone very wrong in his inner life. His embrace of an artificial, almost mechanical approach to study showed that the unconscious force had now entered his volition, his will. That force would soon work its way into the very soundness of his body.

The Specter of Weakness and Decay

After only one month in Divinity Hall, where he spent hour upon hour studying in his damp, crowded room, Emerson's health began to fail rapidly. He suffered a lame hip, a "stricture in the chest," and a stroke of blindness that took the use of both of his eyes. The failure of his eyesight can actually be traced in the pages of the Journal as his handwriting became larger and more sprawling, finally ending in an illegible scrawl. Forced to give up his books and his writing, he made no entries in the Journal after March 1825 and retired to his Uncle Ladd's farm, where he rested during the summer. His eyes required two separate operations before they showed signs of healing. As he worked his way back to health on the farm, he learned to see again, to breathe again. By September Emerson recovered enough to leave the farm and teach school in Chelmsford. Only a few weeks after Emerson opened his school, William, who had recently returned from Germany, announced that he had decided to abandon the ministry and was considering law instead. William's encounter with German "higher criticism" so shook his faith that, despite a meeting with Goethe in which the poet advised him to continue in the ministry, he could not in good conscience preach a doctrine in which he no longer believed. The family was shocked, and Aunt Mary was particularly dismayed. After hearing William's news, she wrote to her nephew, "Ah, my dear Waldo, prepare (sight or no sight) to preach this divine medicine to a thoughtless ambitious world."[8] With Edward and

William both aiming at careers in law, and Charles tending in that direction as well, Waldo was the last hope for a minister in the family. Yet the very survival of the family seemed in crisis that fall. Edward's health, unable to sustain the relentless pace of work that the ambitious young apprentice had set for himself in Webster's law office, had begun to weaken at about the same time Emerson lost his eyesight. Edward was forced to abandon his school over the summer as his health continued to deteriorate, and soon after William's return in October the younger brother left for Europe to recover. Waldo, still weak and walking with a cane because of the worsening pain in his hip, closed his own school in order to take over Edward's.

Emerson's hiatus from his Journal lasted for almost a year; he did not pick up his pen again until January of 1826. When he finally returned "with mended eyes to my ancient friend and consoler," he seemed the better for his long rest from reading and writing, calling himself a "more cheerful philosopher." He was loathe to pester himself with questions of death and evil, but was "rather anxious to thank Oromasdes than to fear Ahriman."[9] He gave the name of Ahriman, the Persian god of darkness and fire, to the fear that he had experienced and wished to thank Oromasdes, the Persian god of light, for his recovery. In a certain sense, his ability to name the force that confronted him should have signaled his victory over it. But only a few months after his recovery, the "specter of weakness and decay" returned and the feeling of fear again emerged. "My years are passing away," he wrote in March of 1826; "Infirmities are already stealing on me that may be the deadly enemies that dissolve me to dirt, and little is yet done to establish my consideration among my contemporaries, and less to get a memory when I am gone."[10] Edward's broken health only served to heighten Waldo's anxiety over his own illness. As the weeks passed, he became increasingly devoted to the ministry, as if somehow he could accomplish a lifetime of work by focusing every last bit of strength in its service for the short time that he felt was left him. Indeed, the fear of failing to accomplish his mission became ever more real. His rhetoric regarding the church elevated to a feverish, almost fanatical pitch. In a passionate letter to his Aunt Mary, he expressed his rage that the great glory and depth of Christianity, of the apostles and the martyrs, should "pass away and become ridiculous" after eighteen centuries, an object of scorn for every scoffer, atheist, and drunkard who cared to try his tongue against them; yea, "it were base treason in his servants tamely to surrender the cause" and "vile and supine to sit and be astonished without exploring the strength of the enemy." He wished to help save the church, the institution of Christianity, at any cost.[11]

To this end, despite continued poor health and comparatively brief studies, he was approbated to preach in October of 1826. He accepted several invitations to local pulpits and preached at his father's church in Boston. It seemed at last that he would be able to fulfill the promise Aunt Mary had seen in him, yet a new and even greater threat loomed. The pain in his lungs redoubled its attack, and the signs of consumption, coming so soon after the terrible blindness, panicked the family. Emerson began to sag into despondency and helplessness: "I shape my fortunes, as it seems to me, not at all. For in all my life I obey a strong necessity, and all that sacrifice of time and inclination which certain of my fond friends regard as virtue, I see and confess to be only a passive deference to the course of events."[12] He gathered the courage to rail against such despair, shouting out, "Die? what should you die for? Maladies? What Maladies? Dost thou not know that Nature has her course as well as Disease? . . . Die? pale face, lily liver! go about your business, and when it comes to the point, then die like a gentleman."[13] Yet in spite of what resistance he could muster, the pains in his chest worsened as the damps of autumn came on. The threat of consumption became so serious that had his uncle, Samuel Ripley, not intervened and funded a trip south to Florida for the winter, the family was convinced that he would have died. The actual reasons for this illness and that of the previous year lay much deeper than dampness and close rooms, for even the best doctors in Boston could not divine the nature of it.

In a certain sense the trials that Emerson had experienced earlier in his life manifested in his physical illnesses. The laming of the will caused by mechanical study had a correspondence in his lame hip; the coldness of his emotions observed at the finishing school, in the constriction of his lungs that threatened full-blown tuberculosis; and the hollowness of intellections experienced while studying at Harvard, in his blindness. These diseases reflected the effects of the three steps of Ahriman's attack. All three of Emerson's forces of soul became permeated by fear and he felt his soul forces—the qualities of thought, emotion, and will—become divergent. Emerson was aware that his was not a "regulated soul," and he perceived the discord with alarm, for he had an "instinctive dread of the tendencies to harmony in the Universe . . . which betoken some future violence to root out this disorder. If the string cannot be made to accord, it must be broken."[14] He wrote, on January 30, that "God secures the execution of His moral laws by committing to every moral being the supervision of his own character." Whereas up to this point his qualities of soul had been regulated for him, maintained in a steady equilibrium and harmony according to the laws of the Universe, they now began to separate and fall apart, as if the responsibility for regulating them, for good or ill, were left entirely in his care.

The journey to Florida in the winter of 1826 proved essential to the opening up of Emerson's inner life. He had always felt a certain sympathy with nature, but the warmth of love could not penetrate the deepest regions of his heart, and he still described himself as a cold, frigid being. In Florida he met Napoleon Achille Murat, the first of two people who would pry him from the shell that separated him from the world. The son of the infamous general of Napoleon who had become King of Naples fascinated Emerson, for Murat was as eager and ready of thought, as eloquent, and of even greater power of mind. He was also agnostic, a quality that puzzled Emerson in a man of such exceeding value. The two men spent long hours in conversation, including many days shut up together in the hold of a ship during a storm that struck during one leg of Emerson's journey back north. Emerson felt, for the first time in uncounted years, the warmth of human relation. Even more, he idolized his friend, for he was, beyond his keen and active intellect, strengthened to action, the lack of which Emerson often lamented in himself. He later stated that the prime responsibility of the Great Man, above all other things, was to do the good. His first example was Achille Murat.

When Emerson returned from Florida in January of 1827, he wrote very little in the journal and yielded to the necessities of his delicate constitution. He wrote a letter to one of his brothers in the spring describing how he was "living cautiously, yea, treading on eggs to strengthen my constitution. It is a long battle, this of mine between life and death. . . . So I never write when I can walk, and especially when I can laugh." On a fine afternoon, he would shut up his books, put on his old clothes and old hat, and head off into the woods and hills. He took great joy in his walks and valued them even above his intellectual pursuits. He wrote only a sermon a month in the way of work and spent the remainder of his time in rest and relaxation. He looked back on the near-fanaticism of the previous year with disapproval, giving himself a stern reminder that "the whole object of the universe to us is the formation of character. If you think you came into being for the purpose of taking an important part in the administration of events, to guard a moral province of the moral creation from ruin, and that its salvation hangs on the success of your single arm, you have wholly mistaken your business."[15] He also viewed the calling of the ministry differently. He felt that it had become dull and degenerate but for Dr. Channing. In Channing he saw a spark that promised there was "much in man that operates to postpone the convulsion, or guide the ship in the event of a storm." Channing, the staid, humanistic theologian, increasingly replaced Milton as Emerson's model. Rather than stand forward in full armor as champion of the community of believers, he now only wished to preserve whatever corner of the church might remain standing after the storm struck.

In December, 1827, an event occurred that transformed this suspended waiting and touched his heart. He met Ellen Louisa Tucker and fell in love. Ellen's beauty and grace pierced to the quick the coldness that had so long made its home in him, the coldness from which, as he observed in a letter to his aunt, only a very few persons had ever encouraged him to emerge. His world became filled with pure light and joy. He called Ellen his angel. She was his ideal, and she wrought a change that swept his entire being, making him happier and stronger than he had ever been. When they first met in Concord, he thought the event so momentous that he addressed the reader of the Journal directly, perhaps the only time in sixty years of writing that he did so, in order to inform whoever followed his words that he had never before been in love, and that now the unimaginable had happened to him. He wrote that in the few shades of different tones of feeling that made up his day, one was the "sweet asylum" of his happiness, which he kept in sight when disasters befell him. It was in this sweet asylum that he spent the year of his recovery, 1828. Indeed, it is probably the influence of Ellen that caused him to adhere to his policy of relaxation so diligently. In a very real sense, her love healed him.

The pervasive ambition native to his brothers and himself was much on Emerson's mind in the spring of 1828, and when news came that William had fallen seriously ill, he dashed off a letter of reproval to his elder brother. "You naughty boy how dare you work so hard?" he chided. "Have you forgotten that all the Emersons overdo themselves? Don't die of the leprosy of your race—ill weaved ambition." Waldo, full of the exuberance of a young man in love, presented himself to his brother as a prime example of the value of rest, for he was now mending from his wasting illness "and am said to look less like a monument & more like a man." His new-found ease was so potent a healer that he wished he could "persuade that wilful brother Edward of mine to use the same sovereign nostrum."[16] Edward's characteristic ambition was, in fact, so strong that his brothers distinguished him by it as the "lion of the tribe." As counterpoint to his relentless drive for success, Edward's health had never been robust. Whereas William and Waldo had made it out of Harvard without any serious illness, their younger brother not only had to go south to rest for a year before he entered college, but had to leave in the midst of his matriculation because of poor health and travel to

Europe in order to recover. After he returned from Europe, Edward had pushed himself even harder. In the spring of 1828, soon after Waldo wrote his letter to William and just before what was to have been Charles's moment of glory as valedictorian speaker, Edward's sanity failed. As Charles delivered his graduation oration, Edward was sitting in the McLean Asylum, where he remained for four months.

In December of 1828, Emerson learned that he would soon be invited to fulfill a post as junior pastor at the Second Church. He and Ellen were engaged to be married shortly thereafter.[17] It is no coincidence that his call to the pulpit and his engagement came at the same time. The presence of Ellen confirmed to him that he was on a path blessed by God, and the pulpit offered the means for him to support a family of his own. The engagement and the pastorship signified the full acceptance of the family calling. Buoyed by the unmixed happiness of his circumstances, encouraged by the recovered health and new prospects of all of his brothers, he reported to his Journal that "my history has had its important days within a brief period." He expressed his gratitude to God and his total dependence on Him for these blessings. Basking in the warmth of this new love, he penned words in his Journal that would have been unimaginable only a year before.

> All that thy virgin soul can ask be thine,
> Beautiful Ellen.   Let this prayer be mine;
> The first devotion that my soul has paid
> To mortal grace it pays to thee, fair maid.
> I am enamoured of thy loveliness,
> Lovesick with thy sweet beauty, which shall bless
> With its glad light my path of life around,
> Which now is joyless where thou art not found.
> Now am I stricken with the sympathy

That binds the whole world in electric tie.
I hail love's birth within my hermit breast,
And welcome the bright ordinance to be blest.

The Family Calling

In January of 1829, three years after the formation of the American
Unitarian Association under Channing's leadership, the Second Church in
Boston sent Emerson a formal invitation to become junior pastor to Henry
Ware, Jr., who, because of health problems, could not fulfill all of his duties.
While it did not share the high prestige of the First Church, which Emerson's father had led, the Second Church nevertheless boasted a long and
venerable tradition, having been under the ministry of two of the giants of
the early Puritan community, Increase and Cotton Mather. It also claimed a
not unreasonable share of Boston's distinguished families. With the invitation of the Second Church in hand, Emerson wrote to his Aunt on the sixth
of January, flush with optimism and encouraged by the blessings that seemed
to crowd in upon him from every side: "Now, when it [success] seems to be
coming, I choose to direct to you this letter which I enter as a sort of protest
against my Ahriman, that, if I am called after the way of my race, to pay a fatal
tax for my good, I may appeal to the sentiment of collected anticipation with
which I saw the tide turn and the winds blow softly from the favouring
west."[19] If Ahriman had not been defeated, Emerson thought, at least he had
been delivered a palpable rebuke. Fear seemed to have been banished.

Aunt Mary was hardly caught up by the festivities of Waldo's heart;
her response to her nephew's ebullience was chiding in its tone. She returned
once again to her old criticism of his character, one that he still did not seem
to grasp, saying, "you do exaggerate (notwithstanding the modest & gracious

stole of moderation is thrown so gracefully on) your success— It is *common* for such as you—and thousands less deserving. . . . One would think to hear you all vapour about your changes that the contrast was to be as poetic as the fisherman's of Galilee—and that the world was to bear the marks of your destiny to the end of time." It was Waldo's practiced habit of connecting the whim of fortune with real spiritual advancement that so raised her spleen. Though she could feel happy for Waldo and "sympathise most warmly with those whose golden spoke the white fates have turned up—and would fain hail your ascent—were it such," she could not abide the outer show that belied the real state of his soul, for "the appointments of *enjoyment* are fixed beyond the power of circumstances—that indeed its preponderment belongs to a mediocrity of talent and virtue while virtue is in an exiled state."[19] Once again she saw that fatal flaw against which she had warned him so many years before, and again she called him on it.

Emerson himself had suspicions about the deficiency of virtue to which his aunt referred and felt a certain unease with the moral authority that came with the position of minister. In 1827 he had written that, though he considered himself a moral agent designed to contribute to the welfare of others, he did not feel he had the right to point the way to others when he himself was a "castaway." Channing's increasing influence on him had helped alleviate this feeling, or, rather, obscure it. Emerson determined that the role of the Christian minister was not to preach the great Day of Judgement, not to fill each member of the congregation with a loathing for his or her own sin and depravity, but "to show the beauty of the moral laws of the universe; to explain the theory of a perfect life; to watch the Divinity, in his world; to detect his footstep; to discern him in the history of his children by catching the tune from a patient listening to miscellaneous sounds; by threading out the unapparent plan in events crowding on events."[20] Concerned that his view of the role of the minister might not mesh with the realities of leading a congregation, Emerson met with the senior pastor of the Second Church, who encouraged him to persevere. Still unsettled by some of the finer points of Unitarian belief, Emerson expressed reservations about the pre-existence of Christ; the Reverend Ware told him to "leave it alone; it is a thing of small consequence." Thus reassured, Waldo sealed his commitment to the Second Church. The only doubt that lingered in his mind concerned Ellen, who had coughed blood twice that winter and whose health had deteriorated to the point where her care might require a move south. He accepted the call to the pulpit after her doctor assured them that the tuberculosis was not too far advanced and would go into remission with care in Boston. That September he and Ellen, his beloved Jewel, were married.

The thin film of joy brought by circumstance soon broke. Only a year after accepting the call to the Second Church, Emerson's uncertainties about Church doctrine and the duties of the minister became bona fide doubt. "That man will always speak with authority who speaks his own convictions," he declared; "that which, true or false, he hath perceived with his inward eye." It became clear to him that the truth of inner conviction stood in contradiction to his role as a minister. According to Unitarian belief, absolute authority rested only in the divine words of Christ and the teachings of his disciples. The active thinking, conscious of itself, that emerged in the Journal somehow had to be reconciled with the unequivocal authority of scripture as divine revelation and absolute truth. Early in his ministry, apparently sensing this struggle, several parishioners complained to Reverend Ware that the Junior Pastor did not give due attention to the Holy Word. Emerson responded to Ware's query into the matter in no uncertain terms: "I shall certainly take great pains to remove any such impression. I consider them [the Scriptures] as the true record of the Revelation which established what was almost all we wanted to know, namely the Immortality of the Soul—& then, what was of infinite importance after that was settled, the being & character of God."[21] As time went on, however, this certainty began to fade, and the struggle to fit the words of his sermons into a mode acceptable to the congregation began to place an increasing strain on him. The fact was that there *was* something more beyond the being and character of God that he wished to know—namely, his own character and the dimensions of the Self. He began to feel mastered by the topics set for each Sunday, since the subject that the Church required him to speak on was often at odds with what he pondered in the musings of the Journal. Sunday inevitably came, however, and the sermon had to be given. He settled for the traditional topic and privately complained that he was not free to write in the way "best and most level with life."[22] As the months wore on, Emerson began to couple the idea of reliance on the self, of speaking about what he had personally experienced and had apprehended as truth, with the seedling of the idea that maybe he did not belong where he was at all: "The elm is a bad oak, but a beautiful elm."[23] The minister began to suspect that his calling was not the blessing he had once extolled. The realization began to dawn on him that he had actually entered a trap.

On a Tuesday morning in February, 1831, Ellen Tucker Emerson, age twenty, died of tuberculosis. They had been married only seventeen months. Ellen's death—so long foreshadowed in droplets of blood and the wasting cough, so hopefully combated with fresh air and long rides in the country—struck Emerson as a hammer-blow. Its effect on him was catastrophic. The one human being in the world who represented to him all purity and truth, the one who showed him what love truly was, was cruelly taken from him in the flower of her youth. He at first floated in a kind of euphoria that Ellen would no longer suffer from her bleeding lungs and had finally found rest in heaven, but this feeling soon succumbed to an increasing frustration at not being able to talk with her any longer, at not having her by his side. "Will the dead be restored to me?" he mourned; "shall I ever be able to connect the face of outward nature … with the heart and life of an enchanting friend?"[24] He was shattered and broken, longing for the dead to return to him, seeking ever after his angel and finding her nowhere and yet everywhere. "The mourner reads his loss in every utensil in his house, in every garment, in the face of every friend," he sorrowed. "The dead do not return." He bewailed his inability to speak with her, to hear her voice even one last time. Finding no one among the living to whom he could say a true word or in whose presence he could feel joy, he longed to retire to the hills, alone with his books and the memory of his beloved. Her sweetness and purity were matchless in the world, and deep within a desire stirred that he might die as well and join her. His depression grew as the winter wasted away, and he visited her tomb every morning. On March 29, 1832, he wrote a lone sentence on a page of his journal: "I visited Ellen's tomb and opened the coffin." There is, in the end, no way to interpret this action as sane or reasonable. It arose from the anguish of his heart. The depression that settled on Emerson after his wife's death is actually the greatest testament of the degree to which Ellen opened up the untouched regions of his inner life. He mourned not for the future of his career, or for the loss of his health, or for his inability to study with manic efficiency in order to make a name for himself in the eyes of his ancestors. He mourned for a human being whose love had fled from the world.

IV.

HITCH YOUR WAGON
TO A STAR

Crossing the Water

A fter Ellen's death, Emerson began to attack the ministry and its readymade rituals, the "cold and cheerless" religious shows of the institution that he had once so ardently wished to preserve. He became bitter at his imprisonment within its forms, frustrated that the demands of others constantly drew his energies towards them and away from his private thoughts when he only wished to surrender himself to lamenting Ellen's passing. Five months after her death he wrote, "I suppose it is not wise, not being natural, to belong to any religious party. In the Bible you are not directed to be a Unitarian, or a Calvinist, or an Episcopelian. . . . A sect or party is an elegant incognito devised to save a man from the vexation of thinking."[1] Feeling the bonds of the church steadily tightening, he at last burst out, in December of 1831, "Whatever faith you teach, live by it." He decided that he must conform to his own principles, for none could inform him of how to live but himself. "It is the best part of the man," he wrote in another passage, "that revolts most against his being a minister. His good revolts from official goodness. If he never spoke or acted but with the full consent of his understanding, if the whole man acted always, how powerful would be every act and every word."[2] Emerson's responsibilities as a minister, which had already proved difficult, now became onerous. Compounding his difficulties with giving set sermons was the duty of visiting sick parishioners, who sometimes complained that he treated death with "unbecoming indifference" and did not sympathize with them by making their suffering his own. Emerson was helpless to respond to this charge with much more than a long rationalization in his Journal about how he did not fear death, and how those who do fear it are mistaken owing to their uncertainty of what comes after death.

The problem with his ministry was essentially the same one that thwarted his efforts as a teacher at the girls' school: the discrepancy between his thoughts and action brought him dangerously close to hypocrisy. It is a strange minister indeed who sits with his Journal and contemplates the unspeakable beauty of the individual soul and the jewel of thought, that God is within, and then tells a sick parishioner he is simply mistaken to fear death. For one such as Emerson, the only thing worse than trying to formulate a unified theory of education and then calling your own students unteachable geese was accepting a position in which people have asked you explicitly to care for their spiritual health and well-being and thinking that all you have to do is preach a little on Sundays. Eventually he could not even do that to his satisfaction. Contrary to his youthful presumption, adopting the form of the thing had not filled him with the substance of it; rather, it had left him empty and wanting. The god of fire had triumphed.

What Emerson had seen as a victory over Ahriman was really the final victory of the dark force that had pursued him through hollowness, coldness, mechanical thought, and fear as he walked confidently into the open prison of the tradition of his fathers. By all rights Emerson should have remained there in the ministry, trapped, feeling frustrated and unfulfilled for the rest of his life. What is difficult to understand is the impulse that led Emerson to decide that he had to abandon his ministry. It was no simple thing to simply leave his post. He had accepted a calling, had been made much of as the son stepping forward to fill the father's place. The community expected an Emerson from an Emerson, and Aunt Mary argued that dissatisfaction with his position meant only that he should pray and preach harder. Ellen's death was indeed a great personal tragedy. Yet her passing acted effectively as an inspiration to move him in a new direction, a powerful surge of longing that could not only counter, but untie the millstone of ancestral tradition. What he saw as her failure to return in body, and as his own failure to re-establish a connection with her beyond the grave, was in fact her active presence working within him as an impelling force, urging him to seek more direct knowledge of the spiritual world to which she had gone. The beleaguered minister came up with many reasons as he sought an exit, but in truth it was not possible to think himself out of the trap he had thought himself into. The relation between Emerson's physical illnesses and his spiritual trials suggests that Ellen's death may well have been a sacrifice that rescued Emerson from his failure. Ellen Tucker Emerson, his angel, had died of the worst illness that had threatened her husband's life: tuberculosis.

In July of 1832, Emerson announced to his congregation certain controversial views that he held on the administration of communion, which centered on the idea that Jesus had meant the first communion only as an observance for his disciples and not as a ritual to be performed in the churches generation after generation. After submitting a written request to the church that he be excused from performing the communion service, as it was against his conscience to do so, Emerson undertook a journey into the mountains in order that he might look down upon the bustle and noise of the town from a distance and "obtain a just view."[3] Family and friends, even the majority of the congregation, encouraged him to hold the course, to set aside his differences and serve his flock; yet Emerson was listening to a new voice, one that arose from deep within. The trip into the mountains was an outward expression of a powerful spiritual event in Emerson's inner life in which he not only rose up and looked down upon the town "at such a distance as may afford a just view," but on himself and his actions as well. He looked upon himself as a stranger might, viewing his deeds and passions with an impartial eye. When he returned to his congregation on September ninth, he again expressed his views on communion and offered his resignation to the Second Church. His official reason for leaving the pulpit had nothing to do with his suspicion of the institution itself nor with his grief and frustration at the death of Ellen. Rather, his ideas had not recommended themselves to the congregation; that is, they had not been able to accept a new evaluation of the ritual of communion. After month upon month of tortured thought, the care-worn Emerson had come to the simple conclusion that "in order to be a good minister, it was necessary to leave the ministry. The profession is antiquated. In an altered age, we worship in the dead forms of our forefathers."[4] While in the White Mountains, he had realized that he could not, in conscience, remain as the leader of a group of people who did not share his principles, and he could not force them to accept or even to listen to ideas contrary to their professed beliefs, no matter with what tenderness or affection he might regard them. His congregation did not want to let him go, but finally voted to accept his decision with reluctance. He wrote out his resignation on white silk.

On October 9, 1832, Emerson, having recently resigned from the pastorate that he had worked his entire life to attain, wrote a poem in the Journal entitled "Self-Reliance." He had been working with the idea of Self-reliance for two years, and the poem represented the final expression of the principle itself after accomplishing the one action that he never could have carried through without it. Something deep within him repudiated his life's calling. Truly free of expectations and commitments for the first time in his life, facing an unknown future and an uncharted course, Emerson shaped this new guiding principle into verse.

> I will not live out of me.
> I will not see with others' eyes;
> My good is good, my evil ill.
> I would be free; . . .
> I dare to attempt to lay out my own road.
> . . . . .
> Henceforth, please God, forever I forego
> The yoke of men's opinions. I will be
> Light-hearted as a bird and live with God.
> I find him in the bottom of my heart,
> I hear continually his Voice therein.
> . . . . .
> The little needle always knows the north,
> The little bird remembereth his note,
> And this wise Seer never errs.
> I never taught it what it teaches me, I only follow when I act
>   aright.

On Christmas Day Emerson set sail for Europe. His decision to go to the Continent was uncharacteristic, made suddenly while he was considering a visit to Edward in Puerto Rico, where his brother had gone to nurse his broken health. Instead Emerson booked passage on a brig heading for Malta, putting his affairs in order and setting out without a backward glance. He was plagued by a severe diarrhea that had wasted his body for almost five months, an unexplained malady that had started around July twenty-second and had persisted, with only a few brief respites, until his departure five months later. He boarded the brig *Jasper* in a wretched condition that was only exacerbated by a storm that caught the ship as soon as it set sail. The small crew weathered the storm and rough seas for the first week of the voyage, and all were so seasick that they were forced to stay in a tiny cabin whose conditions made sleep impossible. The floor was always wet, and there was no heat. Strangely, when the storm finally ended, Emerson had completely recovered from the diarrhea. He regained his appetite, and was hardy and sound in body.[5] On this journey through the Holy Nights in the dark hold of a ship, the wasting illness that had plagued him for half a year ended. More importantly, he was rid of the shadow of tuberculosis for the rest of his life.

Emerson's aim in going to Europe was to find a Master who could instruct him in this new exhilarating freedom, who could guide him on a new course now that he had loosed all moorings, but before he even set foot on foreign shores he discovered that he would not succeed in doing so. On January 3, 1833, on the first fine day after the storm had passed and his illness disappeared, he stood on the deck of the ship and fell into a reverie as he gazed at the heavens. He remained there for some time, apparently transfixed by what he saw. The world, which had been devoid of all glory since

Ellen's death, came alive again, and spoke. After his juvenile fumbling about for a source of inspiration, after a tortured and fruitless search through elementals and gods for some small notice from the spiritual world to enliven his thoughts and his pen, here before him was the very source of artistic endeavor, presenting itself to him in its full glory. He found a teacher in nature, and the teacher instructed him to seek the answers to his questions within himself. When he finally roused himself, he went to his Journal and tried to describe what he had experienced. "The clouds were touched / And in their silent faces might be read / Unutterable love," he wrote.

> They shone with light that shines on Europe, Afric, and the Nile, and I opened my spirit's ear to their most ancient hymn. What, they said to me, goest thou so far to seek—painted canvas, carved marble, renowned towns? But fresh from us, new evermore, is the creative efflux from whence these works spring. You now feel in gazing at our fleecy arch of light the motions that express themselves in arts. . . . This strong-winged sea-gull and striped sheer-water that you have watched as they skimmed the waves under our vault, they are works of art better worth your enthusiasm . . . strictly eternal because now active, and ye need not go so far to seek what ye would not seek at all if it were not within you.[6]

In this powerful vision, Emerson experienced not a true inspiration, a heard voice—though he used language that approximates hearing—but rather a powerful imagination. In the vision he saw a "creative efflux" working down out of the arc of light and manifesting in the works of man. More significantly, Emerson saw this creative efflux manifesting within nature and the earth itself—within the clouds, the sea-gulls, the water. The creations of the transient world somehow became eternal because of the activity of the spirit within them. He seized upon this theme, that the eternal can only be found in the activity of the spirit in the present moment, as a central principle.

After landing in Malta, Emerson began a tour of the great cities of Italy, including Syracuse, Florence, Naples, and Rome, following closely in the footsteps of the great men of literature and culture, of Cicero, Dion, Archimedes, Byron, and Napoleon. He made his way through the temples, ruins, and caves, through the streets and corridors of the past. These were the roads that the men he had first met in the library of Harvard had walked, the mountains they had looked upon, the fields they had fought upon. He found much to awe him, much that was beautiful in sculpture and architecture, far beyond what the infant culture of America could offer, but the vision on the Atlantic lived within him. In the works of other men he sought only himself, for "wherever we go, whatever we do, self is the sole subject we study and learn . . . Myself is much more than I know, and yet I know nothing else." "Self" he used not "in the low sense, but as self means Devil, so it means God. I speak of the universal man to whose colossal dimensions each particular bubble can by its birthright expand."[7]

Several months later, having left the quiet towns of Italy, Emerson found himself in the midst of the noise and bustle of modern Paris. There he visited the Jardins des Plantes, the Cabinet of Natural History, a museum that housed a vast collection of plants and animals from throughout the world, classified and ordered according to the natural system developed by Jussieu. The displays of the Cabinet, arranged to emphasize the physical interconnectedness of the species, implied whole realms of possibility never before considered by this casual observer of nature's beauty. Though the bright colors and various forms dazzled his eye, it was rather the universal laws that undergird them which provoked his mind, and he wrote, "Not a form so grotesque, so savage, nor so beautiful but is an expression of some property inherent in man the observer,—an occult relation between the very scorpions and man. I feel the centipede in me,—cayman, carp, eagle, and fox. I am moved by strange sympathies; I say continually 'I will be a naturalist.'"[8] Beneath the purely physical interconnectedness of animal bodies, he saw a hidden relation between man and nature that he would call, later that year, the language of nature. To know the words of that language was to have access to a great book, writ large upon the world, that revealed the hidden secrets of the self, for "There is not a passage in the human soul, perhaps not a shade of thought but has its emblem in nature." Were one "under the influence of strong passion" to go into the fields, one would readily see "how every thought clothed itself with a material garment, even as every spirit clothes itself with a body."[9] Under the influence of these mighty thoughts, he began to formulate the principles for a little book for which he had already found a title: *Nature*.

Emerson's study of nature focused on the relation between the phenomena of the natural world and their simultaneous appearance as properties or principles in man. Though too young in his thought to draw explicit correspondences, he knew that any deeper insight beyond this first sympathy required a new kind of thinking. As Emerson developed this insight, he realized that comprehending Nature in connection with the being of Man required the use of a kind of perception that could overcome the subject-object dichotomy. Realizing that an eagle or owl was a counterpart of something within himself was one thing, but actually overcoming the intellectual separation of *I* from *that* and perceiving the correspondence itself was something else entirely. Years earlier he had examined this problem in heavily religious terms as the contrast between the man of Knowledge and the man of Genius. He had extended and defined this difference through Coleridge's *Aids to Reflection*, which he had read in 1829, as the difference between two kinds of thinking: that born of Understanding and that born of pure Reason.[10] Like Coleridge, all of the Romantics accepted the primacy of Imagination as the vehicle of Truth, but it was only they, who maintained an inexplicable relation to it, who could use its power. They could never give others the practical means to develop this faculty. Emerson, however, entered the Romantic worldview not through definition or by extended effort of thought, but through experience. Emerson's use of a method of study that fostered Reason above Understanding began to ennoble and enliven the mechanical thought that had stifled his creativity while at the Divinity School. In the second stage of his recovery, the dark force that had lamed his volition, or force of will, could now be opposed by an organic thinking arising out of the use of Imagination and poised to discover the mysterious connection between Man and the world.

The last portion of Emerson's tour of Europe was spent in England visiting the leading men of the times whom he had crossed the ocean to see, the now-aged founders of the Romantic school in England, Wordsworth and Coleridge. He felt drawn to them out of necessity. With Coleridge, who talked for over an hour and barely let Emerson get a word in edge-wise, he had no earnest conversation. Wordsworth was very kind to him and even recited to him three sonnets that he had just composed, though the old poet did not overly impress him. For the most part they could only discuss ideas and opinions formed years before and entrenched by age. He had already sucked them dry. They had no room in their old age to entertain a new friend, a young minister from America. Their great ideals he carried with him already. To see the men themselves in their aged and declining state taught him to be just to wise men. It also convinced him that he and others like him were now the caretakers of the future growth of these ideals, the new bearers of the Spirit of Romanticism.

At the end of his journey, Emerson visited the outspoken Scotchman, Thomas Carlyle, with whom he had long and involved conversations. In spite of their perfectly opposite personalities, they formed an instant connection that was to last a lifetime. Emerson spent twenty-four hours with Carlyle in their first meeting, a good portion of the time spent walking over the bare hills of Dunscore and talking "upon all the great questions that interest us most."[11] Carlyle spoke often of Goethe, who had died the year Emerson set sail for Europe, and emphasized that it was Goethe who had inspired him to take up writing in earnest. He spoke of his intimate correspondence with the poet and encouraged Emerson to learn German that he might enjoy the "mastermind of the German people" to the fullest. It is said that Emerson read the whole of the fifty-five volume set of Goethe's writings, in the original, because Carlyle asked him to. Emerson called this meeting with the fiery and often contradictory Scotchman "a white day in my years." He thought that he would have been in danger of going the whole trip without saying a true word if it had not been for Carlyle. Emerson later professed that he loved Carlyle almost from the moment they met, and the feeling was no less returned by Carlyle himself, as well as his wife, Jane. What most impressed the young American about his new friend was the entire alignment of his character with all that he spoke. In the short sketch that Emerson wrote of Carlyle at the end of his life, he observed that Carlyle "is not mainly a scholar, like the most of my acquaintances, but a practical Scotchman, such as you would find in any saddler's or iron-dealer's shop, and then only accidentally and by surprising addition, the admirable scholar and writer that he is." The influence of Carlyle's strong practicality could not have come at a better moment for Emerson. He had left America looking for a Master and found instead two directions that he could pursue: the path of the poet, laid out in the vision on the Atlantic; and the path of the naturalist, hinted at in the Jardins des Plantes. What was he to do with two visions of such depth and power? In Carlyle he met another writer at the beginning of his career, young enough in his habit and thought and energy that he could open himself to Emerson as a friend, yet far enough advanced in his public career that he could serve as a model to one whose life was changing so rapidly that anything beyond the date that he would sail home for America was obscured by a hazy atmosphere of uncertainty. Carlyle was not the Master that he had looked for; he was, however, a true friend.

On his homeward journey, an entirely different matter preoccupied Emerson. His decision to leave for Europe had been spontaneous and foolhardy in the eyes of his family. He had sold all of his furniture and cut all ties to his old life. While he was traveling in Italy and France, he received the news that Ellen's sister had died and, later, that her mother had died as well. It seemed that all earthly links to his beloved were broken asunder. He had no ministry to return to, no occupation to resume. A small inheritance from Ellen ensured that, at least for the first few years, his choice of a new vocation would not be forced upon him by an immediate need for money, but this prospect raised more questions than it answered. The feeling of freedom lived undeniably within him, broad, almost terrible, confirmed by his outer experiences. Returning to his native country, one thought occurred ever again to his mind: "I wish I knew where and how I ought to live." The Jardins des Plantes had given him the hint to answer this question: "There is a correspondence between the human soul and everything that exists in the world." The "only adequate symbol" for the great spiritual truths, the "laws of the Law," was the material laws of nature found in astronomy, physics, chemistry, biology. To unravel the mysteries of the laws of nature and elucidate their correspondence to the laws of the human soul was no small matter; to form those insights into a practical means of shaping a moral life and sound character was a greater undertaking still. Riding the surface of the great still ocean, Emerson learned to read a script written in a hand that was new and yet very old. "That which I cannot yet declare has been my angel from childhood until now," he wrote. "It has separated me from men. It has watered my pillow. It has driven sleep from my bed. It has tortured me with guilt. It has inspired me with hope. It cannot be defeated by my defeats. … As long as I am here, I plainly read my duties as writ with pencil of fire. They speak not of death; they are woven of immortal thread."[12] Shedding the mission of his fathers, he had the first intimation of his own. What was needed was a teacher, a whole race of teachers, not to explain the moral and eternal law, but to point out the means needed to discover that law for oneself. He pledged in the pages of his Journal "to demonstrate that all necessary truth is its own evidence, that no doctrine of God need appeal to a book."[13] The man who had missed the fundamental point of his position as a school teacher, the man who had sadly misunderstood his role as a pastor, now finally grasped what it meant to be a true minister to his fellow human beings. He would be a teacher of the principle of Self-reliance.

Awake, thou Godlike that Sleepest!

Two weeks after making landfall in New York, Emerson wrote in his Journal that this new type of teacher "must occupy himself in the study and explanation of the moral constitution of man more than in the elucidation of difficult texts."[14] To this end, it seemed clear that the subjects for his first speaking engagements should be the laws of the natural world and their significance to the being of man. In November of 1833, he delivered a lecture to the Boston Society of Natural History entitled "Uses of Natural History" and a second on "The Relation of Man to the Globe." He also lectured on "Water" to the Mechanics Institute and on "The Naturalist" to the Boston Historical Society. The lives of great men provided a goldmine of material as well. In January of 1834 he began to prepare biographical materials for a lecture on Michelangelo that he would deliver the next year, part of a series of six lectures that included Martin Luther, Milton, George Fox, and Edmund Burke. Not only did the opportunities to lecture give him great freedom in subject matter and style, but they also offered a forum in which he could expand and shape the torrent of thoughts on the individual, the universe, and the teacher that he poured into the Journal. Neither was he finished with the ministry. He seemed ready and willing to face the challenge of bringing these same ideals into the context of the church, reflecting his conviction that whatever the role of the teacher were, it somehow had to be a transformation and elevation of the old role of the preacher. On the second Sunday after he returned from Europe he preached in his old church in

Boston, and once more that winter. Though he was reluctant to accept a permanent position anywhere and turned down several offers from established congregations, he began to enjoy traveling throughout New England to fill the pulpit of a church for a Sunday, or even for a month. He preached nearly every Sunday in 1834 to congregations in Waltham, Fall River, and Providence. Those churches that did invite him for a few Sundays or even to a permanent position did so either in spite of or because of what had happened at the Second Church, or they simply did not care; there were those who still took notice, however, for one church cancelled its invitation for him to speak after the parishioners found out who he was. He no longer had to worry about tailoring his message to the habitual beliefs of the congregation. November of 1835 saw him begin a stint as temporary pastor of the small church in East Lexington. Every Sunday for the next several years, he either preached there himself or found a substitute. At this church he found a warm welcome and open acceptance. One parishioner there commented that "we are very simple people here, and don't understand anybody but Mr. Emerson."

Though Emerson enjoyed the role of itinerant pastor, it could not serve as a true vocation. A building sense of excitement and conviction paralleled the ever-expanding reach of his thought and his experiments with lecturing. Every new thought, each new aspect of the eternal law that he discovered only deepened his sense that he had to *do* something with these insights, to make of them a way of life, for "it were well to live purely, to make your word worth something." He could not help but thrill that every new opportunity to speak afforded "an opportunity of communicating thought and moral excitement that shall surpass all previous experience, that shall constitute an epoch, a revolution, in the minds on whom you act and in your own."[15] Something deep within him seemed to quicken with the coming of spring, and in April of 1834 it broke through like a seed pushing its cotyledons through the soil to the light for the first time: "Awake, arm of the Lord! Awake, thou Godlike that sleepest! Dear God that sleepest in man, I have served my apprenticeship of bows and blushes, of fears and reverences, of excessive admiration." He realized a pivotal truth of his life: he had been asleep for thirty-one years.[16] He recognized the events of his life for what they were: an apprenticeship, a preparation that had brought much pain but had not been without beauty. Ellen was the light that shone in his heavy slumber. The lectern granted him even more freedom than the pulpit, for the only limitation was that the topic had to fall within the general interest of the institute or society who sponsored him. By August he made a final decision: "Were it not a heroic adventure in me to insist on being a popular speaker, and run full tilt against the Fortune who with such beautiful consistency shows evermore her back?"[17] Emerson overcame the pull of the hereditary vocation, transforming and renewing it through the individual experience of his rightful mission. He would be a lecturer.

The idea of being truly awake was fundamental not only to Emerson's concept of his own development, but also to the way that he thought of his audience. The cardinal thought that governed his approach to lecturing was that Truth and Beauty could not be taught because they had to be discovered by the individual for himself or herself. He would not fall into the old trap of indoctrination. The subject matter of the earliest of Emerson's lectures, those on natural science in the winter and spring of 1833 and 1834 and the series on biography in the winter of 1835, was entirely consistent with this aim. Emerson thought that natural science could accomplish such an awakening by revealing what the experience in the Jardins des Plantes had shown him. "It is in my judgement the greatest office of natural science to explain man to himself" he declared in his lecture on "The Uses of Natural History." Even more to the point were the lectures on biography. Were it true that the ultimate reason for studying science is to learn about the self, then it was also true of the study of other human beings. Emerson approached biography as a miner would a bed of rock, searching for archetypes of character as if they were veins of gold hidden within these personalities. He listed his possible subjects according to the chief value that might be discovered in them, "Demosthenes for the sake of his oratory and the related topics; Alfred for his human character; Sam. Johnson for his genuineness."[18]

By late autumn of 1834, the *how* of his life was answered by the profession of lecturer, but the *where* begged a solution. His instincts led him to Concord—the town that his ancestor had founded seven generations before, the town where his grandfather had built the family home—and he moved in with his uncle in October. He had barely time to settle in. News of Edward's death in Puerto Rico arrived. Word of his passing was not unexpected; there was little hope remaining among the family that he could regain his health in any permanent way, though he was only twenty-nine. Edward, once the great intellectual lightning bolt of the Emerson family, valedictorian of his class at Harvard, had spent the last months of his life in a clerk's office doing routine work at an assistant's desk. Emerson summed up his brother's life, in a phrase, as "a tragedy of poverty and sickness tearing at genius." Granted little time to grieve his brother's inevitable sad passing, Emerson traveled to Brooklyn for a scheduled speaking engagement in early November. On the fifteenth of the month he returned to the Emerson ancestral home, the Old Manse, built over half a century before by Emerson's grandfather, the Reverend William Emerson, the same grandfather who had served as a minister of the Continental army during the Revolutionary War. The house stood less than one hundred paces from the North Bridge, where was fired "the shot heard round the world." On the very ground where his grandfather had watched the War for Independence begin, a stone's throw from the field where Ralph Waldo had played as a little boy, Emerson wrote, "Hail to the quiet fields of my fathers! Not wholly unattended by supernatural friendship and favor, let me come hither. Bless my purposes as they are simple and virtuous." On this first day back in Concord he also took a vow: "Henceforth I design not to utter any speech, poem or book that is not entirely and peculiarly my own work."[19] It was a vow that rounded out this stage of healing and new beginning, a statement of absolute freedom that repudiated the last vestiges of Ahriman's near-fatal attack. Here was his own ringing shot of independence to answer that of the heroic embattled farmers. Emerson himself stood forth as an individual, unencumbered by the past and the call of his ancestry, original in thought and action for good or ill. Three weeks later the decision to move to Concord seemed to be confirmed: "I do not cross the common without a wild poetic delight," he wrote, "notwithstanding the prose of my demeanor. Thank God I live in the country."[20]

On January 24, 1835, he sent a letter proposing marriage to Ms. Lydia Jackson, whom he had met in the spring of 1834 when he delivered a lecture in her hometown of Plymouth. Having discovered a new place and new profession, he found a new life's companion as well. She responded in the affirmative within a week. Almost immediately the question of where to live was raised. Lydia (whom Emerson called Lidian thereafter) wished to remain in Plymouth and pointed out that there were no real responsibilities tying Emerson to Concord. Emerson, however, had become deeply attached to his grandfather's town, and on February first wrote Lidian that "under this morning's severe but beautiful light I thought dear friend that hardly should I get away from Concord. I must win you to love it." Concord was the town for a poet, and a poet he professed to be—a poet "in the sense of a perceiver and dear lover of the harmonies that are in the soul & in matter, & specially of the correspondences between these and those." It was nature, above all, that was so dear to him: "a sunset, a forest, a snow storm, a certain river-view, are more to me than many friends & do ordinarily divide my day with my books. Wherever I go therefore I guard & study my rambling propensities with a care that is ridiculous to people, but to me is the care of my high calling. Now Concord is only one of a hundred towns in which I could find these necessary objects but Plymouth I fear is not one. Plymouth is streets; I live in the wide champaign [sic]."[21] Lidian eventually agreed. In July Emerson bought a house not far from the center of Concord on the main road to Boston. On September fourteenth they were married in a small ceremony, and on the fifteenth moved into the new house. The *where* of his new life was settled.

After the marriage, the new house quickly became a lively center of activity. Charles, who had been living at the Old Manse for the last year, now moved in with the Emersons. Four years earlier, in 1831, a sudden turn in Charles's health had forced him south with Edward to Puerto Rico in order to recover, but he had returned to graduate from law school and fell deeply in love with Elizabeth Hoar. The two had set a wedding date for the following September and were looking forward to moving into rooms that Emerson was adding to the new house for them. Charles and his elder brother grew closer than they had ever been, spending long hours together talking and reading the Greek tragedies in the original. Emerson's Journal began to fill with Charles's thoughts, opinions, and observations. That fall Bronson Alcott, a brilliant conversationalist and founder of the Temple School in Boston, became a regular visitor at the house. Alcott had often gone to hear Emerson speak in the early days of his lectures in Boston, but had never approached the author of those beautiful lectures until one evening in Philadelphia, when Emerson paid a visit to a woman living in the same apartments as he. The two formed an instant friendship, and Emerson invited Alcott to Concord. He now read Alcott's journal for 1835 and his manuscript book on the incarnation and growth of the immortal soul during childhood, entitled "Psyche." Emerson was working a little on a book of his own, which he had been writing off and on since his return from Europe, but he made little headway. As an added joy to the energy and bustle surrounding the newly established Emerson household, Lidian became pregnant in January of 1836.

This busy happiness was not to last. Throughout the winter, Charles's already delicate health steadily weakened. Elizabeth Hoar had premonitions that she would never be married. Charles's lungs finally betrayed him in the warmth of spring; he died suddenly on May ninth. His death was the fifth to take from Emerson a loved one in the five years since the tragic loss of Ellen, deaths which included Ellen's mother and sister; his best friend, George Sampson; and his brother Edward. The loss of Charles was even more heartrending than that of Edward. Charles, mild-tempered and introspective, was "beautiful without any parallel in my experience of young men . . . Clean and sweet his life, untempted almost, and his action on others all-healing, uplifting and fragrant." Emerson felt that he had entered a "new and gloomy epoch" of his life, one bereft of his greatest friend and confidant. In the vast emptiness of his grief he wondered, "who can ever supply his place to me? None. . . . The eye is closed that was to see nature for me."[22] Yet somehow the closing of Charles's eye opened his own, and he began to see nature for himself. His inspiration came through Alcott. After two weeks of helpless mourning following Charles's death, something began to change. He read Alcott's *Records of Conversations on the Gospels* and met several times with this master of conversation in June. After these meetings he went to his Journal and wrote out long passages that, almost unchanged, became the last two chapters of the little book that he had begun to prepare while in Europe three and a half years before. *Nature* seemed to flow out of him in one piece. On September ninth, it was published—anonymously.

The book was unprecedented, both in the life of a minor New England minister who was trying to make a name for himself in the Lyceums and in the development of a young nation that had little native culture to speak of. Almost all of Emerson's energy since his return from Europe had been focused on the task of transforming the vocation of minister into that of the lecturer. In the winter of 1835 Emerson had shifted from the lectures on science and biography to a series on English literature, in which he expounded at length on the achievements of the English in poetry and prose and closed with an optimistic look at the possibility of a great American literature. His careful review of the history and development of the greatest works written in English represented an initial preparation in the realm of literature for what he would attempt in *Nature*. His first book was a "pure" essay, formed and written out of a central governing thought. Despite its poor sales, the book became widely known, enough so that it became the object of criticism and even parody. Though many could make little sense of the strange ideas set forth in the book's eight sections, the carefully wrought sentences that set forth the Ideal Philosophy were sufficiently powerful to provide the rallying point for a circle of young forward-looking New England intellectuals. They would come to call themselves Transcendentalists.

Young men and women began to seek Emerson out, for they found something in his words that spoke to their better thoughts and resounded in their souls. They came to him one by one, sometimes by introductions, sometimes by traveling up the turnpike from Boston to Concord and knocking on the door of his house, which stood just off the carriage route. One of these young men was Henry Thoreau, a Concord native and son of a pencil maker. In April of 1837, a senior at Harvard in his final term struggling to make the last payments required in order to graduate that summer, Thoreau borrowed *Nature* from a library in Cambridge. While there were connections between the Emerson and the Thoreau families—Aunt Mary had been a friend of Henry's grandmother, and Lidian's sister, Lucy Jackson Brown, was boarding with Henry's parents—the two had never met. *Nature* was Thoreau's first experience of his Concord neighbor, and while there is no record of what the nineteen-year-old thought of the book, he liked it well enough that he inscribed a first-edition copy and gave it as a parting gift to a friend later that spring. Thoreau likely read *Nature* at the suggestion of Lucy Brown, to whom he was quietly devoted, and it was Lucy who began to bring

Emerson samples of Thoreau's writing and poetry. One afternoon in May Thoreau wrote the poem "Sic Vita" on a sheet of paper, wrapped it around a bunch of violets he had picked, and tossed it through Lucy's window. Lucy, enchanted with the poem, took it to Emerson to read. Hearing of Henry's financial troubles—again, most likely, through Lucy—Emerson wrote a letter to the president of Harvard, Josiah Quincy, advocating for Thoreau and asking if something might be done to help ensure his graduation. Quincy, who was hearing from Thoreau's instructors that the young man was indifferent and inconsistent in his studies, was swayed by Emerson's letter; he petitioned the College's governing body, which granted Thoreau the needed funds. That fall, as Thoreau was looking for teaching positions after graduation, he and Emerson began to see each other around Concord. On October 22nd, as they were talking, Emerson asked, "What are you doing now? Do you keep a journal?"; that afternoon, Thoreau made his first journal entry. In December Lidian noted that Emerson "has taken to Henry with great interest and thinks him uncommon in mind and character."[23] Not long after, on a winter afternoon, Emerson and Thoreau struck out on a walk into the Walden woods, beginning a regular tradition of Sunday excursions.

Man-Lecturing

Emerson's method of forming a lecture holds the best clues to what he hoped to accomplish by becoming a popular lecturer. In the early years of his new career, his major effort went into preparing a main cycle of lectures, usually ten or twelve unified by topic or theme, to be delivered over a number of weeks. A few weeks before the annual winter lecture cycle was to begin, Emerson would draw up a very simple outline of the whole course.

This outline usually consisted of single-word titles. He would then work with each individual lecture title and comb the extensive indices of the Journals for entries that related to the topic in order to draw up a list for each lecture. The Journal entries would often find their way into the lecture verbatim. He would next turn his thoughts to the subject as a whole, such as "Human Culture" or "The Present Age," and form an introductory lecture for the whole series. The lectures themselves he would not write until just before they were to be given, in the manner of the minister who prepared the sermon for the week only when it was actually to be delivered. He found he could only spend approximately twenty hours on the actual task of writing a lecture if he were to preserve enough energy to write and deliver the following lecture. This second stage of preparing a lecture involved arranging the collected journal passages according to an organic process that may best be compared to his famous statement about poetry being made, not by meter, but by a meter-making argument: the lectures were made not by outline, but by an outline-making argument. Emerson was adamant that Rhetoric not become "an immethodical harangue." He thought of his task as analogous to architecture, as the "Building of Discourse." Just as the architect must work with the laws of physics to determine the strength and placement of pillars and beams and cross-braces, the lecturer had to use the laws of thought to order his themes and paragraphs and sentences. Emerson characterized his method of writing the lectures in this way: "let the same number of thoughts be dealt with by a natural rhetoric, let the question be asked— What is said? How many things? Which are they? Count and number them: put together those that belong together. Now say *what your subject is*, for now first you know: and now state your inference or peroration in what calm or inflammatory temper you must."[24] Each new lecture did not grow out of the one before it, but out of itself. The effect of writing one lecture at a time, a few days before it was to be delivered, was that he could focus his energy on the architectonics of the discourse, or building the form for what must be said.

One of the finest examples of Emerson's architecture appeared in his first literary work. The argument of *Nature* did not develop according to logic, but rather a kind of dialectical thinking, a method of writing that allowed the thoughts to grow out of each other by coordinating them together rather than prescribing their order through deductive reasoning. The central ideas of *Nature* had their direct source in the imaginations of the Jardins des Plantes, imaginations that had revealed to Emerson the reality of the spirit manifest in nature and the relation, as seal and print, between the laws of nature and the soul of man. In eight chapters, Emerson described the different moods of the worldview of Idealism, introducing the reader to the successive "Uses of Nature," from the most practical commodity of using its resources for heat and shelter to seeing beyond its outer show to the fundamental activity of the Spirit that stood behind and worked through it. With a great upward momentum, Emerson led the reader from the world of phenomena into the world of spirit by moving from the most common outer facts to the central thoughts of the Ideal philosophy and finally releasing him to take his stand and actively create his own world. Emerson led the reader to Idealism and then set him free. This freedom arose, however, not out of the form-*less*ness of the book, but out of a very specific form lovingly created by Emerson to aid the reader in discovering Idealism for himself. The form of *Nature* unfolded organically at each level out of the dialectic of Matter and Spirit. The coarser and lower sheaths of nature, such as Commodity, Beauty, and Language, fall away to reveal ever newer aspects of the Ideal. *Nature,* in its semi-outline format with numbered and titled sections, still resembled both the essays of Enlightenment writers and the sermons of the Puritan tradition. Yet Emerson transformed the language and form of both so that no reader would experience the same limitation and frustration that he had felt as a student at Harvard, ruled by the topics and the thoughts of others, oppressed by the weight of the literary behemoth impending over him. Emerson created a unique form, which may be pictured as follows.

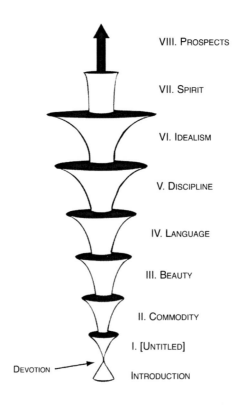

VIII. PROSPECTS

VII. SPIRIT

VI. IDEALISM

V. DISCIPLINE

IV. LANGUAGE

III. BEAUTY

II. COMMODITY

I. [UNTITLED]

DEVOTION

INTRODUCTION

The picture of the form of *Nature* illustrates what Emerson hoped to achieve in each of his individual lectures. Through the use of various architectonic forms, he ever and again strove to accomplish a single goal. The orator was to be "lifted above himself." Because Emerson considered thoughts to be spiritual realities and not mere manufactures of the brain, he believed that if the orator could raise himself to the level of Reason, that is, into the realm of thought realities, he would actually become the channel for the Idea to be communicated to the audience. If he spoke only out of the Understanding, he could do no more than try to explain a thought second- or third-hand. Emerson felt that by opening himself to the intimations of Reason the orator would give the audience the thought itself, would communicate to them words of pure Spirit. He could become the medium of inspiration for his listeners; "I know not how directions for greatness can be given," he wrote, "yet greatness may be inspired."[25] Emerson felt that when he was lecturing at his best, his own personality actually receded into the background, and he became the mouth piece of the Muse or Genius that worked through him. He described the self-surrender of the orator with the phrase "*l'abandon.*" The great orator would utter only truth: "grand truth! the orator himself becomes a shadow a fool before this light which lightens through him. It shines backward & forward; diminishes, annihilates everybody, and the prophet so gladly, so sublimely feels his personality lost in this gaining triumphant godhead."[26] Ultimately the lower self of both speaker and listener would be left behind as their higher selves rose together into the sphere of the activity of the Genius, for "in perfect eloquence, the hearer would lose the sense of dualism, of hearing from another; would cease to distinguish between the orator and himself; would have the sense only of high activity and progress."[27] Emerson's experience of the presence and absence of such an inspiring force attained such a regularity in his youth that he could identify his "thinking seasons," periods when he felt himself so inspired that he could rise to profuse outpourings of eloquent thought. With the departure of this activity of the Genius, however, he was often cast into such depression at his inability to write or think that he thought he might never pen a good word again. One of his goals in becoming a lecturer was to achieve a balance between the ebb and flow of Genius, to deliberately, not accidentally or haphazardly, discover the higher self and "make himself the mere tongue of the occasion and the hour."[28] He no longer sought to bind the muse, but prepared himself as a channel for her activity. In their very selflessness, the lectures were explicitly tied to a path of self-development that culminated in the vow at the Old Manse. To achieve his goal for the Lecture he had to become, not the man giving the lecture, but Man-Lecturing.

Emerson felt that he did not discover the actual subject of his discourse until all of the Journal entries had been numbered, counted, identified, and put together according to kind.[29] What Emerson meant by "subject" was the central thought, and it was this central thought that he saw as the true living element of the discourse, its inhabiting spirit, the sign of the presence of the Genius descending into the form created for it. For Emerson compared writing a lecture to building a temple. Just as gravity is the principle that determines how a building stands up, Emerson used a principle of organization that he called the Order of Wonder to govern how the lecture held together as a Discourse. "If you desire to arrest attention, to surprise," he advised, "do not give me facts in the order of cause and effect, but drop one or two links in the chain, and give me with a cause, an effect two or three times removed."[30] By leaving out the logical connective words, the "therefores" and "thuses" and even whole connective clauses and sentences, Emerson created openings in the structure of the lecture that had to be filled by the active thinking of the listener through the discovery of something that remained unsaid. The attitude of the orator during the lecture itself was vital to the success of the Order of Wonder, for "the eloquent man is he who is no beautiful speaker, but who is inwardly & desperately drunk with a certain belief; it agitates & tears him, & almost bereaves him of the power of articulation. Then it rushes from him as in short abrupt screams, in torrents of meaning." This "possession by the subject of [the eloquent man's] mind," the inspiration and inhabitation of him by the Genius, "ensures an order of expression which is the order of Nature itself, and so the order of greatest force & inimitable by any art."[31]

Emerson once wrote that the only thing of value in the world is the active soul. In terms of lecturing, there was nothing as value-less to him as an inert audience that merely received his words intellectually and went home to dinner. He saw that the great majority of men slumbered in ignorance of their own potential, of their origin in the spirit and the wisdom in nature presented to them every day as a picture of the human being in its divine proportion. Overcoming this ignorance provided the impetus for Emerson to climb into the lectern time and time again. "The whole secret of the teacher's force lies in the conviction that men are convertible," he wrote; "And they are. They want awakening. Get the soul out of bed, out of her deep habitual sleep, out into God's universe, to a perception of its beauty and hearing of its call, and your vulgar man, your prosy, selfish sensualist awakes, a god, and is conscious of force to shake the world." With the Order of Wonder, Emerson sought not to build up walls of thought, but to open doors of perception.[32] The core purpose of the lecture was to ensure that "every man in the presence of the orator [feels] that he has not only got the documents in his pocket to answer to all his cavils & to prove all his positions, but he has the eternal reason in his head."[33] His intent in lecturing was to provide a temple that the people in the audience could enter into, where the Genius could speak to them directly. In every audience he saw something excellent, a capacity for virtue that was expectant. "They are ready to be beatified also," he perceived, and "know so much more than the orators." The key element that united listener and speaker in the Word, however, was always the same: love, and only love, the unutterable love opened in him by Ellen, could accomplish such a thing.

In the midst of the winter lecture series of 1836-1837, Emerson coasted on a wave of energy and enthusiasm impelled by the success of the inspiration working in his lectures: "I seem to vie with the brag of Puck;— 'I can put a girdle round about the world in forty minutes.' I take fifty."[34] On August 31, 1837, one year after the publication of *Nature*, Emerson delivered an oration before the Phi Beta Kappa Society of Harvard College that he later entitled "The American Scholar." The subject of the oration was the accepted topic of tradition for the graduation exercises of the Society and the tenor of the oration was revolution and change. He took his audience into the past, to ancient Greek civilization, then to medieval France, and finally into the present European civilization, noting that in each of these the basis of cultural gatherings and celebrations was "for games of strength or skill, for the recitation of histories tragedies, and odes;" "for parliaments of love and poesy;" and "for the advancement of science." Emerson informed his audience that a greater day was at hand. He declared that "our day of dependence, our long apprenticeship to the learning of other lands, draws to a close. The millions that around us are rushing into life, cannot always be fed on the sere remains of foreign harvests." America would have its literature, its poetry—would become something more than a land of commerce and industry. At the height of this crescendo came the prophecy: "Who can doubt that poetry will revive and lead in a new age, as the star in the constellation Harp, which now flames in our zenith, astronomers announce shall one day be the pole-star for a thousand years?" Emerson, in one comprehensive stroke, connected the sweep of human history and the development of poetry to the laws of nature and the divine plan embedded in the wisdom of the cosmos. This grand introduction led to Emerson's central theme: the American Scholar, Man-Thinking, who would bring forth this age of poetry through the influences of nature, books, and experience upon him, and the content of his character. For Emerson, the time for the American Scholar to appear was not off in the near or distant future, but there and then, in the immediate present. Oliver Wendell Holmes, who attended the oration, wrote that on that August day Emerson had delivered "our intellectual Declaration of Independence." In that hall, for a brief space in time, Emerson created a temple, a dwelling place for the spirit that would inspire a new American culture.

V.

THE TRANSCENDENTALIST

The Siege of the Hencoop

As the sons of the men who had founded Unitarianism came of age, the sons too of Harvard, they began to feel that their fathers had missed something vital. The first whispers that the elder Unitarian radicals may not have gone far enough reached the ears of the young men through Herder, Schiller, and Goethe; through Coleridge, Wordsworth and Carlyle; and through Sampson Reed, the great exponent of the Swedenborgian Church in America—through writers whom the "old school" had summarily dismissed with the charge of obscurity. In cautious reviews published in The Christian Examiner, the official Unitarian journal, the new school began timidly to push the boundaries of what their fathers were willing to concede, to obliquely suggest where they had gone wrong. They drew strength and confidence from each other. From January of 1832 to November of 1835, George Ripley, Frederic Henry Hedge, and Orestes Brownson published a series of reviews and articles that exposed the first cracks in the

Unitarian edifice. What Ripley began as a general apology for German literature became a close-fisted blow in March of 1833 when Hedge published an article on Coleridge in which he blatantly stated, regarding the charge of "obscurity" leveled by the elders, that "to those only is he obscure who have no depths within themselves corresponding to his depths."[1] Hedge, at the end of his life, described this article as "the first word, so far as I know, which any American had uttered in respectful recognition of the claims of Transcendentalism." In September of 1834 Brownson joined the fray with a review of Benjamin Constant in which he predicted the inevitable collapse of Unitarianism and its intellectualism, and looked for the emergence of a new nucleus "round which already gravitate the atoms of a new moral and religious world."[2] The following year, Ripley launched the shot that split the Unitarians wide open, accusing the elder generation of tricking their congregants with their rejection of Calvinism and original sin while secretly holding the insulting doctrine that human beings could not discover religion for themselves, but depended upon divine favor and the assistance of miracles. Andrews Norton, perhaps the most outspoken and dominating personality of the elder generation, responded with definitive outrage, joining a battle that would play out over the next five years.[3]

This younger generation of radicals gravitated naturally towards Emerson. On September 8, 1836, the day before *Nature* was published, Emerson met with Hedge, Ripley, and another like-minded individual named George Putnam to found the group that would later become known as the Transcendental Club. The purpose of the Club was to provide a forum where those who "found the present state of thought in America unsatisfactory" could gather and hold conversations on a model of open discussion about a specific topic given for the meeting. The topic at the group's third meeting, by way of example, was "What shall nourish the sense of beauty now?", a discussion about the lack of aesthetic or artistic endeavor in the country and what might be done to bring about a new genius in the Arts. The only rule of membership was that no one would be admitted who might exclude any particular line of conversation. Though the club was Hedge's idea, Emerson likely shaped the loose structure, for it bears a striking resemblance to the unnamed literary club that he had helped to found when a student at Harvard. Indeed, the formation of the group was a deliberate shot over the bow of the Unitarian establishment, which had its center at Harvard. The Club officially began on the day of Harvard's bicentennial celebration, and its aim was to foster the impulse that stood behind those same philosophers and writers who had been excluded from the College curriculum. Worse yet for the entrenched aristocracy of Boston and Cambridge, the Club was composed almost entirely of former or active Unitarian ministers and recent graduates of the Harvard Divinity School. Over the next four years the Club met thirty times, hosting anywhere from ten to more than twenty persons at each meeting. The original premise of the Club was open discussion. This quiet idealism soon gave way to vociferous activism.[4]

After leaving the Unitarian Second Church in 1832, Emerson himself had managed to avoid, for the most part, any further public attention, though his friends and particularly his wife sought his participation in a number of causes. The local activism centered on religion, but the national concern was slavery. Despite his exposure to the abolition movement through the newspapers, through Aunt Mary—who took it upon herself to invite a group of abolitionists to the Emerson household just a month after

Waldo and Lidian had married—and especially through Lidian herself, who dedicated herself wholeheartedly to the cause after meeting with the Grimké sisters in September of 1837, Emerson himself had been moved to speak out on the subject of slavery just once. Two months after the meeting with the Grimkés he had delivered an address following the shocking and violent murder of the abolitionist printer Elijah Lovejoy at the hands of a mob in Alton, Illinois. Emerson's feelings about sacrificing his well-guarded privacy to join the public voice on such an occasion may well be summed up in the few lines that he wrote in his Journal six months later, when he bowed to requests from his friends to write a letter to President Van Buren protesting the removal of the Cherokee people from their homeland: "this stirring in the philanthropic mud gives me no peace. I will let the Republic alone until the Republic comes to me. I fully sympathize, be sure, with the sentiment I write, but I accept it rather from my friends than dictate it. It is not my impulse to say it, and therefore my genius deserts me. No muse befriends, no music of thought or word accompanies. Bah!"[5] With these words he abandoned the role of social activist altogether.

Yet the debate on religion came home to Emerson on a personal level and began to draw him out. While he avoided the polemics that his friends in the Transcendental Club engaged in, he began to foment a private rebellion in the pages of his Journal. His thinking on Christianity and on the person of Jesus was stirred by the meetings of the Sunday Club, a group of Sunday school teachers that met regularly in his home, and by the new pastor of the church in Concord, one Barzillai Frost, whom he found especially distasteful. In March of 1838 he wrote, "I regret one thing omitted in my late course of Lectures: that I did not state with distinctness and conspicuously

the great error of modern society in respect to religion . . . Christ preaches
the greatness of man, but we hear only the greatness of Christ."[6] Again in
March, after a day at church that made him want to say that he would not go
again, his thoughts turned to his old office: "There is no better subject for
effective writing than the Clergy. I ought to sit and think, and then write a
discourse on the American Clergy, showing them the ugliness and unprof-
itableness of theology and churches at this day, and the glory and sweetness
of the moral nature out of whose pale they are almost wholly shut."[7] Then
in April he got his chance. The seniors of the Harvard Divinity School, after
meeting with him to talk about theism, invited him to address the class at
their graduation in July. Emerson accepted.

Though there were many topics that he could have chosen for such a
function, there was only one thing that he had to say to a group of young
ministers who were still exploring what it meant to be a minister of Christ.
The older men to whom his discourse would also be directed, however, were
men that he knew, men that, in some cases, had been his teachers and men-
tors. He knew they would view him as the son who had turned on the father
that nurtured and raised him. In the Journal entries just before the Address,
Emerson carefully explored and weighed the reasons why the clergy needed
to be opposed. The main thrust of his argument was that the proper examples for the modern age were human beings, not gods, and that idolizing
Jesus did a great injustice both to Christ and to man's own moral nature.
Christ he took as the only Man in history to have been fully awake, fully God.
Emerson considered Christ to be the greatest exponent of Character that
the world had ever seen. He believed that a Christianity in which the individual held a relationship to Christ through a line of tradition and ritual, that

maintained an earthly connection with the person and time of Jesus through a kind of relay race in which the right to know Christ was handed from generation to generation, was a profanation. Such knowledge came from the memory and not from the soul, thus destroying the power of preaching. God is, not was; speaketh, not spake: "That which shows God in me, fortifies me. That which shows God out of me, makes me a wart and a wen." The current ministers of the Gospel taught a dead religion; they had caused a famine in the churches. The only true religion, Emerson felt, is one that teaches that God lives and speaks in the heart of every individual. "In how many churches," he asked, "by how many prophets, tell me, is man made sensible that he is an infinite Soul; that the earth and heavens are passing into his mind; that he is drinking forever the soul of God?" The true preacher had to abandon all creeds, books, and rituals, all prophecies and miracles, and teach the soul and the infinitude of man by following the voice within: "cast behind you all conformity, and acquaint men at first hand with Deity" would be his advice to the students. Although the reasons to oppose the clergy were plain, the question occurred to him, why he was giving the speech at all. There was no good, solid, intellectual reason that he should give the address. The truth was that he held no grudge against Harvard, and he in fact admitted an instinctive reluctance "to take away titles of even false honor from Jesus." He knew very well that delivering the address could cause shock and controversy among family and friends; "but when I have as clear a sense as now that I am speaking simple truth," he wrote, "without any bias, any foreign interest in the matter,—all railing, all unwillingness to hear, all danger of injury to the conscience, dwindles and disappears."[8] In the midst of this strange sea of people and events, a single star shone in Emerson's heaven, and he chose to navigate by it. On July 15th, he delivered his fell stroke to Unitarianism and formal religion.

Word of the controversial Address at the Divinity School quickly spread, and the response from the religious establishment was swift and condemning. At the Phi Beta Kappa celebration in August, a month after the Divinity School "Address," there was already talk of Emerson being ostracized. Paragraphs against him began to appear regularly in the newspapers. Even Aunt Mary thought that a devil was speaking through her nephew. By October of 1838 the attacks on Emerson were so pervasive that even the integrity of Carlyle and the reputation of Goethe were threatened, for the heretical lecturer had acted as agent in America for the books of the former and was known to support and publicize the works of the latter. On the eighteenth of October, Emerson wrote Carlyle asking him to postpone his visit to America until "this storm in our washbowl" had passed. He did not entertain illusions that the effect of the campaign of criticism would spare his own career as a lecturer. He was thinking seriously of learning to fish and hunt so that he would not be a burden on his friends and family if he were cast out of society.

Members of the Transcendental Club came out publicly in support of Emerson, and several of them wrote replies to Andrews Norton and other attackers in the local papers. Emerson's reaction to his advocates may seem strange: "I hate to be defended in a newspaper. As long as all that is said is said *against* me, I feel a certain sublime assurance of success, but as soon as honied words of praise are spoken for me, I feel as one that lies unprotected before his enemies."[9] To engage in the kind of polemic and argumentation that George Ripley and Orestes Brownson relished in the early days of Transcendentalism was not only contrary to Emerson's style and personality, but to his deepest spiritual goals as well. On September 16, 1838, he returned to the Old Manse, to the Concord battlefield, and "renewed my vows to the Genius of that place." Four years before he had vowed not to write or speak anything that was not "entirely and peculiarly my own work;" now he was experiencing the reality of what it meant to follow that star unerringly. Emerson's vow was a vow for truth, not the truths that everyone accepts when they are spoken, but the hard truths that refute core assumptions and deny the easy comfort of resting in the prevailing opinion of the hour. Emerson held such truths to be indefensible, that is, they were beyond argumentation. Any effort to argue, Emerson felt, was an admission that what had been said was not Truth, but merely a new round of polemic banter. His refusal to acknowledge criticism and honied praise alike was the Janus face of the principle of Inspiration that was central to the goal of his lecturing. The well-intentioned efforts of his friends on his behalf made him shrink and affected him as much as the attacks. Likewise, when later that year his old mentor, Henry Ware, Jr., wrote him a letter inviting him to defend or amplify what he had said in the "Address," he refused. It was the renewal of the vow that gave him strength, for the vow was the kernel of Self-reliance. Shortly after arriving in Concord and making his original vow four years earlier, he had written out an aphorism in his Journal: "It is very easy in the world to live by the opinion of the world. It is very easy in solitude to be self-centered. But the finished man is he who in the midst of the crowd keeps with perfect sweetness the independence of solitude."[10] Emerson now experienced the true hardship of that principle and the peril that lay in being rudely dragged from his position as an innocuous lecturer onto a public stage where he was ridiculed by the establishment and fawned over by young admirers. Both, he said, disrupted his equanimity and made him unfit for writing or working.[11]

Emerson's problems with the Concord Circle went beyond what he viewed as their misguided attempts to defend him. "If you rail at bodies of men," he wrote, "at institutions, and use vulgar watchwords, as bank, aristocracy; agrarianism; etc., I do not believe you. I expect no fruit. The true reformer sees that a soul is an infinite, and addresses himself to one mind."[12] The members of this Transcendental Club could become tedious in their own right. Henry Thoreau could be stubborn and eccentric, and he seemed perpetually shy of fulfilling his own potential. Alcott, he had to agree at times, was "one-toned, and hearkens with no interest to books or conversation out of the scope of his one commanding idea." Sometimes he simply would not shut up about himself. He also lacked the ability to undertake any project without continuously asking for money and time. Young Jones Very refused to accept any of Emerson's suggestions for editing his poems since he felt that the words came to him directly from God, and of course it would not do to edit God. Emerson was at times so disenchanted that he attempted, perhaps half-heartedly, to disassociate himself from the Transcendentalists altogether. On a lecture tour that took him to Rhode Island he wrote his mother, "I am reckoned here a Transcendentalist" and "carried duly about from house to house" by the citizens, but "in vain I disclaim all knowledge of *that sect of Lidian's.*" Emerson almost seemed to stand outside of the Concord Circle, watching with a sort of bemused frustration, seeming to be a third party not only to their ideas of activism but to their affections as well. Few of his friends could learn as quickly as did Alcott on his first visit to Emerson's house how delicate a gift this friendship of Emerson's was, and how far its boundaries extended: "Emerson must never know that where he had given only his admiration, his strong and faithful help, his wise council, and the partnership of his deep poetic mind, Bronson Alcott had given no less than his whole heart."[13]

In the fall of 1839, while criticism still churned in the wake of the year-old Divinity School "Address," Emerson expressed doubts about giving another course of lectures after the coming winter.[14] As he prepared himself for his sixth season of lecturing, he wrote, "once more I must renew my work, and I think only once in the same form, though I see that he who thinks he does something for the last time ought not to do it at all."[15] His objection did not stem from a dissatisfaction with the lectures themselves, so much as with the forum in which he had to give them, the Lyceum circuit and the system of ticket-selling upon which it was based. The Lyceum was a loose affiliation of lecture houses that was formed to promote popular education through public lectures, and it was on this circuit that Emerson had originally found the ideal vehicle for his lectures, a hall that had neither the doctrinal niceties of a church nor the topical restrictions of a scientific society. In the Lyceums, the integrity of the thought itself became the motivation for speaking, the reason to stand before an audience, and Emerson had accepted selling tickets as a concession to "the concatenation of errors called society." The economic necessity of lecturing, coupled with the past year of controversy, cast a shadow on the creative process of preparing the lectures. Collecting Journal passages and writing itself became laborious. Instead of shaping his thoughts according to their natural order and preparing a temple for the Genius, he began to experience the Lyceum as an institution that demanded he write lectures because his pocketbook required it, a building full of people who expected their money's worth. When he finished the lecture series in February of 1840, it became apparent that the problem he had faced in October had taken on new dimensions. Not only had his preparation for the lectures been beset by problems, but the temple itself, the form whose construction was the entire purpose of his preparation, had collapsed. In his account of the series he wrote,

> These lectures give me little pleasure. I have not done what I hoped when I said, I will try it once more. I have not once transcended the coldest self-possession. I said I will agitate others, being agitated myself, I dared to hope for exstasy[sic] and eloquence . . . Alas! Alas! I have not the recollection of one strong moment. A cold mechanical preparation for a delivery as decorous—fine things, pretty things—but no arrows, no axes, no nectar, no growling, no transpiercing, no loving, no enchantment.

He felt that he had not achieved the l'abandon that he considered the height of the art of lecturing, had failed in uniting himself and the audience through the eloquence excited within him by the presence of Genius. "I seem to lack constitutional vigor to attempt each topic as I ought," he wrote; "I ought to seek to lay myself out utterly—large, enormous, prodigal, upon the subject of the week." The reason he could not do so, he thought, was that in order to have the strength and faculty to prepare and deliver the next lecture expected of him, he could spend only twenty-one hours on each lecture, on the average. The result, "of course, I spend myself prudently; I economize; I cheapen; whereof nothing grand ever grew."[16] His "cold mechanical preparation," marked by a lack of strength and perseverance, could not produce a vessel fit for habitation by a muse. Even if he succeeded in putting words and sentences on a page and getting up in front of an audience, even if his audiences applauded and praised him, there was no life, no heart, no voice.

The failure of the lectures would affect Emerson throughout the remainder of the year. After the Boston lectures he continued his usual tour to other New England towns, but his heart was not in it. In Providence he was warmly welcomed and invited to deliver additional lectures, but he declined. He became wistful. He did not read. In a strange way, he was reliving his experience teaching at the girls' school fifteen years earlier; the disillusionment, the displeasure at performing his job poorly, the sense of being held back by a mechanical routine had all returned. Above all, the coldness that had consumed him and penetrated his heart had come back with new force, touching with a chilled finger the lectures themselves. When he closed the Boston lectures, he complained that he had "not once transcended the coldest self-possession." The familiar coldness had lain dormant for so many years; it now returned, and he was overcome by a listlessness that lasted into spring. The flaw was not in the lectures, but in his character. For all of the progress that he had made since returning from Europe, there was still a significant defect within that rose to the surface through his vocation and yet could not be mended by it. It was not a virtue that he could teach himself. He needed the loving touch of a friend—of many friends. He wanted to turn earnestly to writing essays but the failure of the winter lectures extended to his writing as well. The page, like the podium, was still and cold.

His own resources exhausted, Emerson finally attempted, for the first time since the death of Charles, to allow another human being to become close to him. Margaret Fuller, a forceful, brilliant intellectual whom he had known since 1836, became his favorite correspondent, his confidante, his best friend. The basis for their deepening friendship was the launch of the *Dial*, a literary magazine that grew out of the discussions of the Transcendental Club. Fuller agreed early in 1840 to be the *Dial*'s editor, and she turned to Emerson for assistance in preparing each issue. Throughout that spring and into the summer, Emerson found more and more of his time taken up with reading and judging the essays and poems that Fuller sent him, as well as soliciting friends and acquaintances for new material. Essays by Thoreau, poems by Ellery Channing, "Orphic Sayings" by Alcott and contributions from many others, all had to be carefully read and edited. Emerson also devoted much energy to his own contributions, writing an introduction to the first issue, a companion piece to Channing's poetry, several essays, and many poems. The bulk of Emerson's correspondence in 1840 was to Fuller, and the majority of these were at least partly or wholly devoted to discussing the *Dial*, or "Dialling" as he and Fuller called it. Though he sometimes grumbled that the intensive work took him away from his own studies, it was clear that he had found a fresh source of energy and creativity.

In the summer of 1840 Emerson grew close to three other people as well: Samuel Ward, Anna Barker, and Caroline Sturgis. Friends had started to gather around him as early as 1836, just before the publication of *Nature*, but Emerson had always looked at these new seekers with a sense of wonder, never quite comprehending how it was that such affection and devotion could be directed towards him with so little apparent reason. In 1840 this sense of awe deepened as these four friends sought to become ever closer to him. To Fuller he wrote, "I do not know how I have ever deserved any friends. I behold them as they approach with wonder. If they depart from me I shall not wonder more."[17] He became so immersed in the mystery of relationships, in the invisible laws that drew human beings to love each other and work together in one time and place, that he devoted more and more of his time to these four friends. He came to think of these months as his "summer of friendships," spending much of his time writing letters and visiting. After his usual habit, he gathered material to write an essay on friendship in order to explore that strangely elusive phenomenon of human interaction. Above all, he opened himself up to his friends' feelings, let them wash over him, and attempted to let himself live within them. He felt himself drawn into a new heaven and swore to Elizabeth Hoar that he was "sufficiently disposed to drink the last drop, if such there be, out of this horn of nectar which the new Hours offer me. Have I always been a hermit, and unable to approach my fellow men, & do the Social Divinities suddenly offer me a *roomful* of friends? Please God, I will not be wanting to my fortune but will eat this pomegranate,—seeds stem and leaves—with thankfulness."[18]

Within the world of friendship, unlike in the world of thought, Emerson was a stranger. He had spent much of his life forsaking his own health in pursuit of his father's vocation. Too often he had loved another human being only to have them snatched away by death. It required a conscious effort on his part to receive friendship. At times he almost pleaded for insight, writing to Fuller, "give me more tidings of your friends. They are as pleasant to me as the south wind over myrrh and roses."[19] Margaret, for her part, sought an ever-deepening friendship with Emerson, touching upon topics of emotion and thought that he had long buried deep. Though he willingly gave what he could, there remained a certain reserve that began to frustrate his friend. In August of 1840, as the summer of friendships drew to a close, Fuller reprimanded Emerson for his selfishness, accusing him of "inhospitality of soul." While he agreed with her that reservation on the part of a friend was perhaps a denial of real friendship, he wrote that "a friend is not made in a day nor by our will."[20] Unsatisfied with this answer, Margaret pushed for more, but Emerson demurred. She had drawn him into a world of friendships from which, he mused, he could "never quite go back to my old arctic habits," yet he could not feel that they were one thought in the Divine Mind, as she desired them to be, but "two thoughts, that we meet and treat like foreign states... whose trade and laws are essentially unlike." At the end of September, he was willing to accept that they would be a puzzle to each other, willing even to "make out a case of difference & ... open all my doors to your sunshine and morning air."[21] Fuller denied that she would make too much claim on him: "I am no usurper," she wrote, and if he could not find the common ground on which to meet her then "you are not the friend I seek."[22] Emerson brought the discussion to an abrupt halt on the twenty-fourth of October, chiding her that "I ought never to have suffered you to lead me into any conversation or writing on our relation." Fuller wanted the same thing that Brownson and Ripley wanted of him—a total commitment, an offering of all of his love, his passion. Emerson, however, had to be himself; he could not be what his friends wanted him to be.

Despite the bonds of friendship he had forged that summer, he seemed further from the Transcendentalists than ever that fall. There is perhaps no better example of this distance from his contemporaries than the Journal record in October of a meeting in which George Ripley and his wife Sophia, Margaret Fuller, and Alcott tried to convince him to join Brook Farm, a social experiment in sustainable community living that sought to foster individual and artistic freedom. Although he wished "to be made nobly mad by the kindlings before my eye of a new dawn of human piety," he may as well have been in the next room for all that their ideas concerned him. "And not once could I be inflamed," he wrote the next day, "but sat aloof and thoughtless; my voice faltered and fell. . . . I do not wish to remove from my present prison to a prison a little larger. I wish to break all prisons. I have not yet conquered my own house. . . . Shall I raise the siege of this hencoop, and march baffled away to a pretended siege of Babylon?" The reason he could not devote himself to their idea was that it did not agree with his own, for by going to live at Brook Farm "it seems to me that so to do were to dodge the problem I am set to solve, and to hide my impotence in the thick of the crowd." Emerson did not feel that he could ever come to their way of thinking: "I can see too, afar,—that I should not find myself more than now,—no not so much, in that select, but not by me selected, fraternity. Moreover, to join this body [Brook Farm] would be to traverse all my long trumpeted theory, and the instinct which spoke from it, that one man is a counterpoise to a city,—that a man is stronger than a city, that his solitude is more prevalent and beneficent than the concert of crowds."[23]

A hundred reminders that a man is a counterpoise to a city could not lessen the seriousness with which he regarded the effort to revitalize American culture, nor could it serve as a reason to abandon the many who relied on him for guidance. He realized that the like-minded, the ones who shared his interest in core principles and thoughts, would not be sent to him. Disappointed in his companions but recognizing the essential purity of their intentions and their striving, he concluded that he had to "let his music be heard, let his flowers open, let his light shine, believing that invisible spectators and friends environ him. . . . Moreover, when once he attains a spiritual elevation sufficient to understand his daily life and the ministry to him of this motley crew, this galling prose will be poetry." His comfort in the midst of the loneliness brought on by the company of the Transcendentalists was that their presence actually represented part of the design of the "invisible friends and spectators," the angelic and spiritual beings whom he considered to be the patrons of the work that he had dedicated himself to. The divergence between Emerson's public persona and his private self became pronounced as a conflict emerged between what others demanded of him and what the higher law he had chosen to follow required of him. He resolved to treat this "motley crew" in the way that Alcott had perceived: "Give them your conversation; be to them a teacher, utter oracles, but admit them never into any infringement on your hours; keep state: be their priest, not their companion, for you cannot further their plans, you cannot counsel them on their affairs, and you have never pledged yourself to do so by confounding your relation to them."[24] He signed a peace treaty with the Transcendentalists.

The summer of 1840 drew to a close, and the circle of friends began to break up as Anna and Sam married in October and moved away. Emerson turned to his essays. The warmth of friendship had not fully dissipated the old coldness, which returned to attack his essay writing with new vigor: "My genius seemed to quit me in such a mechanical work [of writing the essays], a seeming wise—a cold exhibition of dead thoughts." The Genius did not return, and there was little encouragement for the success of the project, yet he forged ahead. Preparing the essays for publication occupied so much of his time that he laid aside his lecturing for the winter and devoted himself to shaping the twelve pieces that were to make up the first volume of his essays. He adopted a sedentary lifestyle, often shutting himself away in his study and receiving few visitors. He pored over his voluminous Journals and sorted through old lecture material, reworking the material sentence by sentence, then recasting it yet again and adding still more new material.[25] The weeks upon weeks of slow and painstaking work at last yielded results. When Emerson sent the Essays to press on the first of January, 1841, he was still dissatisfied with them, but conceded in his Journal, "what remains to be done to its imperfect chapters I will seek to do justly. I see no reason why we may not write with as much grandeur of spirit as we can serve or suffer. Let the page be filled with the character, not the skill of the writer."[26] Indeed, the writing of the essays became a matter of character. He certainly did not carry through the project because of the ease with which the material came to hand or because the sentences wrote themselves, which in the past they had often seemed to do. Writing became a matter of almost pure will, of discipline and application, offering no reward of inspiration, of elevation in the moment of delivery in a crowded lecture hall. The only reason to finish them was for the sake of the act itself. The completion of the book of essays, more than any literary or artistic achievement, signaled his development of the lonely virtue of perseverance.

The Fall of the Morning Star

Lidian was pregnant with their first child when Emerson wrote the greater part of *Nature*, and the beautiful boy was brought into the world the month after his father's first book was published. The coincidence of the two events had a special significance for Emerson. Little Waldo was for him the child of *Nature*. He experienced all of the brightness and promise of human life through his son, received glimpses of the divine through the babblings of an infant who insisted that his father's work had to be less important than hitching up his rocking horse. There was something in little Waldo's every gesture, in his simple and penetrating questions and observations, in the studied insistence of his play that was perpetually communicant with the Original and innocent, with the First Cause. "I have seen the poor boy," he wrote, "when he came to a tuft of violets in the wood, kneel down on the ground, smell of them, kiss them, and depart without plucking them."[27] The touch of his small hand could draw Emerson out of deep or idle speculation and cause him to rest in simple wonder. Waldo was the sum of Emerson's hopes, the affirmation of the beneficence of the Universal soul and the very proof that Love bound together the cosmos and caused the woodland flowers to bloom.

In his strong attachment to his son, Emerson seemed to want very much not to be the frightening presence his own father had been. He harbored an abiding hope for the boy's future. As he later confessed to Carlyle in a letter, after the Emerson family had further grown with the addition of two daughters, "we have two babes yet, one girl of three years, and one girl of three months and a week, but a promise like that Boy's I shall never see. How often I have pleased myself that one day I should send to you this Morning Star of mine, and stay at home gladly behind such a representative."[28] The poem "Threnody," his poem to his child, reveals exactly what he wanted Waldo to represent:

> Not mine,—I never called thee mine,
> But Nature's heir,— . . .
>   . . . .

> For flattering planets seemed to say,
> This child should ills of ages stay,
> By wondrous tongue, and guided pen,
> Bring the flown Muses back to men.

The future he imagined for Waldo was no less than the fulfillment of the mission that he had dedicated himself to when he returned from Europe, the reawakening of mankind to the prospects of the Spirit that he had prophesied in *Nature*. The father could fool himself into thinking that he recognized nothing of himself in his son, but in the end he still saw this small child as the future representative of all that he worked towards. His son even had his name.

In many ways Waldo was the child of Transcendentalism. Many of the women who came to the house delighted in the boy, especially Elizabeth Hoar, Margaret Fuller, and Caroline Sturgis. Little Waldo had one other friend among his father's who was especially close. In April of 1841, Henry Thoreau, then twenty-four, moved into the Emerson household to help plant a garden and orchard on the Emerson property in exchange for room and board. The arrangement was much to the advantage of both men. Emerson, in a weakened state owing to the extended effort he had put into preparing the *Essays*, needed the air and exercise that the garden promised in order to work his way back to health, but he did not have the strength to tackle the project alone. Thoreau the young scholar and aspiring poet, was having difficulty earning a living, wondering what to make of himself and turning over the idea of becoming a farmer after his efforts at starting a school with his brother John had ended in disappointment earlier in the spring. Just when Thoreau's hopes had reached their nadir, Emerson opened his home to him.

The two worked side by side through the spring, and Emerson regained his strength as the garden took shape. Drawn into the Emerson family circle, Thoreau formed an instant friendship with little Waldo, who tottered playfully about the yard while the two men worked. Emerson remarked on their unusually fast relationship: "Henry Thoreau . . . charmed Waldo by the variety of toys, whistles, boats, pop-guns and all kinds of instruments which he could make and mend; and he possessed his love and respect by the gentle firmness with which he always treated him."[29] The friendship was quite natural; the boy who seemed attended by the woodland spirits played with the man who seemed able to teach Emerson the language of nature. Thoreau accompanied Emerson on his favorite walks, pointing out the various flora and fauna, unraveling the mysteries of the ecology of Concord's woods and fields. On a boat trip in June, Emerson described how "the good river-god has taken the form of my valiant Henry Thoreau here & introduced me to the riches of his shadowy, starlit, moonlit stream."[30] Yet Thoreau also frustrated Emerson: "I told Henry Thoreau that his freedom is in the form," Emerson wrote later that fall, "but he does not disclose new matter. I am very familiar with all his thoughts,—they are my own quite originally drest. But if the question be, what new ideas has he thrown into circulation, he has not yet told what that is which he was created to say."[31]

On January 11, 1842, Henry Thoreau's brother John, with whom he was very close, died of lockjaw. In the week that followed, Henry developed a sympathetic illness and himself began to show severe symptoms of the disease that had killed his brother. When Emerson returned home from his winter lectures on January twenty-second, Henry's symptoms were at their worst. By Monday morning, however, Emerson could write that the symptoms had subsided enough to dispel worry. That night his son came down with scarlet fever. Three days later, on January twenty-seventh at fifteen minutes after eight, little Waldo died. He was just five years old. Henry was stricken by the death, particularly after the events of the previous two weeks. He too had seen the ineffable unity of Waldo with nature: "He died as the mist rises from the brook," he wrote to Lidian's sister, "which the sun will soon dart his rays through. Do not the flowers die every autumn? He had not even taken root here. . . . Neither will Nature manifest any sorrow at his death, but soon the note of the lark will be heard down in the meadow, and fresh dandelions will spring from the stocks where he plucked them last summer."[32]

Emerson could find no such brave words. The grief that he felt at the passing of his first child was like what he had experienced after Ellen's death, though with the loss of Ellen he had at least held the hope that they would meet again in the spirit beyond the gates of death. With Waldo he discovered not even this consolation. All that the father knew was burned up, and he was left in a world he did not recognize. His ideal, his Morning Star, had fallen into the sea. Waldo had been tied to nature itself, and his death left in its wake a world stripped of soul. On the Sunday after Waldo's passing Emerson woke at three o'clock to hear

> every cock in every barnyard . . . shrilling with the most unnecessary noise. The sun went up the morning sky with all his light, but the landscape was dishonored by this loss. For this boy, in whose remembrance I have both slept and awaked so oft, decorated for me the morning star, the evening cloud,—how much more all the particulars of daily economy.[33]

Emerson wrote to Caroline soon after little Waldo's death, "I chiefly grieve that I cannot grieve; that this fact takes no more deep hold than other facts, is as dreamlike as they."[34] In truth grief hollowed him out, left him empty and bereaved to such a depth that his heart was stricken with numbness. Having thundered forward into this new career, having regained hope and vitality and purpose of life, having achieved a victory over Ahriman, here was the old hollowness again, consuming, now made bitter by unspeakable sorrow. Waldo's death was a portal to emptiness and oblivion.

The necessities of life did not allow Emerson pause to grieve. The day before Waldo came down with the fever, Emerson had been reckoning his accounts after closing the winter lecture series in Boston, a series of eight ambitiously entitled "The Times." Though the lectures had been successful, they had not made enough to offset his debts from the previous year, and he reluctantly settled on the need to carry the lectures to Rhode Island. Not two weeks after his son's death he was in Providence to give five lectures over seven days, hoping the series would bring in enough to make a third trip that winter unnecessary. The audience was small, however, and there was little choice but to schedule a third extended engagement. He was home with his grieving family only a week before departing for New York City, where three or four hundred people came to hear him deliver six lectures from "The Times" over the course of eleven days in March. Save for a handful of single lectures near home, it would be his last trip until December.

The signature lecture of the New York series was "The Poet." Emerson had lectured only a half dozen times the previous winter, while he was finishing the *Essays*, and had not prepared new lectures for over a year and a half before he had started composing this lecture in October. "The Poet" was not a description of an abstract principle of what a poet should be, but a kind of prophecy of an individual who would one day appear and shatter the old conventions, bringing about a revolution not only in poetry but in culture and society as well. When Emerson returned to writing lectures after his long confinement in what he felt was the more cramped and formal style of the essay, he was charged with new enthusiasm for the unique possibility of the lecture to act as a form for a governing thought that could descend at the moment of eloquent delivery and exalt all who were gathered to hear. In "The Poet" Emerson advanced further towards the goal of constructing such a temple. A reporter named Walter Whitman, who was in the audience the day Emerson gave the lecture in New York, described it as "one of the richest and most beautiful compositions, both for its matter and style, we have heard anywhere, at any time." "The Poet" was in many ways the encapsulation of all the hopes and dreams Emerson had invested in his own son. When he had written the words the previous fall, the reality of what he was describing must have seemed eminent and apparent in the person of his first child. There was something profoundly sad in his standing before that audience in New York to describe a future of which he was now bereft.

The lecture was Emerson's prophecy, his unqualified description of the poet who would one day appear as the master of all language, benefactor of the world, the interpreter who sees and comprehends nature and society and turns it out again as his best report to his fellow human beings. He began the lecture by indicating the inviolable source of poetry as a muse or angel who sits among the hierarchies of angels. He then identified the act of expression as the relating of those highest spiritual facts to his fellow man through the use of symbol and metaphor, employing the smallest things to express the greatest truths. Emerson did not see the poet to come as dwelling high above in the unreachable aeries of the muse, but down among the rough or painful or joyous facts of existence. The poet would be equally at home in rich men's palaces or poor men's huts, related to all things and expressing all things, the tragic, painful, sorrowful, and fearful as well as good cheer, love, and beauty. Emerson described how the facts of the world down to the lowest and most common would form the poet's dictionary, how the poet would shape these according to his intellect and perception to express new and higher facts. He predicted the end of rhymed verse as the poet invented new meters to clothe new images, for "new topics, new powers, a new spirit arise, which threaten to abolish all that was called poetry, in the melodious thunder of the new."[35] He closed the lecture where he began, with the "Genius of the times," that spirit which is perpetual and large, which works through and governs all aspects of culture, society, and daily life. The appearance of the poet was inevitable, Emerson stated, because the actions of this resistless spirit demanded expression. Lest those gathered to hear him think his prophecy spoke of a time in the far distant future, he ended with words directed out towards the audience: we are all poets at last, eternal and immense, though we recognize this only in the high and solemn moments of life. The poet is the one who sees and celebrates this marvel whilst we sleep.

In April, left to his own thoughts after the end of the lecture season, Emerson began to write a poem on the death of his son. It ached with the father's loss—

> The South-wind brings
> Life, sunshine and desire,
> And on every mount and meadow

Breathes aromatic fire;
But over the dead he has no power,
The lost, the lost, he cannot restore;
And, looking over the hills, I mourn
The darling who shall not return.

. . .

The hyacinthine boy, for whom
Morn well might break and April bloom,
The gracious boy, who did adorn
The world whereinto he was born,
And by his countenance repay
The favor of the loving Day,—
Has disappeared from the Day's eye;
Far and wide she cannot find him;

. . .

Nature, who lost, cannot remake him;
Fate let him fall, Fate can't retake him;
Nature, Fate, men, him seek in vain.

The poem continued, the pain gaining depth and breadth through 174 lines. But Emerson could not finish it. He arrived at a point in his grief beyond which he could not go, beyond which he saw no renewal. For two years he would not be able to pick up the poem again; for two years his sorrow would not mitigate. He could find "no experiences nor progress to reconcile me to the calamity," no words to capture the unfathomable and unwelcome mischief of Fate that had shredded hope.[36] The reminders came twice a year, on Waldo's birthday and on his death day. There was no harmony in the fact, no continuity that fit any theory, ideal, or plan. He had secretly dreamt that Waldo would be everything the Transcendentalists seemed to promise, but without their flaws, their eccentricities—the herald of the procession of Soul without the Transcendental peculiarities. Waldo's death—the death of beauty, the death of hope, the death of his Ideal—threatened to overwhelm him with grief.

Serving the Concord Circle

The day that Emerson returned home from lecturing, he received a letter from Margaret Fuller saying that she could no longer edit the *Dial* because the magazine was failing and her health was too poor for her to sustain it. Emerson first responded that he could not accept the responsibility of carrying the *Dial* beyond one more issue. As he pondered over the course of the next few days, he turned restlessly between the void of his son's death and this great burden that Margaret had placed on his doorstep. On March twentieth he wrote, "I comprehend nothing of this fact [Waldo's death] but its bitterness. Explanation I have none, consolation none that rises out of the fact itself; only diversion; only oblivion of this, and pursuit of new objects."[37] He admonished himself that "a new day, a new harvest, new duties, new men, new fields of thought, new powers call you, and an eye fastened on the past unsuns nature, bereaves me of hope, and ruins me with a squalid indigence which nothing but death can adequately symbolize."[38] He finally came to realize the inevitable: "the *Dial* is to be sustained or ended, and I must settle the question, it seems, of its life or death." The next day, March twenty-first, he wrote to Margaret saying that he would edit the Transcendentalist's magazine and take full responsibility for it. From the grim outlook that the *Dial* might see only one more issue, his confidence grew into optimism about an indefinite run: "We will hope that our Dial will one day grow so great & rich as to pay its old debts."[39] When Emerson decided to become editor of the *Dial*, he effectively became what he never could have dreamed of becoming, what he would previously have run from with all the speed left in his legs: the figurehead and leader of the American Transcendentalists, the editor of their symbolic hub, the chief representative of those who had gone to Brook Farm for those who had remained in Concord and those others who were scattered throughout New England and beyond.

Emerson's interactions with the Transcendentalists that spring seemed marked by a new willingness to accept responsibility for ensuring that their endeavors succeeded. The same day he agreed to edit the *Dial*, Emerson wrote a letter of introduction to his old friend Carlyle on behalf of Alcott. He had agreed to finance Alcott's trip to England in order that his friend might visit a school that was named after him and founded on his principles of education. Emerson's letter to Carlyle concerning Alcott's impending visit contained an entreaty: "If you have heard his name before, forget what you have heard," he wrote; "Especially if you have read anything to which his name was attached, be sure to forget that; and, inasmuch as in you lies, permit this stranger, when he arrives at your gate, to make a new and primary impression."[40] Emerson learned quickly that he would have to receive everyone who came within his compass as he wished Carlyle to receive Alcott. His prejudices would not govern how he interacted with them. On October twenty-first, Alcott returned home from England with the two men who had founded the English school, the Fourierists Charles Wright and Henry Lane. When the men arrived in Concord, it was Emerson who organized a summit of the "triumvirate" with the Brook Farmers in his own house in order that they could discuss the new socialist ideas. Open-mindedness did not come easy to Emerson; it was a perpetual struggle. Just after the Fourierist summit, Alcott came to him with an idea to start a farm as an experiment in pure and innocent living and the hope that the land for the farm and the crops might be bought for them by similarly idealistic well-wishers. Emerson's first reaction was to strongly reject it.[41] Yet two days later

Emerson wrote to Henry Hedge, one of the original founders of the Transcendental Club, of Alcott and his friends: "they talk of buying a farm in these parts to realize their high ideas. May they prosper."[42]

The Transcendental Club was just over five years old at the time of little Waldo's passing, and his friends had always viewed Emerson as its heart, its patron. Ideas for this social experiment or that political protest were always brought to him, and he would give his opinion and often monetary support. His friend, Oliver Wendell Holmes, characterized Emerson's role in the cultural revolution of Transcendentalism by saying "Nothing is plainer than that it was Emerson's calling to supply impulses and not methods. He was not an organizer, but a power behind many organizers, inspiring them with lofty motive, giving breath to their views."[43] In a toast made at the Phi Beta Kappa dinner in 1837, Charles Henry Warren had stood and saluted Emerson, "I give you *the Spirit of Concord; it makes us all of One Mind.*" Emerson was the bearer of an inspiration, one that began to work in him while in Europe. This inspiration, associated with a cultural movement that traveled from east to west, appeared in the philosophy and literature of German Idealism and in the poetry of English Romanticism. When it appeared in America, it retained its character of *Sturm und Drang,* of rebellion and reform. Ripley had to found Brook Farm, even though it ruined him financially for the larger portion of his life. Alcott nearly starved his family in pursuit of his ideals. And Emerson had to deliver the Divinity School "Address," even though it made him a pariah.

There have been many efforts to define what Transcendentalism is, and in a certain sense all of these must stop short at Emerson's essay "The Transcendentalist." In this essay he stated that "there is no such thing as a

Transcendental *party*." There can be no Transcendental party because the essence of Transcendentalism is freedom. True freedom arises out of the "transfer of the world into the consciousness," the testing and measuring of all things against the Self and the expression of this Self in the powers of thought: "I—this thought which is called I—is the mold into which the world is poured like melted wax." This characterization of the Transcendental Movement helps to clarify the great problems that Emerson's friends encountered when joining together for any kind of concerted effort. Their individualism was so powerful that at times they could perhaps better be called the Concord Tangents than the Concord Circle. Emerson also viewed Transcendentalism in a positive light as "Idealism as it appears in 1842," the unfolding in the mid-nineteenth century in Boston of a world-historic governing Idea that Emerson also associated with the Stoics of ancient Rome. What Emerson encountered in the Jardins des Plantes in Paris, what struck him as the insight into the hidden relation between nature and human beings, was Idealism as a world-historic idea untethered by place and time, and for this reason he could trace it to Germany in the age of Goethe or to Rome nineteen hundred years before. The Spirit of Idealism inspired Emerson and worked through him; indeed, he was the primary agent through which it unfolded its activity in America. He spent his hours and days seeking this spirit so that it might touch his essays and lectures, yet after the death of little Waldo he began to recognize its presence in the very friends that crowded around him.

In the winter of 1842, his own financial situation still in perilous straits, he paid the costs of the ailing *Dial* out of his own pocket. The flagship publication of the Transcendentalists had till then demanded only the commitment of time, a precious commodity to Emerson; now it asked of him treasure as well. He did what lecturing he could that winter to try to make up for the money that he increasingly poured into his friends' projects. In addition to the endless hours spent soliciting, collecting, and editing material for the *Dial*, Emerson also made it his duty to take the young Ellery Channing under his wing and build his reputation as a poet. For several years Emerson had collected Channing's poetry for publication in the *Dial*; he now made it his task to edit a book of the younger man's poetry that would go to the publisher that spring. In addition to these projects, he was still providing Thoreau with roof, board, and a job as gardener, and he continued to act as the chief agent for the American editions of Carlyle's books. In March Emerson was again on the verge of abandoning the *Dial*, but a few words of encouragement from Carlyle were sufficient to renew his commitment to sustaining the publication. Channing's book of poetry finally appeared the first week of May, at about the same time that Alcott and Lane purchased a farm where they would try out their utopian ideas. The same week Thoreau moved out of Emerson's house to go and tutor William Emerson's children in New York. In October, Emerson added the responsibility of serving as the curator of the Concord Lyceum and arranging for lecturers for the coming season. Shortly after Thoreau returned from New York in late November, Alcott's farm—dubbed "Fruitlands"—fell into financial crisis. In desperation, Lane wrote to Emerson asking him to buy the property and be his agent. Already tapped to his limit, Emerson could do nothing. The small community was forced to abandon the land in early January. In April of 1844, unable to sustain it any longer, Emerson put out the last issue of the *Dial*, sad and disappointed that it had not drawn more recognition and created more of a stir. Everywhere he looked his friends were departing, most of them for Europe. The Concord Circle was breaking apart. In October he published the capstone of his contribution to Transcendentalism, the second series of *Essays*. Emerson would not write another essay devoted to the themes of Transcendentalism for the remainder of his life.

Emerson had poured his time and money into supporting the Transcendentalists and their projects, but the opportunity for him to facilitate the culminating event of Transcendentalism cost him very little. Sometime in March of 1845, Thoreau approached Emerson and asked permission to squat on a few acres of land that Emerson owned by Walden Pond in order to build a cabin in which he wished to live alone by the shore. The previous September Emerson had purchased the land, some fourteen acres of pine grove and field on the edge of the pond, which had been a familiar walking ground for years. The request could hardly have come as a surprise to Emerson, who for the last several years had worked closely with his young friend not only as mentor, guide, editor, and critic, but as employer and agent. Thoreau had considered the idea of retreating to a cabin on some lonely hill or by some pond since before he had moved into the Emerson household. When Thoreau broached the idea to his friends, they could only stare at him in bewilderment and ask what useful employment he could hope to find alone in the woods. Only Emerson, who had made it his task to sustain the young man materially until he found that defining moment that would enable him to spring forward with irresistible force, appreciated Thoreau's restless and often frustrated search for the marrow of life. His employment of Thoreau as his gardener, the stint he had given Thoreau as editor of the *Dial* in 1843, the job he had arranged tutoring his brother's children, the numerous poems and essays he had edited, promoted, and distributed—all had been but preparation for the moment at hand. Emerson gladly agreed to allow his friend free use of the land for as long as he wished. Thoreau's friends and his biographers, unable to take Thoreau at his word, have speculated broadly on why Thoreau went to Walden Pond that spring, offering reasons from his desire to escape family and noisy boarders to his need for a quiet place to work on a book he was writing to his scheme for forwarding runaway slaves. Thoreau himself recorded the true impulse in his Journal that summer: "I wish to meet the facts of life—the vital facts, which are the phenomena or actuality the Gods meant to show us—face to face."[44] Here in this one simple and economical act, this bold experiment, was the fulfillment and realization of the ideas set forth in *Nature*, in "The American Scholar," and in Emerson's essay "Self-Reliance." In late March and April, Thoreau did the preparatory work of clearing land and digging a foundation for the cabin. In May, Emerson, along with Alcott, Ellery Channing, and several other Concord neighbors, raised the frame. Thoreau moved into the cabin on July 4th, Independence Day. Emerson's faith in his friend's endeavor was unqualified. He wrote a will soon thereafter and made Thoreau heir to the land by Walden Pond.

VI.

TO THE MOUNTAINTOP

The Uses of Great Men

Even as the Transcendentalists' efforts at social and cultural reform slowly faded away, another movement gained new strength: that of abolitionism. Numerous antislavery societies and a solid core of prominent antislavery politicians and businessmen had emerged in the 1820s, but the abolitionist movement itself found its first catalyst in a passionate and hitherto unsuccessful printer named William Lloyd Garrison. Whereas the majority of slavery's detractors were temperate and intellectual in their arguments for gradual emancipation, Garrison was bold and uncompromising. He launched a new antislavery weekly, the *Liberator*, in 1831 with the declaration that on the issue of slavery "I will be harsh as truth and as uncompromising as justice ... I am in earnest—I will not equivocate—I will not excuse—AND I WILL BE HEARD." Garrison gained his reputation for radicalism—and, his opponents charged, insanity—by promoting his "doctrine of immediate emancipation," which was based on the belief that slavery was an abomination to God and therefore all Christians were under the obligation of a religious imperative not only to free the slaves, but to train, educate, and employ them in order to raise them to the level of equals. A core of radical abolitionists began to coalesce around the *Liberator*, and in 1833 Garrison took the lead by writing the founding document of the American Anti-Slavery Society, a declaration outlining a program of "moral suasion" that aimed to convert citizens of the North and the South to accept immediate emancipation by adopting four nonviolent tactics: founding newspapers and societies, organizing petition campaigns, sending out speakers, and challenging slaveholders in the churches. By 1837 the impact of moral suasion could be measured not only in the thousands of converts and hundreds of new antislavery societies that had sprung up across the Northern states, but also by the violent backlash against the abolitionist cause in both the North and the South. Many Northerners believed the abolitionist program could only lead to economic disaster and the dissolution of the Union. Angry mobs invaded abolition meetings and attacked the property and persons of abolitionists and free blacks alike as police stood by and judges declared the actions of mobs exempt from the rule of law. In response, one wing of the American Anti-Slavery Society began to urge that the Society become involved in politics and put forward abolitionist candidates for office; but Garrison opposed any involvement in elections as a concession to a system infested with the sin of slavery, denouncing both secular government and organized religion. The resulting schism in 1839 broke the national abolition movement into three camps, but left Garrison in control of the Society. Garrison's Society, now ideologically purified, included prominent female abolitionists such as Lucretia Mott and the Grimké sisters; many leading black abolitionists and freed slaves, such as Frederick Douglass; and Boston aristocrats, such as Wendell Phillips and Edmund Quincy. As Northern hostility to abolition spread in the early 1840s and it became apparent that moral suasion was having no effect on the policies of the federal government, Garrison took the radical position that the Constitution itself must be opposed as a slave-holding instrument and "an agreement with hell." A new slogan adorned the masthead of the *Liberator*: "No Union with Slaveholders!"

For seven years, ever since his address protesting the murder of Elijah Lovejoy, Emerson had avoided being drawn into the public debate over slavery. For seven years he had privately mulled over his abhorrence for the institution of slavery and his distaste for all that it represented. In the spring of 1844 he remained aloof, concluding that "abolition Societies & Communities are dangerous fixtures," and he was increasingly impatient with meetings of public protest and debate, after which he found himself wishing "to be shampooed & in all other ways aired and purified."[1] Indignation meetings and Antislavery Societies could be no answer to the problems of the nation, he thought, but only individual reform and development of the character. "I am always environed by myself," he wrote in March; "what I am, all things reflect to me. The state of me makes Massachusetts & the United States out there." He felt that he could not join the reform movements of the day because he "had another task nearer." This higher purpose, the "siege of the hencoop," was what he would later call his "bias," the one idea that he continually returned to and found most congenial to his soul. His inner compass alone could point him to his true north, and he could not find his bearings without it. He could see no route through direct action that would lead to the desired social change and so felt that the most direct attack on the problems facing the country was "to mind the work that is mine, and accept the facilities & openings which my constitution affords me."[2] Yet Lidian was a proud and staunch supporter of the abolitionist cause (as a protest against the slaving provisions of the Constitution, she draped the gates of the house in black on July 4th), and her influence helped to soften Emerson's poor opinion of the "indignation" meetings held by such reformers. That summer, the Women's Anti-Slavery Association, of which Lidian was a member, invited Emerson to give an address on the occasion of the tenth anniversary of emancipation in the British West Indies. More than just another gathering to rail at slaveholders and the misguided policies of the government, here was an opportunity to mark one of the great events of the time that stood as evidence of the inexorable advance of the spirit of freedom against oppression and tyranny. Emerson accepted.

On August first, having spent hours poring over histories and accounts of the emancipation of the slaves in the British West Indies, having collected notes, organized his thoughts, and prepared a lecture, Emerson apprehensively eyed the gray sky that hung over the Old Manse. Town officials, who disapproved of the event, had barred the meeting from taking place in the churches. Nathaniel Hawthorne, now living in the Emerson ancestral home, assured the Association that the large lawn in front of the Manse was free for its use; but the skies opened, and a steady rain prevented a gathering on that ancient and famous ground. In need of a hall, the organizers of the anniversary commemoration finally settled for the town courthouse. Throughout Concord the citizens heard a knock at the door and answered to find Henry Thoreau standing outside, exhorting them to come down to the meeting. Just before the speakers were scheduled to begin, the sexton of the First Parish Church announced that he would not ring the bell to gather the crowd; Thoreau, taking matters into his own hands yet again, ran to the church and rang the bell for all the town to hear. The audience finally settled in, rewarded not only by an address from Emerson, but also from Frederick Douglass, who was on hand, no doubt, to give an account of his escape from slavery and the unimaginable punishments that he had seen and endured. Emerson's address rose to meet the power of Douglass' famous eloquence and presence, and many in the audience were moved to tears by his invocation of the horrors of slavery and his gruesome description of its sordid history. One member of the audience noted that it was not Emerson who addressed them, but the spirit of Liberty herself, who had taken possession and spoken through him.[3] Emerson's rhetoric rose to fever pitch, and he announced, "Here is the Anti-Slave. Here is Man; & if you have man, black or white is an insignificance. The intellect, that is miraculous, who has it has the talisman, his skin & bones are transparent, he is a statue of the living God, him I must love & serve & perpetually seek & desire & dream on: and who has it not is superfluous."[4] He concluded by announcing the first of August to be a sign to the nations, that Right and Freedom cannot long be detained by injustice and tyranny. "There is a blessed necessity," he ended, "by which the interest of men is always driving them to the right; and, again, making all crime mean and ugly.... The Intellect, with blazing eye, looking through history from the beginning onward, gazes on this blot, and it disappears."[5]

Emerson's speech was welcomed by many abolitionists, who were pleasantly surprised that the aloof Concord essayist had decided publicly to support the cause, as many of his literary colleagues—including Whittier, Longfellow, and William Cullen Bryant—had for years. Yet even as he was preparing the Emancipation address, he was grumbling in the Journal, asking, "Does not he do more to abolish Slavery who works all day steadily in his garden, then he who goes to the abolition meeting & makes a speech? The antislavery agency like so many of our employments is a suicidal business."[6] Speeches against slavery were a "pleasant oxygenation" of the lungs, he thought, but as for the individuals involved in the movement, he wished they would do their own work instead of rushing blindly along after the latest reform. The August address was well enough received that Emerson consented to allow Thoreau to arrange its publication, but as fall came on, Emerson's hope for reform in the social sphere swung back to his faith in the individual, that the private man, by looking to his own character, can awake a hero; "then is one a match for a nation." By December he was once again frustrated at the futility of sitting in meetings and listening to speech after speech; "let us however, says Prudence, attempt some what practicable: why should we call meetings to vote against the law of gravitation, or organize a society to resist a revolution round the sun?"[7] The feeling that he did not prosecute reform because he "had another task nearer" returned: "He who does not his own work, is a slave-holder."

In January of 1845, an event occurred that pulled Emerson back into action. For the past two winters Wendell Phillips, a powerful and controversial abolitionist orator who, Emerson had declared, could give lessons in eloquence to Webster and Everett, had spoken in Concord. There had been opposition to allowing him to speak, despite the strong antislavery sentiment in the town, because of his more radical statements that the sin of slavery was to be laid at the door of the religion of the country and its twenty-thousand pulpits, and that the "curse of every honest man should be upon [the] Constitution" for its protection of the peculiar institution; despite the opposition, he had still been allowed to speak. When the ladies of Concord wished to invite Phillips back for a third time, the Curators of the Lyceum refused to honor the request and said they would close the doors of the lecture hall to him. Emerson pressed the two Curators to allow the speech "because I thought in the present state of this country the particular subject of Slavery had a commanding right to be heard in all places in New England in season & sometimes out of season."[8] The Curators resigned in protest when, on March fifth, the invitation was extended to Phillips regardless, and Emerson, along with Thoreau and one other man, were appointed in their place. Phillips spoke on March eleventh.

As the spring of 1845 wakened the earth around him, no new projects came to hand, no new thoughts, and Emerson's writing and reading seemed to labor on with no positive goal in sight. The inspiration of the Spirit of Idealism that once flowed through him seemed to have all but fled. Emerson had placed himself in the service of this spirit, had sought to make himself a vessel through which it could speak, but this spring the only use that the "country people" could imagine for him was "to ask him to deliver a Temperance Lecture, or to be a member of the School Committee." The months-old political conflagration over whether to annex the Republic of Texas as a new state was eating the nation alive; yet Emerson found he had "no voice or counsel to give in America—only the coarse party cries are heard." He must have sat at his desk for days upon days, trying to eke out some new thought from his pen, when finally, in April, he abandoned the effort. He lamented that he had only enough energy to walk in his garden and to work in the study; if he so much as stretched out a hand to help a neighbor, he found, the Genius would fly and make him pay for his poor attendance by being two or three days prostrate on the couch. "These are costly experiments to try," he chided; "I grow circumspect & disobliging beyond the example of all the misers."[9] Almost in desperation that the Muse would not stay a little longer, and concluding that things could not have come to such a pass unless he were trying to do other men's work and not his own, he tried to renew the vow of self-reliance: "I decline henceforward (ah would God it were so!) foreign methods & foreign courages. I will do that which I can do: I will fight by my strength, not by my weakness."

The vow that had propelled him to become a lecturer and later sustained him during a time of intense attacks from critics now failed of its purpose. Neither did the feeling of melancholia abate with the warm days of summer. The cause of abolitionism, of pauperism, of all the other "soup societies" gave him no pleasure, though he could not do otherwise than help their adherents out of a "sincerity and honesty of character." Whatever dark days, waiting, untuning cares, bad company he suffered, he refused to "submit to the degradation but will bear these crosses with what grace I can," for he knew that "with every self truth come mysterious offsets for all that is lost;" that the compensation for these distractions and demands that pulled him away from his work would surely be "some pearl of great price."[10] Plucked up by this resolve, he gave a second address to commemorate the anniversary of emancipation in the British West Indies on August first and attended a protest meeting in late September on the annexation of Texas at which he heard Garrison, Phillips, and many other orators of the abolition circuit. As the winter lecture season approached and he made out his schedule of engagements, he was informed by a friend that the Lyceum of New Bedford, in which he lectured frequently, had adopted a racist ticketing policy that excluded blacks from buying memberships and sitting with the subscribing members in the hall, forcing them into a segregated gallery. Emerson sent a letter to the Lyceum committee asking if the rumor were true and stating that if it were he would feel so embarrassed by the unkind and unlooked for policy that he could not speak there. When he received a letter in reply confirming the decision of the Lyceum committee, Emerson followed through and withdrew his name from the program. Charles Sumner, a noted abolitionist speaker, also withdrew. The *Liberator* followed these events closely throughout December, and at the request of those who opposed the Lyceum's action, Emerson allowed his initial letter of protest to be printed in the January issue of Garrison's paper. Though the abolitionists hailed him, Emerson saw it as a small thing, more distraction than triumph. He was a lecturer, not an icon of protest.

Emerson embarked upon the Lyceum circuit that winter with a new set of lectures, the first version of "Representative Men." The previous January, just as he had become involved with the uproar surrounding Wendell Phillips, he had been working on a lecture on Napoleon and had envisioned the list of men who should be included in a "Pantheon course of lectures": Plato, Swedenborg, Montaigne, Shakespeare, Napoleon, and Goethe. Soon thereafter he had discovered the topic for the introductory lecture, "On the Uses of Great Men," and had plunged into intense research on his subjects, especially Napoleon. He was in search of the archetype of Universal Man, whom he knew to be Christ, but he felt himself unequal to the task of such a portrayal. Instead he examined individual aspects of the one great arche-type: the Philosopher, the Mystic, the Skeptic, the Poet, the Man of the World, and the Writer. His frustration throughout 1845 over his waning inspiration arose directly from his work on these lectures. As he struggled to understand the role he should play in his own time, he wrestled with these men to discover how they had found access to the living spirit in theirs. He had chosen the chief "heads" in human history, the men who seemed to be the lightning rods of their age, who seemed a direct conduit of a higher thought. Significantly, all of the men that he chose were Europeans. There was not one American among them.

The winter lecture season proved to be unusually busy and carried well into the early months of 1846. On March eighth, as Emerson was deliv-ering a lecture on "Domestic Life" in Hartford, a small army of about twenty-five hundred men under the command of General Zachary Taylor marched out of Corpus Christi, Texas, and moved towards the Rio Grande. President Polk had approved the annexation of Texas the previous year, and the months since had been spent, Polk's critics charged, in maneuvering to provoke a war with Mexico that would lead to the acquisition of territory in California and New Mexico. Unable to get a rise out of the Mexican army at Corpus Christi—the Mexicans had to start the fighting, for the United States could not appear to be the aggressor if war were to gain popular support—Taylor advanced his forces and began to build a fort opposite the Rio Grande, where it would be more convenient for the Mexican army to strike at the invaders. In early June the Mexican army besieged the fort, and on June twelfth the United States declared war on her neighbor to the south. In Congress, Representative Abraham Lincoln of Illinois charged that the thinly veiled land-grab was part of the Slave Power conspiracy to extend slavery beyond its current boundaries and gain a permanent majority in the Congress. Emerson, who had thought the annexation of Texas looked like "one of those events which retard or retrograde the civilization of ages" and had attended several protest meetings against the annexation in 1845, now predicted that "the United States will conquer Mexico, but it will be as the man swallows arsenic, which brings him down in turn. Mexico will poison us." His indignation at the actions of the government drew him once again towards the abolitionist cause. He gave a speech on July fourth at Dedham in which he proclaimed that the abolition party was the true successor of the Church, of Calvinism and Puritanism—that this "fervent, self-denying school of love and action" was consecrated by the blood of martyrs. Yet he felt the need to qualify his admiration for this "party of freedom": "I am glad, not for what it has done, but that the party exists. Not what they do, but what they see, seems to me sublime."[11]

The perception and ideals of the abolitionists were at last praiseworthy to Emerson, but overt action was another matter. Thoreau—who was more deeply involved with the abolition movement, and whose family's house was a way station on the Underground Railroad—followed the dictates of his conscience and, towards the end of July, refused to pay his poll tax in protest against the state of Massachusetts and the war with Mexico. He spent one night in jail before an unknown person paid the tax for him. Emerson at first supported his friend, noting that the "rabble at Washington" could count on the Governor of Massachusetts and Daniel Webster to fall in line with the war, but they could not count on Thoreau; even the abolitionists, though they opposed the war, paid the tax. Yet over the next few days Emerson grew increasingly upset with Thoreau's action, and he gave his friend a lecture in his Journal, admonishing him not to "run amuck against the world" but to wait for a true cause, a "good difference" with the state that would have an impact and that he could well die for, like the cause of Socrates. Part of his anger was an outgrowth of the feeling he had towards the abolitionists, the feeling that there was something hypocritical underlying their protest. He could not fully articulate the hypocrisy, but he pointed out the fact that refusing to pay the tax did not have as direct an effect as would boycotting cotton clothes, sugar, and books, which all paid for the war—and these his friend did "not stick at buying." For all of the arguments he stacked up against Thoreau, in the end he simply could not understand why Henry—who was supposed to be, like himself, a scholar and poet who reserved himself from the world and cultivated his character and art as the greatest benefit to the universal reform of mankind—would take such extreme measures. When he finally confronted Thoreau and asked him why he went to jail, Thoreau replied, "Why did you not?"

Over the Christmas holiday in 1846, Emerson published a small book of sixty-one poems. He had planned the volume in the summer of 1845 and had done intensive work on the poems in the spring and summer of 1846, at the same time that he was re-forming the lectures on "Representative Men." Indeed, as the *Poems* went to press, Emerson was delivering the expanded and revised series of biographical lectures for the second time. There were, of course, poems such as "The Humble Bee" and "The Snow-storm," which took up the theme of nature in a distinctly American way, as well as poems that embodied the practical themes of Emerson's Transcendental lectures, such as "Each and All," "Tact," and "Compensation." The majority of the latter he had written before 1844, and he now polished them for the new collection. The remainder of the poems that he wrote during this year and a half, perhaps a third of the pieces in the volume, were closely related to "Representative Men," but instead of seeking to know the chief heads of the ages, the poems sought to give voice to the spirits of the nations. The first poem, entitled "The Sphinx," led the reader back to ancient Greece and Egypt, as did "Eros," "Hermione," "Bacchus," and "Xenophanes." He approached Spain in "Alphonso of Castille;" embarked to ancient Britain in "Merlin I" and "Merlin II;" and invoked ancient Asia Minor in "Mithridates." The traditions of Islam, Judaism, and Hinduism found voice in "Uriel" and "Hamatreya," the latter inspired directly by the Vishnu Purana. Emerson even included translations of two medieval Persian poets, Hafez and Saadi. This assemblage of voices from the pen of a man who had dedicated ten years of his life to shaping American culture and proclaiming foreign harvests to be sere and dead seemed both surprising and out of place. Many of the new poems were masterpieces of imagination and so shaped by his own voice that often the title was the only clue to the poem's roots in a foreign culture. Even today many of these poems hold their place among the greatest of Emerson's achievements as a writer. This outpouring of creativity in the poetic genre, derived from a refreshing surge of imaginative vision, helped to restore his sagging spirits.

A Whip for My Top

Throughout 1846 Emerson had recopied a passage in his journal with such frequency that it became almost a mantra: "By always intending my mind." It was the answer Newton had given to the question of how he had achieved his discoveries. Through Newton's method, Emerson sought to focus his resources, draw on inner strength, and accomplish his daily work. As the new year commenced, Emerson felt a cautious optimism and tried to lay out a plan for a new series of lectures; but as the weeks wore on into March he felt his reservoir of inspiration drying up. He seemed to be losing direction rapidly and felt he had no mission, no goad, no "whip for his top" to keep him in the advancing attitude, with one foot forward. He wished for a professorship to give him direction and became so depressed in March that he wrote in his Journal, "Much as I hate the church, I have wished the pulpit that I might have the stimulus of a stated task." Standing in front of his audiences, he felt all he had to offer them was gold dust when they wanted ingots and blamed himself for using Intellect as a puppet show. To make matters worse, the "name of Washington City" seemed to grow blacker every day and the government, as the Mexican War dragged on, seemed to be capable of no act except to be as "wicked as they dare." Invitations to lecture in England had come, and in his dark mood he thought he might accept, though his real inclination was to run away to Canada and "withdraw myself for a time from all domestic & accustomed relations & command an absolute leisure with books—for a time."[12] In May his mood became so dark that even the days themselves seemed to "come and go like muffled & veiled figures sent from a distant friendly party;" but they said nothing and carried their gifts away. Even his garden turned against him. He had a dream that he stooped to pick a weed behind the corn and found four thousand and one more—then woke to find that he was a weed himself. On a page of his Journal he wrote out a heading, *Insufficient Forces*, and underneath it recalled what his doctor had said to him in his boyhood: "'You have no *stamina*.'"

In August of 1847, Emerson had a moment of clarity and recognized that "men run away to other countries because they are not good in their own; and run back to their own, because they pass for nothing in the foreign places. Achieve a mastery in any place, and it is good in all." Yet England was looking more attractive by the day; he laid plans for his departure and began to take lessons in French. America had its proper glory, he thought, though "shrouded and unknown." By going to Europe, he "would let it shine." In reality, he seemed more intent on pursuing the Spirit that had inspired him for so many years, and which now seemed to be lifting from America's shores. It was almost as if he hoped that by returning to Europe, where he had first experienced the visions that had sent him back to America with mission and purpose, he could find that inspiration again. On October fifth, Emerson set sail. He knew not what awaited him on the other side of the ocean, but he knew at least that whatever lay ahead, he was speeding away from the worries and troubles of home. On October twenty-second the ship arrived at Liverpool, and Emerson set foot on English soil for the second time. He had made his great escape.

As soon as he stepped off the ship, Emerson became the quintessential observer, taking note of the build of the men, the gait of the women, the structure of the buildings and pervasiveness of industry, as if he were Tacitus come back eighteen hundred years later to see how Roman Britain had come along since he had written his *Agricola*. The character of the Journal underwent a sea change. Gone were the introspection, the doubts, the complaints. All that remained was England, mighty, industrious England and her people. In the fifteen years since his last visit, the industrial revolution had transformed the cities. He was overawed by the wealth and bustle, and he remarked in his Journal that "if I stay here long I shall lose all my patriotism, & think that England has absorbed all excellences."[13] He asked questions, took down measurements of textile mills and iron works, paced out the public spaces, and wrote out lists of the strange inflections and turns of phrase to be heard in the British tongue. Between his meetings with diplomats, poets, politicians, scientists, and writers, he had very little time for study or, indeed, for much beyond jotting out his impressions of the people and their conversation. He reunited with Carlyle; met Thomas DeQuincey, Charles Dickens and George Eliot; and paid a short visit to Wordsworth, who was in the final years of his life. He heard the scientific lectures of Richard Owen and Michael Faraday, met the mathematician Charles Babbage, heard a recital by Frederic Chopin, viewed Turner's paintings, and dined with the nobility. When he did find time to pick up a book, it was invariably some history of the island or of the Anglo-Saxon race.

Emerson was famous in his own right throughout Great Britain, and he began lecturing in November in such cities as Manchester, Edinburgh, and Glasgow. Many of the lectures were drawn from the "Representative Men" series, which he now reworked for the third time. He also gave lectures on "Eloquence," "Domestic Life," and "Reading." On March second he arrived in London and began to make his way into the high society of the great city. The heavy social calendar, however, preempted all lecturing, and at the beginning of April he reported to Lidian that he had not made a single pound since he had been in the capital city. He did not have any new lectures to give, he wrote, though he had been working on some new writing that was "a kind of 'Natural History of Intellect.'"[14] The question of how he was to continue to pay for the trip was pressing. The "Natural History" material was still rough and lacked the structure necessary for a series, but it would have to do. In the first week of May he accepted a proposal to give a series in London. The engagement was to begin on June sixth, leaving time for a visit to Paris before he began the lectures. His timing was impeccable. Just one week after he arrived in the city, he sent a letter to Lidian describing the revolution he had witnessed in the streets—the speeches of the ringleaders that he had heard in the clubs, the streets swarming with bayonets, and the final defeat of the uprising by the National Guards. In the midst of this turning point in France's history, Emerson began the process of shaping the new lectures into final form. On June third he returned to London in order to give his last six lectures before returning home.

Emerson's final title for the London series was "Mind and Manners in the Nineteenth Century." The first three lectures of the series, which he gave on the sixth, eighth, and tenth of June, were based on the "Natural History of Intellect" material that he had described to Lidian. He had been making bare sketches of ideas relating to this project early in 1847, but had not drawn them together or come up with a coherent organization. Now he worked on them furiously, outlining and writing them almost as he gave them. The fresh excitement that warmed his pen and sped it across the page stood in stark contrast with the slog that had been "Representative Men." His biographical lectures had been intensively, even laboriously researched and had comprised almost his total repertoire for the last three lecture seasons as he tried to hammer the stubborn thoughts into a satisfactory form. Every paragraph was a hard-fought battle, every lecture a campaign. The new lectures returned to a favorite topic that actually predated "Representative Men," as well as the bulk of the writing he had published over the last decade, picking up on an idea he had formulated in 1837 and which he had explored through threaded themes in his 1839 lecture series on "The Present Age" and the 1841 series "The Times" (of which the lecture "The Poet" had been a part), as well as the essays "Intellect" and "History" from his first book of *Essays*. Inspiration, so long in abeyance, struck like a bolt of lightning. After the frustrations and anxieties of the last two years, after the feelings of isolation and despondency that almost crippled his will, making it hard for him to even get up off the couch at times, here was Emerson back in stride. He was confident, energetic, unstoppable.

The lectures flowed from his pen: "Powers and Laws of Thought;" "Relation of Intellect to Natural Science;" "Tendencies and Duties of Men of Thought." His fundamental assumption in attempting a subject as grand and apparently intangible as a "Natural History" of "the Intellect" was that systematic study could discern the activity of the Intellect, that ultimate source of the ideas that inspire art and science and direct the course of human history. A natural history was a workable metaphor for what he wished to attempt: the study of a single species of flower or insect in a woodland could render little useful knowledge about the complex plan of the ecosystem in which it existed, but a comprehensive survey of all of the flora and fauna and their interactions could begin to reveal the unifying principles of the delicate ecology. Likewise, a studied observation of the great thoughts and ideas, their interaction and relation, could reveal the intricate activity of the universal Intellect. In "Powers and Laws of Thought" he set forth the study of the Intellect as a science, noted the universal interest that such a pursuit had to all people, and then enumerated the hindrances that existed for one who wished to pursue this interest. He then laid the basis for making such a study practicable by describing the predictable and discernable laws that govern the Intellect, dispelling the need for mesmerism or other dark arts to descry the mysteries of the universe. The next lecture, "Relation of Intellect to Natural Science," took up the discovery of these laws in more detail by exploring the identity of thought with nature, the idea that the laws of the mind correspond to the laws of nature. The third lecture, "Tendencies and Duties of Men of Thought," explored the significance of the discovery of such laws to the scholar, the poet, the scientist, or any other individual who seeks to become a student of the Intellect. In the presence of such laws, Emerson illustrated, there would be a powerful instinct towards right action, an ethics of thought based on the probity of the Intellect. The fundamental question of life, of how to act, resolved itself into the theme of the series: men of conscience in the present day who recognize the laws of the Intellect have a duty laid upon them to realize the good by acting in accordance with the oracle of Instinct, of Self-reliance.

The Reluctant Abolitionist

The strange journey that Emerson had been on since 1845 was a journey to the mountaintop, a quest to find the pinnacle of perfect solitude from which the poet could look down upon society, find undisturbed inner peace and perfection of character, and enter into the pure flow of inspiration, such as he had experienced when writing the "Mind and Manners" lectures. The jolt that caused such disruption in his feeling life, the cause of his recurring depression, was the discovery that the mountaintop was actually barren, that his careful efforts to protect himself from the transient heats and concerns of society had brought him no closer to the muse. True inspiration had come in places far removed from his ideal of the poet's solitary retreat—amidst the buzz of London society and the revolutionary mayhem of the Paris streets. Set adrift on the Atlantic, pulled away from the distractions of high society and the bustle of London and left to himself for the first time since he had landed in England, he felt suddenly isolated, bemoaning "these lackluster days [that] go whistling over us." Once, on his first voyage across the Atlantic, the vast ocean and sky had opened to him and revealed the source of all artistic endeavor as the creative efflux of the spirit manifest in the beauty of nature; once he had gazed on the clouds from the deck of a ship and seen his mission in life laid out before him. Now he cursed the sea as "one long disgust." He returned to the quiet streets of Concord in August to find his woodlot burned, rubbish and lumber lying about the yard, and his grass and trees all wanting attention, drawing him away from the demands of "the gods." "Can I not have some partner," he wrote; "can't we organize our new society of poets & lovers, & have somebody with talent for business to look after these things, some deacons of trees & grass & cranberries, & leave me to letters & philosophy?" The old impulse to retreat, to run fast and far was still there, but he seemed to have learned something new, for "the nettled gods [said], No, go to the devil with your arrangements. You, you, you personally, you alone, are to answer body & soul for your things."[15] As for his friends, however, he felt perhaps more distant from them than ever, writing that he and they were "fishes in their habit." He was particularly upset with Thoreau, of whom he wrote that he "should as soon take the arm of an elm tree" as that of the recalcitrant individualist.

One friend in particular provided Emerson with an incalculable benefit. On the last day of September, 1848, he struck out on a walk with Ellery

Channing through the apple orchards around Concord, where they found acres and acres of hardy trees and heaps of apples strewn upon the ground. The trees seemed "to grow for their own pleasure; they almost lost price." As the autumn days progressed, he and Ellery began taking regular walks together through the country, and his friend's ebullience and quick wit combined with the beauty of nature began to have a healing and rejuvenating effect on Emerson's soul. A soothing quality encompassed his work as lecturer and scholar; not long after the September walk he wrote in his Journal, "Our philosophy is to *wait*." "I obey the beautiful Necessity," he continued; "the powers that I want will be supplied, as *I* am supplied, and the philosophy of waiting is sustained by all the oracles of the Universe."[16] Emerson's inner turmoil still showed itself,—one day in October he wrote that he would quickly dismiss the "chatterers" that visited him, but he was never sure that his inspiration would be there for him after they left, so he suffered them to stay,—but an inner change was having its effect on him. On October twenty-eighth, Emerson and Channing went for a walk on which nature seemed so glorious that "it needs the pencils of all the painters that ever existed, to aid the description." Nature's splendor inspired conversation to match it, and Emerson did the best he could to record the lakes and trees and rivers as well as the conversation of the "Saturday afternoon professors," but always found it impossible to capture the import and essence of what had been said. "In walking with Ellery," he wrote, "you shall always see what was never before shown to the eye of man."

When Emerson laid out the London lectures on "Mind and Manners in the Nineteenth Century" and prepared to revise them for the winter lecture season, the prospect of hitting the circuit once again and trading thoughts for money held no more luster than before: "Again must I make cheap what I adore, / And play the mountebank one winter more." His aims for the series, however, were high, perhaps higher than any he had set for himself before. "In my chapter on Intellect," he wrote, "I should wish to catalogue those high commandments which in all the mental history elevate themselves like towers; as, not until our own day, did Herschel go to the Cape, & publish the catalogue of the stars of the Southern Hemisphere." Like Herschel's, it was a "catalogue" that would attempt to describe what had always been present but never accurately described—namely, the hidden activity of spiritual causes in the actions of the great individuals of history. Despite the enormity of the undertaking, he was certain "that this almanack of the soul may be written as well as that of Greenwich."[17] He embraced the project fully, and it became the main focus of his lecturing activity. He expanded the "Mind and Manners" series into six lectures and delivered the lecture cycle five times the course of the next two years.

Emerson's attempt to describe the Intellect as it appeared in history deepened his insight into the lectures on Napoleon, Goethe, and the others. He began to view these men as the towers of strength, exemplars of the deeds of the Intellect. In December, as he was reworking the "Mind and Manners in the Nineteenth Century" lectures, he notified his publisher that he was preparing a book on *Representative Men* and had made significant progress with several of the chapters. The summer of 1849 found Emerson back at work on *Representative Men*, researching, taking notes, and struggling anew with Plato, Shakespeare, and Napoleon. He took two breaks from the work: to give another address on the anniversary of Emancipation in the British West Indies, and to prepare a collection of his earlier works entitled

Nature, Addresses, and Lectures, published on September eleventh. The final version of *Representative Men,* the product of almost five years of labor, appeared in late December. Emerson's book of archetypal men had started under the influence of Idealism as the heroes of Europe, but it took final form in direct conjunction with the new lectures on the "Natural History of Intellect." Emerson completed his presentation of the men of conscience, the leaders of humanity who had brought the Intellect into their lives and had acted as its conduit into the world. "It is natural to believe in great men," he opened the book. "Nature seems to exist for the excellent. The world is upheld by the veracity of good men: they make the earth wholesome." "Our religion is the love and cherishing of these patrons," he wrote; they pointed to the new moral religion whose dawning was yet beyond the horizon.

An event occurred in the spring of 1850 that startled Emerson from his routine. On the seventh of March, Daniel Webster—whom Emerson had considered, since he was a young man, to be the lion of the country, the great icon of American culture whose very words had passed through the fire of Intellect—gave his famous speech in the Senate in support of Henry Clay's compromise, which included the Fugitive Slave Law. The heart of the issue splitting the Congress was the fate of the vast lands, from New Mexico to California, acquired in the successful war against Mexico. A block of incendiary Southern Democrats was threatening secession if provisions outlawing slavery in the new territories were passed; the compromise was intended to save the Union by leaving the status of slavery in New Mexico and Utah to popular sovereignty and granting greatly expanded powers to slaveholders to recapture runaway slaves. Many Abolitionists were outraged at the bill, but they were even more incensed that Webster should put his weight behind it. Emerson was deeply disappointed. This event convinced him that the idol of his early years had sold out and could be had "for any opinion, any purpose." To make matters worse, the cream of Boston society gathered a thousand signatures on a letter of support that they sent to Webster at the end of March. Emerson could feel nothing but cold disdain for these "aged & infirm people" of his class, "who have outlived everything but their night cap & their tea & toast." What surprised him most was that a number of young people had signed as well. But for his sincerity, his summation on the turn of events was almost melodramatic: "The badness of the times is making death attractive."[18]

Then a disaster struck that caused Emerson to lose all interest in the darkening clouds enveloping the country's politics. On July nineteenth, Margaret Fuller, now Margaret Fuller Ossoli, came within sight of the American shoreline for the first time in three years. She was returning from Italy with her new husband and son, almost two years old, when a gale struck up in the night and drove the ship aground just four hundred yards from the beach on Fire Island. The ship was dashed to pieces and the entire family died. Emerson, in great distress, sent Thoreau to the seaside to see if anything of hers might be recovered, but his friend found nothing. Emerson eulogized Margaret for days in his Journal as he recalled all of her best qualities, all of the things that had endeared her to so many friends. "I have lost in her my audience," he mourned. Her death was a sharp reminder, an admonishment that he had "few days left" and had to hurry to his work. William Henry Channing, Ellery's cousin and a long-time member of the Transcendental Club, suggested that a life of Margaret should be written. Emerson, along with

Channing and Samuel Ward, took on the task of collecting and editing her journals and letters.

The Fugitive Slave Law received President Fillmore's signature on September eighteenth. Efforts on the part of Southerners to take advantage of the Bill were almost immediate, and slave hunters from Georgia descended on Boston like hounds. Emerson himself was confident that Massachusetts would never bend to such a law, that his fellow citizens would resist it with such strength that it could not be enforced. For a few months, it seemed that he was justified in his belief. A core of abolitionists formed the Boston Vigilance Committee to resist any attempts to capture slaves in the city. In October Emerson attended a meeting with Wendell Phillips, Garrison, Charles Sumner, and others at which the group discussed the case of William and Ellen Craft, two slaves with warrants outstanding against them. The Crafts were successfully spirited out of Boston and escaped to England. Short months later, in February of 1851, a black member of the Vigilance Committee formed a party of twenty black men who broke into a courthouse and freed Shadrach, a waiter who had been seized as a fugitive slave. The group fled Boston and took refuge in Concord before heading north to Canada. The Southerners responded to this and other similar events with heated threats, warning that if the law were not upheld the Compromise of 1850 would be dead, and they would split with the Union. Consequently the Northern authorities redoubled their efforts to see the law carried through, and when Thomas Sims was arrested in the first week of April, the doors of the courthouse were secured with great iron chains and a heavy guard was posted. An intense legal battle ensued, but on the morning of April thirteenth a phalanx of guards led Sims through the streets of Boston and placed him on a ship bound for Savannah, where his owners publicly whipped him. It was the first successful application of the Fugitive Slave Law in Massachusetts, the state that was the very heart of the abolition movement.

The re-enslavement of Sims shattered the confident dream that had enveloped Emerson for so many years, the dream that the Intellect, with blazing eye, would gaze on slavery, as dark and terrible a crime as could be imagined, and cause it to disappear. He was, at last, genuinely outraged. His anger at the government, at Massachusetts, at his own race, at Webster in particular, poured forth in an unquenchable torrent that coursed in a continuous passage unequaled in length anywhere else in the Journals. He vehemently swore that "all I have, and all I can do shall be given & done in opposition to the execution of the law." He felt nothing but disgrace to be associated with Boston. "This slavery shall not be," he thundered in unison with Garrison's rallying cry; "it poisons & depraves everything it touches. There can never be peace whilst this devilish seed of war is in our soil. Root it out. Burn it up. Pay for the damage & let us have done with it."[19] He made good on his oath almost immediately. Two weeks after the Sims affair, he delivered a new address on the Fugitive Slave Law in which he painted Webster as a morally bankrupt traitor at the beck and call of Southern planters and urged his listeners to follow the directive of a higher law by opposing the immorality of Congress. Opposition to the law became almost his sole thought, attested to by the fact that he took a step that would previously have been unthinkable to him. He took his speech on the road and began stumping for the abolitionist John Gorham Palfrey, a Free Soil candidate seeking the governorship of Massachusetts. Emerson, who had studiously avoided public controversy since the storm of the Divinity School "Address," descended into the ring. In the end Palfrey lost the vote, but Emerson had stepped boldly into the public eye and captured the attention of the newspapers. His critics painted him as a new voice in the campaign to establish a political foundation for the abolition movement.

Events had placed Emerson in the midst of the turmoil, but with the arrival of June the Fuller memoir demanded his undivided attention. There were letters to collect, journals to read, anecdotes to document. He began a new notebook dedicated to the project and relieved himself—perhaps, he thought, only temporarily—of the vow to oppose the Fugitive Slave Law. The summer days wore on, and late in August he wistfully looked back on those whirlwind days of spring, which seemed an age away, and made a note to himself to record in his memoirs "that I always find myself doing something less than my best task. In the spring, I was writing politics; now I am writing a biography, which not the absolute command, but facility & amiable feeling prompted."[20] In October he turned down an invitation to speak at a Women's Rights convention in Worcester, pleading that he was too involved with the *Memoir*. When the book was finally published in February, 1852, it outsold all of his own books.

VII.

SOMETHING LESS THAN
MY BEST TASK

England, England, England

Even with the publication of the *Memoir* and the end of the lecture season in April of 1852, Emerson did not find his way back into politics. Just before his forty-ninth birthday, he began a new project, one that he had been contemplating since his return from England three years earlier. The first phase of the project involved organizing the voluminous notes from his trip to England. Up until this time Emerson's habit was to keep his journals more or less chronologically, writing in one regular journal volume at a time. There was some overlap between volumes, but usually not more than a few weeks or a month. In typical fashion he began a new journal that April to open the England project, but in June he started a second, and by spring of 1853 a third and a fourth. The project began to take on a life of its own, and it grew so consuming that one August night in 1852 he woke suddenly, realized he had abandoned the antislavery cause, and "bemoaned myself, because I had not thrown myself into this deplorable question of Slavery, which seems to want nothing so much as a few assured voices." But when daylight came again, he was able to soothe his conscience and "recover" himself, saying, "God must govern his own world, & knows his way out of this [problem of slavery], without desertion of my post which has none to guard it but me." He had other slaves to free, he wrote, "imprisoned spirits, imprisoned thoughts, far back in the brain of man."[1]

The "English Traits" marathon continued throughout 1853, with a break only in the early months of the year for a lecture tour west to Ohio, Missouri, and Illinois. The railroads were opening the West to Emerson, allowing him to reach new audiences who had till then only read his published essays and poems. Many of his lectures in the winter of 1852-53 focused specifically on England. In Springfield, Illinois, where he gave one lecture on the "Anglo-Saxon" and two from his new "Conduct of Life" series, Abraham Lincoln sat in the back of the hall and listened to this "master of wonderful style and thought," as the local newspaper called him. Then Emerson journeyed back to the East and toured New York, Philadelphia, Maine, and Massachusetts to finish out the season. As soon as he settled into his study at home, he took up the England project again. He filled hundreds of Journal pages with notes and began work on a chronology of British history and literature from the time that the Romans left the island in 426 A.D. The subject of the hour, the new heart of the Journal, was England, England, England. The project had grown beyond any mere travel diary. Emerson was now delving into the very roots of English history, her social customs and leading individualities. He happily agreed with Montesquieu, that only the English people possess true common sense. England, he concluded, was the greatest among the nations.

By now his resolve to oppose the dark blot of slavery seemed distant, and his ire against the Fugitive Slave Law had receded so far into the background that it seemed to die with Daniel Webster in October of 1852. When he did write about slavery in the Journal, it was usually to make strange, intellectual comments on the history and fate of races. In the midst of the England project in 1853 he stopped to write out a poem, then rewrote it three more times before he was happy with it. The poem opened wistfully, almost mournfully:

> Once I wished I might rehearse
> Freedom's paean in my verse
> That the slave who caught the strain
> Should throb until he snapt his chain.

The poem continued:

> But the Spirit said, "Not so
> Speak it not or speak it low,
> Name not lightly to be said
> Gift too precious to be prayed
> Passion only well exprest
> By heaving of the silent breast.

Turning his face away from the slave's plight, the goal of the poet was once again the mountaintop:

> Yet wouldst thou the mountain find
> Where the deity is shrined.

The poem ends with the poet eschewing his role in events, uniting with the mountain deity and becoming the crux between heaven and earth:

> Or if in thy heart he shine
> Blend the starry fates with thine

Draws angels down to dwell with thee
And makes thy thoughts archangels be,
Freedom's secret, wouldst thou know?—
Right thou feelest, rashly do.[2]

However rash it may have been, Emerson could not help but speak out once again, early in 1854, when debate boiled over concerning the legalization of slavery in the territories of Kansas and Nebraska as they sought admittance to the Union. On March seventh, the anniversary of Webster's famous oration, Emerson delivered a new address on the Fugitive Slave Law to the New York Anti-Slavery Society, but it gave him little satisfaction. Soon afterwards he began a new notebook entitled "Liberty" in which he documented the swirl of events and recorded his thoughts on slavery, freedom, and the abolition movement. He was already beginning to have doubts about the ability of Garrison's crowd to handle the events they had set in motion. He had the feeling that the ringleaders of the Abolition movement "may wake up some morning and find that they have made a capital mistake & are not the persons they took themselves for."[3] Phillips seemed the mere mouthpiece of a party, and the Liberator a scold rather than a sibyl. As the Kansas-Nebraska Act took shape it became apparent that the Missouri Compromise, which had kept slavery below the latitude of 36°30' for more than three decades, might be overturned. Emerson noted the country's lack of leadership and commented that "there is nobody in Washington who can explain this Nebraska business to the people,—nobody of weight."[4] The audacity of the Southerner Congressmen to introduce measures that sought to nullify long-established law caused Emerson to pause in mid-step and reconsider the role he should take. In the spring of 1854 it became apparent to him that a man who thinks he can "know this or that, by words & writing" is living in a delusion, for "it can only be known or done organically. He must plunge into the universe, & live in its forms,—sink to rise." After the Kansas-Nebraska Act was signed into law in May, Emerson warmed to this thought and followed it through to its logical conclusion: that the Scholar was to be the "new Potentate," and that what he uttered should be the instruction of nations.

For the lecture season that winter Emerson carried this discovery into action and took with him only two lectures: his address on the Fugitive Slave Law and a new lecture entitled "American Slavery." Phillip Randolph approached Emerson after hearing the latter lecture on February eighth, 1855, and expressed surprise to find him speaking out on antislavery politics, since it seemed a breach of faith for a generalist to speak out on such "temporary heats." Emerson replied that though it was "becoming in the scholar to insist on central soundness, rather than on superficial applications," it was his duty "to give a wise & just ballot, though no man else in the republic doth. I am not to compromise or mix or accommodate. I am to demand the absolute right, affirm that, & do that."[5] The Spirit that had asked him to stand apart and remain silent seemed to cease its plea and fade into the background. A new Spirit, one apparently connected with the country itself, now came forward and required him to stand in the lectern and affirm the ground that no other would stand on.

At about this time Emerson took a great step forward in his relationship not just to his country, but to his friends. Together with Lowell, Alcott, Richard Henry Dana, and Frank Sanborn, he helped to found the Saturday Club in December of 1854. The new Club was the successor of the Town and Country Club, which had been founded in March of 1849 in Alcott's rooms in Boston. The Town and Country Club had been a sophisticated, larger, and more cosmopolitan successor of the Transcendental Club, with a membership that eventually reached around one hundred. The Club had been intended as a café and reading room in the city where scholars could gather for relaxation or to join in conversations on important questions, but it had been disbanded after just two years because of the inability of its members to support it financially. The Town and Country Club had been primarily a forum for Alcott, and Emerson had not always been happy with it. The new Saturday Club, however, fostered an atmosphere of conversation that was especially congenial to Emerson's soul. The camaraderie of the group of intellectuals and poets provided him with much-needed refreshment and new creative impulses for many years to come.

The Poet Arrives

In the second week of July, 1855, Emerson received a small package in the mail. When he opened it, he found a slim volume bound in green covers, entitled *Leaves of Grass*; it bore a picture of the author inside, but no name or mark of authorship. Emerson duly read the volume, which opened with a preface containing all of his best thoughts on poets and poetry, but so heated, so agitated that they seemed to bridle against being confined in sentences and so filled with restless energy that they seemed ready to break the bounds of their paragraphs.

> The Americans of all nations at any time upon the earth have probably the fullest poetical nature. The United States themselves are essentially the greatest poem. In the history of the earth hitherto the largest and most

stirring appear tame and orderly to their ampler large-
ness and stir. Here at last is something in the doings of
man that corresponds with the broadcast doings of the
day and night. Here is not merely a nation but a teeming
nation of nations.

The sentences must have rung with double significance since Emerson's own eye had been turned so long and so longingly on England. For page after page the anonymous author went on, announcing the poet, celebrating the nation and its people, luxuriating in a new image-filled language. Only recently having come to terms with his own duties as a scholar to his country, Emerson read on:

The American poets are to enclose old and new for
America is the race of races. Of them a bard is to be com-
mensurate with a people. To him the other continents
arrive as contributions . . . he gives them reception for
their sake and his own sake. His spirit responds to his
country's spirit . . . . he incarnates its geography and natural life and rivers and lakes.[6]

Then came the resounding first lines of poetry:

I celebrate myself,
And what I assume you shall assume,
For every atom belonging to me as good belongs to you.

There was no rhyme, no regular meter to the poetry, and every line was infused with the persona of the poet, large, demanding, unabashed. It was like nothing that had ever appeared in American literature. It signaled a revolution.

Legend has it that Emerson walked through the streets of Concord with the book in hand, waving it over his head like a flag. He could not contain his enthusiasm, and he began to recommend it to all of his friends. Emerson's excitement was not merely for a good book and a few remarkable words, but for being witness to a cardinal event in history; "All that we call sacred history attests that the birth of a poet is the principal event in chronology," he had once written.[7] Emerson had been searching for such a sign for years upon years in his friends and neighbors, in the towns of New England, in lecture halls from Maine to Illinois. At long last, it had arrived in his mail. He wanted to write a letter to the author, but he could not be sure his missive would reach its goal until one day he saw an advertisement for *Leaves of Grass* in a newspaper. Still lacking a name for the person he was writing to, he began the letter with "Dear Sir" and proceeded to spill out a paragraph of praise more effusive than any he had previously written.

> I am not blind to the worth of the wonderful gift of "Leaves of Grass." I find it the most extraordinary piece of wit & wisdom that America has yet contributed. I am very happy in reading it, as great power makes us happy. It meets the demand I am always making of what seemed sterile & stingy nature, as if too much handiwork or too much lymph in the temperament were making our western wits fat & mean. I give you joy of your free & brave thought. I have great joy in it. I find incomparable things said incomparably well, as they must be. I find the courage of *temperament*, which so delights us, which large perception only can inspire. I greet you at the beginning of a great career, which yet must have had a long foreground somewhere for such a start. I rubbed my eyes a little to see if this sunbeam were no illusion; but the solid sense of the book is a sober certainty. It has the best merits, namely, of fortifying & encouraging.

Emerson concluded the letter by saying that he wished "to see my benefactor, & have felt much like striking my tasks, & visiting New York to pay you my respects." He sealed the letter and mailed it, to the book's publisher, on July twenty-first.

A year before Emerson received the first edition of *Leaves of Grass* he had pointed out in his Journal that the "theory of Poetry is the generation of matter from thought … [but] the brains are so badly formed, so unheroically, brains of the sons of *fallen* men, that the doctrine is most imperfectly received." "Poems!" he had exclaimed, "we have no poem. The Iliad is a poor ballad grinding—whenever the Poet shall appear!" Now he had in hand the book to make the Iliad pale. He was still praising it in September to whoever would listen when he received a visit from Moncure Conway, the son of a slave-owning Virginia planter and now a Unitarian minister and abolitionist. Conway, an admiring student of the elder essayist, was so swept up by Emerson's enthusiasm that he set out for Brooklyn the next day to meet the author of *Leaves of Grass* with a new copy of the book in hand to read on the way. When he arrived, not knowing anything but the poet's name—which apparently had been made known by this time—Conway spent most of the day searching Brooklyn until he finally found Walt Whitman sitting, in an accustomed pose, in front of a case of type. Conway told Whitman about his meeting with Emerson the day before, about the words of praise the essayist had for the poet, and Whitman, who apparently had not yet received Emerson's letter, said he hoped to see Emerson and hear more of his views on *Leaves*. Whitman probably received the letter towards the end of September, and he promptly submitted a copy of it to Horace Greeley's *Tribune*, which published the letter in its entirety—without Emerson's knowledge or permission—on October tenth.

Emerson learned of the publication of his letter not long after from indignant friends in Boston. Emerson himself did not seem offended by the poet's audacity. Indeed, if it had not been for Emerson's plaudits, his repeated insistence that his friends read the book, and his tolerance of Whitman's shameless self-promotion, Whitman's book probably would have found an early grave, for it was universally panned by the literate classes and newspapers as obscene and profane. James Greenleaf Whittier, who also received a complimentary copy of the book, threw his into the fire. Emerson, however, saw something in the unconventional poems that was invisible to everyone else; more than that, he was drawn to Whitman himself. On December eleventh, Emerson lectured at the Brooklyn Atheneum and afterwards made his way to Whitman's home on Ryerson Street. The lecture Emerson gave that day was the only one in New York that season, and it is possible he had arranged it with this meeting in mind. He knocked gently on the door. Whitman's mother answered to find the gaunt, hawk-nosed lecturer standing politely outside the door, and Walt, in the other room, heard the words, "I came to see Mr. Whitman." Emerson invited Whitman to dinner at the Astor House, the posh hotel where he was staying, and they fell into a wide-ranging discussion that, as Whitman remembered it towards the end of his life, "would get hot, stormy (for us): we differed sharply in some things—never hesitated to express our differences—doing so this day rather loudly." After the Astor House, Whitman took his new friend to Freeman's Hall, a "rowdy dive" of a social club, where the poet, quintessentially "one of the roughs," would have felt more at home.

Whitman had seen Emerson before, though Emerson did not know it. In March of 1842, Whitman had been a reporter in the audience when

Emerson delivered a lecture in New York on "The Poet," the same reporter who had written the review describing it as "one of the richest and most beautiful … we have heard anywhere, at any time." This lecture had been Whitman's first experience of Emerson's ideas. Whitman later described how his own ideas "were simmering, simmering, and Emerson brought them to a boil." For the two principal actors in this drama there was no question of how this sympathy of thought and motive had come to be—there was only the shock of recognition. The lecture on "The Poet" had called for America's Poet to arise, and now, thirteen years later, Whitman answered. Emerson had predicted, those many years before, that a poet would come forth and blow all the old poetic conventions to shreds with the invention of new meters that would bring about the demise of rhymed poetry. Whatever critics might say about the free verse ushered in by Whitman, its originality was not in question. Yet for both men the Poet was far more than one who would create new metrics and new devices. In the lecture of 1842, Emerson had described the Poet as

> the person without impediment, who by the favor of God is sent into the world to see clearly what others have glimpses of, to feel richly what they suspect, to gaze with sound senses and responding heart at full leisure, and in a trance of delight, at the heavens and the earth; a soul through which the universe is poured … the hospitable soul, which entertains in its spirit all travelers, tongues, kindreds, all employments, all eccentricities, all crimes even, in its vast charity and overcoming hope.[8]

Whitman's 1855 preface answered with a sympathetic theme on a heightened note:

> Of all nations the United States with veins full of poetical stuff most needs poets and will doubtless have the greatest

and use them the greatest. Their Presidents shall not be
their common referee so much as their poets shall. Of all
mankind the great poet is the equable man ... He bestows
on every object or quality its fit proportions neither more
nor less. He is the arbiter of the diverse and he is the key.
He is the equalizer of his age ... lighting the study of man,
the soul, immortality—federal, state or municipal government, marriage, health, freetrade, intertravel by land
and sea .... nothing too close, nothing too far off ... the
stars not too far off ... He is no arguer ... he is judgment.
He judges not as the judge judges but as the sun falling
around a helpless thing.[9]

When Emerson reworked his lecture on "The Poet" into essay form, he had

illustrated the role of the poet by describing three archetypal pillars of the

universe that reappear in every system of thought throughout history: the

Knower, who stands for the love of truth; the Doer, who stands for the love

of the Good; and the Sayer, who stands for the love of Beauty.[10] Both Emer-

son and Whitman saw America's Poet as the Sayer, the man of compassion,

through whom the lost art of writing should be born anew, and in whose

verse the new wine of the Poet should ennoble his countrymen and raise

them into the sphere of the soul.

Whitman's arrival helped pry Emerson loose from his obsession with

the folk spirit of England as a replacement for the spirit of Idealism that had

all but abandoned him with the fading away of the Transcendental move-

ment in 1845. Turning to more concrete and local sources of inspiration,

Emerson spent the fall of 1855 looking over the notes and lectures on the

Natural History of the Intellect project that he had laid aside in 1850.

Reviewing the progress he had made, he started combing through the jour-

nals of the 1840s and 1850s, collecting any material that might be relevant

and enlarging upon the old passages with new thoughts, new combinations of ideas. If Whitman's little book brought Emerson joy and fresh inspiration, then Emerson's letter must have brought Whitman to the brink of euphoria. The poet sent no letter in reply, but set to work immediately on a second edition despite the blistering criticism he was receiving. The spring of 1856 found him "determined that I should concentrate my powers [on] 'Leaves of Grass'—not diverting any of my means, strength, interest to the construction of anything else."[11] He dashed out new poems, and the little volume grew to three times its original size.

When the second edition of *Leaves of Grass* appeared in 1856, it became apparent why Whitman had not done Emerson the courtesy of sending a letter in reply: the book *was* his reply. Stamped in gold on the spine of the new edition was a quote from the now-famous letter and Emerson's name. The preface of the first edition was replaced by an appendix, which included the full text of Emerson's letter and an open letter from Whitman to Emerson. The letter began, "Here are thirty-two Poems, which I send you, dear Friend and Master, not having found how I could satisfy myself with sending any usual acknowledgement of your letter."[12] Whitman went on to describe how he had expanded the first twelve poems into thirty-two, how the work of his life was clear to him, to keep making poems to the number of a hundred, even a thousand. His reason for making poems resembled Emerson's momentous vow when he first moved to Concord and stood in the fields of his forefathers: "I say the word or two that has got to be said … and remind every man and woman of something." Whitman launched into the body of his letter to Emerson with a remarkable two sentences: "Master, I am a man who has perfect faith. Master, we have not come through centuries, caste, heroisms, fables, to halt in this land today."[13] The bulk of the letter, which filled several pages, went on to condense and sharpen the ideas of the 1855 preface, to delve into the mystery and grandeur of "These States," explore their potential, and describe the poets and masters of the word who would come to transform their inhabitants into a true nation of men and women.

Whitman closed his letter with the idea that the national character that would form in the future—a character "strong, limber, just, openmouthed, American-blooded, full of pride, full of ease, of passionate friendliness"—would stand upright upon "that new moral American continent without which, I see, the physical continent remained incomplete, may-be a carcass, a bloat—that newer America, answering face to face with The States, with ever-satisfying and ever-unsurveyable seas and shores." Character, to Whitman, was everything—the focus, in the end, of all of the Poet's efforts. The closing two paragraphs rise in sweep and affirmation to match Emerson's letter; they deserve to be as famous, and so should be quoted in full.

> These shores you found. I say you have led The States there—have led Me there. I say that none has ever done, or ever can do, a greater deed for The States, than your deed. Others may line out the lines, build the cities, work mines, break up farms; it is yours to have been the original true Captain who put to sea, intuitive, positive, rendering the first report, to be told less by any report, and more by the mariners of a thousand bays, in each tack of their arriving and departing, many years after you.
>
> Receive, dear Master, these statements and assurances through me, for all the young men, and for an earnest that we know none before you, but the best following you; and that we demand to take your name into our keeping, and that we understand what you have in-

dicated, and find the same indicated in ourselves, and that we will stick to it and enlarge upon it through These States.[14]

A Beeline to an Axe

In the winter of 1855-56, Emerson again went west and lectured in Illinois, Wisconsin, Michigan, and Ohio before returning to finish out the season in Massachusetts, Maine, and New Hampshire. Within weeks of his return home on March fifteenth, the ship of state capsized and began to sink, as many saw it, towards inevitable disunion. It had been the brainchild of Stephen A. Douglas to resolve the question of "slave or free" by dividing the Nebraska territory into two parts and allowing the settlers of the territories to vote upon the question of whether slavery would be permitted. Douglas's implicit wink and nod as he rammed the legislation through Congress was that Kansas would enter the Union as a slave state and Nebraska as free. The Kansas-Nebraska Act had created a tense and dangerous environment in Kansas as Northern free-soilers poured into the territory in an effort to thwart the "Little Giant's" scheme, while pro-slavery "border ruffians" from Missouri, perceiving that the North was backing out on the deal it had made to open settlement of the West, moved in as "temporary citizens" to offset the free-soil settlers in the elections. On May twenty-first, 1856, an army of Southern sympathizers, who had marched across the border from Missouri determined to take revenge for the assassination of a Sheriff, surrounded the town of Lawrence. On the following day they sacked and burned the town. That same day, in Washington, D.C., Preston Brooks, a Congressman from South Carolina, took exception to the epithets Charles Sumner had hurled at the Slave Power conspiracy for its rape of the "virgin territory" of Kansas and beat Sumner with his cane until the abolitionist Senator fell, bloody and unconscious, on the Senate floor.[15] Two days later at Pottawatomie Creek in Kansas, a small band of men, infuriated by the burning of Lawrence and goaded on by the news of Sumner's beating, retaliated by sneaking out on the Creek late at night, luring five proslavery men out of their beds, and massacring them with broad swords. Blood was spilt on both sides.

These events, darker and more outrageous than anything that had come before, affected Emerson deeply. Sumner, a famous and outspoken opponent of slavery who had been elected to fill Daniel Webster's seat in 1850, was a friend of Emerson's. It was he who had joined Emerson in boycotting the New Bedford lyceum and he who had asked Emerson to stump for Palfrey with his speech on the Fugitive Slave Law. On the twenty-sixth of May, four days after the attack, Emerson attended an indignation meeting in Concord and listened as person after person rose to denounce the brutal beating. Each seemed to breathe in the eloquence of the one who spoke before like "sweet nitrous oxide gas," and, for a moment, "the most hard-fisted disagreeably virile & thought-paralyzing companion" turned out to be "the most fluent, various, & effective orator." When Emerson's turn came, he delivered a short but powerful speech in which he proclaimed, "I think we must get rid of slavery, or we must get rid of freedom." Emerson's tendency to look through events to the spiritual facts that stood behind them led him to comment, after the meeting, that "Sumner's attack is of no importance. It is only a leaf of the tree, it is not Sumner who must be avenged, but the tree must be cut down." "Suppose we raise soldiers in Massachusetts," he mused; "suppose we propose a Northern Union."[16] As brave as the idea sounded, the reality of what was happening to the country led Emerson to write despairingly that "the hour is coming when the strongest will not be strong enough." The aftermath of the attack on Sumner was probably the first time that Emerson actually considered the use of force, the raising of troops, to be a valid option in the effort to rid the country of slavery.

Though Emerson had arrived at the idea that an army might be needed to force the conflict in the country to a resolution, he could not think through what must be done with such troops. In the past he had experienced great difficulty understanding the political compromises necessary to keep the tension between North and South from exploding uncontrollably and disastrously. For all of the vilification that Emerson had heaped on Webster's head, the truth was that the old politician had always acted out of the ideal of preserving the Union, even at a time when the loudest abolitionists and their sympathizers were willing to let the South go its separate way so that the Northern conscience would be no longer be burdened with the unpalatable reality of slavery in a nation founded on the ideal of freedom. Emerson was too thickly surrounded by radicals to appreciate Webster's motive, and he began to embrace the fact of disunion as inevitable. Yet Emerson also sensed a certain hypocrisy in the abolitionist position that disunion was the ultimate solution, though he had never been able to fully articulate the problem— namely, that cutting off the South to save the North from slavery's taint would doom an entire race to rot in chains. In one Journal entry Emerson sat on the fence and showed how little he comprehended the implications of an official severance of the Union, and how difficult it was for him to work out a real solution: "Disunion [is] excellent, if it is just disunion enough, but if it go too far, 'tis bad."[17] The newly emerging Republican party, on the other hand, seemed to have a workable plan: contain slavery in the South at all costs and do not allow it to spread West or North. Especially after the events of May in Kansas and Washington, Emerson, who had for many years been disenchanted with the Whigs, gravitated towards the Republicans and lent them his support. The Republican Party offered the best way of bringing the cause of abolitionism to the national political stage. Emerson's involvement in politics reached its height that June as he ran for delegate to the Republican nominating convention, though he lost by a narrow margin. Drawn to the ideals of the Republican platform, Emerson took an active role in supporting John Fremont, the heroic explorer of the Sierra Nevada and former antislavery Senator from California whom the convention selected as its candidate. In the midst of the campaign, on August sixth, *English Traits*, a volume that had taken as many years to write as *Representative Men* and had given him even more trouble and heartache, appeared in Boston's bookstores. The book seemed to belong to another age.

As debate raged throughout the country on the issue of slavery, on how to limit its growth or regulate its expansion, there was one man in particular who envisioned an armed campaign, not simply to drive the South into a pen, but actually to free the slaves. In January of 1857, John Brown came to the East, fresh from the all-out war he was waging in Kansas, seeking money and guns. The gray-eyed captain sought out Frank Sanborn and asked if the Concord schoolteacher could introduce him to rich Boston antislavery sympathizers who might materially support his cause. Sanborn was an Emerson's protégé, a young man whom Emerson had helped put through Harvard and whom he had invited, three years earlier, to teach the small private school that the Emerson children attended in Concord. Energetic, bright, and eager to be in the company of men of such strong character and intelligence, Sanborn was mesmerized by Brown. The schoolteacher became the captain's agent in Massachusetts and introduced him to the wealthiest abolitionists in Boston—William Lloyd Garrison and Wendell Phillips among them. Sanborn, Thomas Wentworth Higginson, Gerrit Smith, and three others became part of a core group known as the Secret Six, the group that acted as Brown's inner circle in planning and funding his war.

Brown toured New England giving speeches in order to raise money. On March fourteenth he arrived in Concord at Sanborn's insistence. Sanborn took him straight to Mrs. Thoreau's, a perennial gathering place for the foremost abolitionists of the day. The grizzled Captain sat down with Thoreau and told him the details of the famous battle of Black Jack, where he had accepted the unconditional surrender of a company of twenty-three men. As they were talking, Emerson, recently returned from a lecture trip, called at the house, where Thoreau welcomed him in and introduced him to the visitor. The three men talked through the afternoon. Some hundred citizens of the town gathered to hear Brown's speech that evening, where he described the "folly of the peace party in Kansas," which discouraged resistance to the raids because they believed their true strength lay in the wrongs they suffered. Brown put the question to the assembly, "if their wrong was greater than the negro's, & what kind of strength that gave to the negro?" This point especially resounded with Emerson. Brown gave a brief account of the battle at Black Jack, careful, as always, not to mention his responsibility for the slaughter at Pottawatomie Creek, and made a plea for money to fund the expensive war against the "institution of the devil." The crowd responded well and gave Brown subscriptions and cash; Emerson, deeply impressed with Brown, donated $25 to the cause—enough for perhaps two or three rifles.[18] The money was a small token of the esteem that he held for the Ohio farmer, whom he later called "the rarest of heroes." Feeling stirred to take real and fatal action in service to the good cause, Emerson retired to his Journal after Brown left and noted, "There are men who are born to go to Kansas, men born to take a bee line to an axe."

Some two months later, on May sixteenth of 1857, Emerson gathered with Longfellow, Lowell, Oliver Wendell Holmes, and James Eliot Cabot to meet with a publisher about starting a new journal. All five of these men had been members of the Saturday Club, and their discussions in that forum led to the idea of establishing a literary journal. Holmes gave it the title of the "Atlantic Monthly," and Lowell agreed to be the editor. Emerson at once compared the new journal to the *Dial* and wrote that there should be this difference—that the new magazine should become "the Bible of the Americans." Emerson hoped that this journal would succeed where the *Dial* and the *Massachusetts Quarterly Review* (a venture with which he had been involved between 1847 and 1850) had failed. He saw a new opportunity for culture and art to provide leadership for America, to give oracles relating to the great political upheaval of the times. "It should be waited for by all the newspapers & journals," and the Abolitionists themselves "should get their leading from it, & not be able to shun it as they do."[19] The planning stages of the *Atlantic*, however, left Emerson doubtful that this was the journal to "guide the age," for its founders did not seem to have the will to adopt an Editor who could select only what was "sterling," who would "defy the public... & go on printing, until the discerning minority of the public have found out that the Book is right."[20] Yet if the magazine could not become the moral compass of the nation, it soon proved its worth by playing a vitally important role in Emerson's career. Unlike the *Review* and the *Dial* before it, the *Atlantic Monthly* had tenacity and staying power. Emerson now had a valuable resource, a nimble vehicle for publishing essays and poems that reached a broad reading public while avoiding the time-consuming and laborious process of assembling a whole collection of essays and editing them into a single volume. The original thoughts that rose to the height of inspiration when Emerson achieved *l'abandon* in the lectern could now flow out on a regular basis to the ever-growing readership of the *Atlantic*.

In February of 1858, the Natural History of the Intellect, the project that Emerson held most dear to his heart throughout the decade, took a great step forward. Emerson had been adding steadily to his cache of relevant passages over the last two and a half years. Feeling he had "a goodly quantity of material that ought to interest goodly heads," he accepted an invitation to give a series of lectures in Boston. He now had four lectures instead of the three he had started with seven years before, and he called the new series "The Natural Method of Mental Philosophy." Privately he referred to the project as "the New Metaphysics." Emerson's approach to the Natural History of the Intellect in the 1848-1850 series had focused on how the laws of the Intellect revealed themselves through nature, and consequently how the study of those laws formed the basis for an ethical and just life. Rather than rework these lectures, Emerson set that theme aside and approached the project from a different perspective. The first lectures of the series revealed his new purpose as he concentrated on describing the powers of the mind that were necessary to perceive and study the activity of the Intellect. He then examined the virtue of self-trust prerequisite to the development of these higher faculties of the human being. Just as we have eyes and ears to observe the physical world and form impressions of it, so too must the student of the Intellect develop such higher faculties as imagination and inspiration in order to find his way in the world of spirit. Emerson delivered the four lectures—"Powers of the Mind," "The Natural Method of Mental Philosophy," "Memory," and "Self-Possession"—on successive Wednesdays from March seventeenth through April seventh. When the course ended, the *Boston Evening Transcript* lauded the series as a success "in the fullest meaning of the term." Viewing the lectures as good "studies" or experiments that "gain much by repetition," Emerson obliged and repeated them a second time in November for what would be his seventh public presentation of his ideas on "The Natural History of Intellect," further honing the second theme of the project: the path of self-trust and the development of the powers of the mind needed to uncover the facts of the spiritual world. Emerson was again in sight of his best task. Yet he still wanted an axe.

VIII.

A NEW POWER OF VISION

The War-Note

Emerson became a household name throughout New England and the Midwest, where he toured regularly every winter to lecture, and his books were widely read throughout the country. He delivered as many as eighty lectures a year throughout the 1850s, and audiences packed the halls where he spoke. He was one of the most famous men of letters not only in America, but in England as well. Reports of his lectures appeared in the major newspapers wherever he went, and few speakers could command the public attention that he did. Fame and recognition were not what Emerson sought, however, nor could they fill the void within him. Despite his great success, something was terribly wrong, deep within his soul. Just after he gave "The Natural Method of Mental Philosophy" lectures in 1858, he ceased writing in the Journal. Month upon month went by, and still he did not write. There is no such extended break anywhere in the sixty years spanned by the Journal except for the year that he lost his eyesight after falling ill at Divinity School, thirty-three years before. His Journal had been his constant companion, his daily meditation for almost his entire life; but he abandoned it now, he wrote, because "I see few intellectual persons, & even those to no purpose, & sometimes believe that I have no new thoughts, and that my life is quite at an end." It was as if the source of his inspiration had finally fled. He simply gave up.

One spring morning in 1859, almost a full year since he had last writ-ten in his Journal, a man visited Emerson's house and sat down to converse with him. There is no record of what they discussed or even what the man's name was. When the visitor left, Emerson ran to his Journal and took up his pen again. "This morning came by a man with knowledge & interests like mine, in his head. Suddenly I had thoughts again," he rejoiced.[1] For his entire adult life, Emerson had felt very much alone. Even though he was sur-rounded by a crush of family and friends who loved him very much, he had had the feeling that he was always waiting for his true friends to arrive— those who were in sympathy with his deepest strivings, who shared his thought, who loved what he loved. The man who came calling that spring morning seemed to let him know that he was not in fact alone and rekindled the power that lay dormant within him. The floodgates were opened. A tide of enthusiasm and fresh energy carried him through the summer. New thoughts filled his head and electrified him with a "joy which will not let me sit in my chair, which brings me bolt upright to my feet, and sends me strid-ing around my room, like a tiger in his cage." It was not the spirit of Idealism, nor the spirit of the country, but the Intellect itself that seemed to have touched him with fresh inspiration. Filled with wonder at the beatitude of the Intellect and this renewal of life, he could not find words sufficient to set down "the thought which thrills me." "What if I never write a book or a line?" he challenged; "For a moment the eyes of my eyes were opened, the affirmative experience remains, & consoles through all suffering."[2]

John Brown came to Concord and spoke again on May eighth, soon after the arrival of Emerson's mysterious visitor, in a renewed effort to raise funds. As before, he concealed from his audience his true intentions, which were now far grander than all but the tight inner circle of his closest supporters could imagine. His admirers in Concord lost track of him over the summer, as did the rest of the country. Emerson began fundraising for Brown in the fall, though he still did not know his whereabouts. On October eighteenth, the news reached Concord. The whole magnificent plan was laid bare in a few days. John Brown of Osawatomie had raided federal property and captured the arsenal at Harper's Ferry in an attempt to incite a general slave insurrection in the South. He was captured by Federal troops and was awaiting trial for his life.

Frank Sanborn fled Concord for Canada the instant the news came, fearing that letters in Brown's possession would implicate him and lead to his arrest. For Emerson, however, this event was the touchstone, the moment of clarity, truth, and courage. He admonished Sanborn to return to Concord at once; what Brown needed now was not jackrabbits, but men who would affirm that his was the right cause. The slaveholder was mistaken, Emerson wrote in his Journal, to think that by capturing and killing Brown he could rid himself of his tormentors, for "no matter how many Browns he can catch & kill, he does not make the number less, for the air breeds them." Emerson, who had ridden the ebb and flow of doubt and affirmation for so many years, who had languished in uncertainty over the role he was to take

in his country's turmoil, who had sought the serene solitude of the mountaintop, now, in a matter of days, of hours, became the exponent of decisive
action. Captain Brown broke Emerson's fetters and showed him that "perfect will is electricity, is unquenchable fire, & burns like the sun, & all
creatures must conform themselves accordingly. There can be no such will
except through the conversion of the man into his will." Brown was a principle made flesh, and "every principle is a war-note. Who ever attempts to
carry the rule of right & love & freedom must take his life in his hand." John
Brown was Emerson's war-note. "There was no need of trumpets," he wrote,
only days after Brown's capture;

> There was no need of banners
> Every zephyr was a bugle
> Every woodthrush sang hosannas
> Sharp steel was his lieutenant
> And powder was his men
>
> The land was all electric
> The mountain echoes roar,
> Every crutch became a pike
> The woods & meadows shouted War
> Every valley shouted, strike![3]

Though the country was stunned, Emerson strode out in front, placing himself boldly before the public, defending John Brown and promoting
his cause to anyone who would listen, and even those who would not. The
only one who worked harder on Brown's behalf was, perhaps, Henry
Thoreau. Most of Emerson's friends thought he had lost his mind to risk his
reputation for such a man, who clearly seemed insane. But Emerson saw
through the surface facts to the true significance of the event. Brown's

speeches before the Court were reported in the papers, and Emerson read them carefully. Provoked by the proceedings of the trial, he drafted a letter to the Governor of Virginia, Alexander Wise, pleading Brown's case and appealing to Wise not "to stand in the most unlucky position which history must give to the Governor who signs his death warrant."[4] Governor Wise seemed determined to earn the distinction.

The entire South was in a wild frenzy, panicked by the rumors of general slave revolts following in Brown's wake, and a great cry went up for the rebel's head. Governor Wise, in response, put the trial on a "double quick time." The unrepentant Captain was sentenced November second, just one week after the trial began, to hang on the gallows. Emerson spoke out for his hero in his lecture on "Courage" on November tenth, after which he was pilloried in the press for saying that if John Brown were hanged it would make the gallows "sacred as the cross." On December second, the fatal day, the citizens of Concord gathered for a memorial service at which were read passages from Wordsworth, Tacitus, Tennyson, Jefferson, and many others. Emerson ascended the podium and read Brown's last speech to the court. In Virginia, John Brown looked out from the gallows at rank upon rank of soldiers standing at attention, their glistening bayonets shouldered high in the air, until the hood was dropped over his eyes. His body hung for thirty-two minutes. On December sixth, Emerson spoke at Music Hall in Boston and eulogized the martyr in his address on "Morals." As a final tribute, shortly after the New Year, he gave a lecture entitled "John Brown." Emerson remained committed to helping Brown's family and continued raising money for the relief fund he had helped to start. That spring, Brown's two daughters came to live with the Emersons and enrolled in Sanborn's school.

While John Brown had been alive, Emerson, like most people, knew little of him and probably had even less knowledge of what was actually happening in Bleeding Kansas—or what Brown's plans really were—despite the fact that he had had almost daily contact with one member of the Secret Six and had known several of the others. When Emerson finally recognized what stood behind Brown, his public deeds in rallying to the martyr's defense—which even Brown's inner circle were afraid to do—and his service to Brown's family brought about a deep inner change. Emerson's decisive actions in the midst of the storm were entirely free of the doubt and introspection that had haunted him for so long. In his new concept of personal Power, "*being* and *doing*, must blend, before the eye has health to behold through sympathy & through presence, the Spirit."[5] The spiritual world, which Emerson had felt slowly drawing away for over a decade, now seemed to offer him a great new gift, an affirmation and extension of the experience he had had when the unnamed visitor had come by the previous spring, when "the eyes of my eyes" had opened and he had been granted a new power of vision. Around the middle of October and about two weeks before the anniversary of Harper's Ferry, the scales again fell from his eyes. He described the experience this way: "It is as if new eyes were opened so that we saw under the lilac bush or the oak or the rock or the tiger, the spiritual cause of the lilac, stone, or tiger, the genius of that kind, and so could rightly & securely use the name for the truth it stood for in the human mind."[6] Emerson told of seeing the origin of what he observed in the physical world and its relation to cosmical laws. The veil of physicality was thrown back, so that even the laws of nature—gravity, motion, growth, decay—appeared against the backdrop of the spiritual beings who were their cause. Emerson called this experience the beatitude of the Intellect, the beholding of the imminent presence of the spiritual world and the real gods that populate it. He saw the eye of the Intellect, blazing forth and burning up all illusion.

Some three weeks later, on the morning of Wednesday, November seventh, word spread across the country that Abraham Lincoln had been elected to the Presidency of the United States. Emerson hailed the "sublime" news as the "pronunciation of the masses of America against Slavery." The Slave Power thought no less. On December twentieth, a special convention in South Carolina decreed "that the union now subsisting between South Carolina and other States, under the name of 'The United States of America' is hereby dissolved." Charleston celebrated in jubilee atmosphere, and one after another of the Southern states called conventions to follow South Carolina's lead and voted for secession. In the first weeks of the new year Southern troops began seizing Federal arsenals on an almost daily basis, and wealthy slaveholders gathered to discuss a new sovereign nation, the Confederate States of America. In the North it was a dangerous time to be an abolitionist. Pro-Union agitators laid this worst of all crises at the door of those who had advocated in favor of the human rights of an enslaved race. The atmosphere in many Northern cities, even Boston, was volatile, but when Wendell Phillips invited Emerson to speak at a meeting of the Massachusetts Anti-Slavery Society at Tremont Temple in Boston, he readily accepted. Emerson had never liked addressing open forums—he was accustomed to the comparatively genteel atmosphere of the Lyceums—and he well knew the danger that might lurk in such a meeting, but he resolved to "do the duty of the day." It was the duty of all thinking men, he wrote in justifying his decision to speak, to assert freedom, to "go where it is threatened,

& say, 'I am for it, & do not wish to live in the world a moment longer than it exists.'" Though he felt he had nothing to say, his respect for Phillips was so great and his resolve to stand before the public and support the cause so firm that he was determined "if I were dumb, yet I would have gone & mowed & muttered or made signs."[7] He was almost forced to that expedient, for a pro-Union knot in the mob roared, groaned, and shouted him down, so that after several attempts to give his speech he was forced to leave the stage.

On April 12, 1861, Confederate batteries—for now there was a Confederacy, complete with government, President, and Constitution—opened fire on Fort Sumter in Charleston Harbor after repeated demands that the Federal government remove its troops from Confederate territory. The fort, undermanned and undersupplied, was forced to surrender the next day. On April fifteenth President Lincoln issued a proclamation declaring an insurrection to exist and calling up the militia of the States to active duty. Emerson greeted the war with cheerful welcoming words and even gratitude, for here at last was a decisive measure that could lead to the extermination of slavery. He saw the war as the great teacher and reconciler that would show all petty quarrels to be ridiculous, and for the sake of ridding the country of the cancer of slavery, it would be "better that war & defeats continue, until we have come to that amputation." He described his fellow citizens as cheerful and jocund that a principled leader had emerged after a parade of inept and corrupt administrations in the pocket of the Slave Power. As if to match the excitement and import of the war, the Journal itself underwent a great change, splitting, as it had when he was writing *English Traits*, into multiple volumes that Emerson kept concurrently, one of which was appropriately entitled "WAR." During the next four years he had at least two journals going, and for much of the time he kept four at once. No longer absorbed with the achievements of a civilization across the sea, the Journal now diverged and expanded to record the events of the times and the heroes of the present day, with whom Emerson sat at table and in the parlor. "We will not again disparage America," he wrote, " now that we have seen what men it will bear."[8]

In January of 1862, Emerson met with the foremost of these men when he traveled to Washington, D.C., to give a lecture at the Smithsonian Institute. His old friend Sumner acted as his guide in the capital and introduced him into the highest circles of government. On February second Emerson met President Lincoln, who greeted the essayist cheerfully and recalled one of Emerson's lectures he had attended years before in Springfield, and what Emerson had said of the manners and air of a Kentuckian—that he seemed to say, "*Here am I; if you don't like me, the worse for you.*" The President impressed Emerson "more favorably than I had hoped." Emerson found Lincoln a "frank, sincere, well-meaning man" who gave clear factual statements mixed with boyish cheerfulness and "jolly good meaning." After a lengthy conversation with the President, Emerson resumed his tour of Washington, D.C., with Sumner and visited both the Treasury Building and the State Department, where Emerson met with Secretary of the Treasury Salmon Chase and Secretary of War Edwin Stanton. Stanton, apparently favorably impressed, invited Emerson to church the next morning, to be followed by lunch at his home, and Emerson accepted. That day he also met Secretary of State William Seward, Secretary of the Navy Gideon Welles, and Attorney General Edward Bates. Lincoln's Cabinet accepted Emerson with open arms, talking with him, joking with him, and discussing policy and the war. That evening Emerson had dinner with Chase and the next morning, as promised, attended church with Seward. Emerson became hopelessly lost in the Common Prayer book; Seward leaned over from time to time to help his companion find his place. After church Emerson accompanied Seward on his usual visit to the President and sat with the two politicians as they discussed markets and foreign diplomacy. He dined with Seward again, then spent Sunday evening at the home of Charles Eames, the former Minister to Venezuela, where he sat with a group that included two governors and Lincoln's personal secretaries, Nicolay and Hay. When he left Washington on Monday, Emerson had not only met the President and his entire Cabinet; he had been welcomed into their circle.[9]

What Emerson could not have known was the role that he himself had played, indirect though it was, in bringing about Lincoln's rise to the Presidency. In his early career, Lincoln had been at best a local politician, never a national figure. Self-educated and lacking the depth of understanding of classical history and culture that his college-educated counterparts made free use of in legislative business and debate, Lincoln found himself swimming to keep his head above the political waters of Washington and left after one term in Congress, disillusioned and smarting from the attacks on his "Spot" speech. Back in his home town in 1847, he began to study the books that would allow him to stand equal to his peers. In every spare moment he could find, Lincoln would stretch out on the too-short office couch and read aloud—he never forgot anything he heard spoken. Lincoln's law partner, Billy Herndon, was an avid reader of Emerson's works, zealously collecting everything he could find written by the New England essayist. When Herndon read a notice of Emerson's praise for *Leaves of Grass*, there was no question that he should buy this unprecedented work of poetry. He obtained a copy in Chicago—the 1856 edition, with Whitman's open-letter reply to Emerson—and set it on the office table, where it sat for some time, the object of occasional debate by the firm's interns. One evening, after hearing Herndon and the law students talking about some of the more controversial passages, Lincoln, his interest piqued, walked over, picked up the volume, and began to read—silently. He read for half an hour, never looking up, never saying a word, and then flipped back to the beginning and started reading again, this time aloud. For weeks Lincoln read *Leaves of Grass* regularly and its style and substance began to transform his oratorical style— powerful and tight, yet logical and mathematical—infusing it with poetic cadence and imagery. It was in this new style that Lincoln delivered his famous "House Divided" speech and the numerous speeches thereafter that inspired the Republican party and caused him to rise past all others to become the party's candidate for President in 1860. It was this same eloquence that carried Lincoln through the grueling campaign and, finally, into the White House.[10]

Emerson returned home from his trip to Washington, D.C., to an ailing friend. Thoreau had fallen mortally ill, at the age of forty-four, with tuberculosis, the same disease that had claimed Ellen's life thirty years before. Emerson found himself able to do little for this best of friends other than sit at his bedside and watch his noble spirit fade from the world. Thoreau was confined to his bed, unable to rise, unable to pace the woods as he had done day in and day out his entire life. Emerson sadly visited Walden Pond alone, and began to take note of the ice on the surface, which seemed to be holding strong unusually late in the season. On April first and second he walked on the frozen water of the pond, which solidly supported his weight, and returned to Thoreau's bed side to give reports on the unusual thickness of the ice. Henry assured his friend that he had seen the ice hold as late as April eighteenth; on April ninth and tenth Emerson walked on the pond again. One week later he heard the purple finch, a favorite of Henry's, sing for the first time that spring, and two days after, on the eighteenth, went down to Walden to check the ice again. The day was very warm, the sun shone strong, but the ice still had not broken; there was, it seemed, a new record. Thoreau's condition worsened, and on May 6, 1862, Henry passed away. Emerson, who so often before had recorded the date and time when those closest to him left the world, wrote no notice of his dearest friend's death in his Journal. Thoreau was buried in Sleepy Hollow cemetery beneath a small stone that said, simply, "Henry," and Emerson delivered the eulogy that would become his greatest biographical essay. In early June, Emerson rowed out onto Walden Pond, where Thoreau seemed to stand before him still, "erect, calm, self-subsistent." For the rest of the year, Emerson regularly took Thoreau's journals off the shelf, reading in them and copying out passages into his own Journal.

The Deeds of the Hero

Lincoln issued the preliminary Emancipation Proclamation that fall, shortly after almost five thousand men from both North and South lost their lives in a bloody battle at Antietam Creek; the single day of fighting claimed an additional 21,000 wounded and missing. The preliminary Proclamation was a shot over the bow of the Confederate States, announcing that on January first, 1863, "all persons held as slaves, within any state, or designated part of a state, the people whereof shall then be in rebellion against the United States shall be then, thenceforward, and forever free." The Proclamation was exactly what Emerson had been waiting for since the opening attack on Fort Sumter. From the beginning he had believed that the very nature of the war would eventually polarize the two sides so that one army must fight for slavery and one against it; until that day came, however, both Waldo and Lidian officially disapproved of the Federal government's stated goals for the war. They would not let their son Edward enlist until the war for the Union became a war to end slavery. The Proclamation, though many abolitionists criticized it and wished it to be stronger, was the document that could irrevocably transform the war into a campaign to exterminate the institution of slavery. Emerson talked with many people who claimed Lincoln really thought emancipation to be "almost morally wrong," who said he resorted to it as a "desperate measure," but Emerson welcomed it as the necessary expedient for the success of the war because it would create an army in the rear of the enemy and make it impossible for Europe to recognize the South. More than that, the Proclamation took up the cause of a universal interest and eternal right, and as such it worked "when men are sleeping, when the Army goes into winter quarters, when generals are treacherous or imbecile."[11]

There is a somewhat peculiar fact about Emerson and the Civil War that is rarely commented upon, which is this: even though Emerson was one of the most consistent journal-keepers in history and the greatest prose stylist of his time, he is rarely if ever quoted by historians who are writing about the War. Soldiers' diaries, generals' memoirs, newspaper columns, citizens' diaries—all are quoted, but rarely observations by Emerson, and for good reason. Once in a while Emerson made a note about General McClellan or a random newspaper report, but for the most part he was useless as a dial of external events. Whereas his contemporaries made detailed notes of the movements of soldiers and cannons, of battles and skirmishes and sieges, of supply trains and rear guard actions, Emerson turned his gaze to a different field. "I know the cosmic results will be the same," he wrote, "whatever the daily events may be."[12] He saw the spiritual background of the war, that slavery was a great disease eating at the moral foundation of the country, rotting its social, cultural, and political institutions. The Civil War had significance not only for the future of America, but for all the nations of the world, who had their eyes turned on the young nation to see if the proposition were sound, that a people could govern themselves without monarchs and lords. A decade earlier, in the midst of the Fugitive Slave crisis, Emerson had noted that Schiller said the Thirty Years War made Germany a Nation; "What calamity," he had wondered, "will make us one?" He now had his answer. Emerson saw the blazing eye of the Intellect turn upon America at that moment in history in order to burn up and consume the disease. The only possible outward effect of such an enormous event in the spiritual world was, in Emerson's view, a war in which hundreds of thousands of young men would die. Like fire, the war would rage and engulf all before it until it found no more fuel and burned itself out. Lincoln later tried to explain the necessity that Emerson anticipated in the sacrifice of so many young lives by saying that every drop of blood shed by the slave-master's whip had to be paid for with the blood of soldiers on the field, both North and South, for no one was innocent of the wrong that had been done.

Emerson saw the Emancipation Proclamation as a great world-historic deed, and when Lincoln finally declared that the war was a war to end slavery, and that there would be no negotiation or surrender until it was eradicated forever, Emerson mustered all of his fame, all of his thought, all of his skill as a lecturer and put them in service of the Northern cause. The Proclamation was still provisional, to be confirmed in January if the Southern states did not rejoin the Union; Emerson put his efforts into ensuring that it would indeed be signed into law on New Year's Day. He had been forced to cancel his lecture season the year before because of the unrest caused by the war, but now he started afresh, with this new theme. On October twelfth he gave a lecture in support of the Proclamation to the Parker Fraternity in Boston, and on November eighteenth he gave a new lecture on the war, "Perpetual Forces," again to the Parker Fraternity. This lecture crystallized Emerson's view of the war. He began by describing the natural world, drawing out the rhythms and cycles of Nature and the power of its forces, such as gravitation and electricity. In the midst of this great circle of Nature, he introduced the human being, who, naked and unarmed, appeared very small and defenseless against the tigers and jackals. Despite the human being's apparently pathetic endowment, Emerson pointed out, he had achieved a complete mastery of the natural world through the power of Reason. One may imagine in the center of the circle of Nature a small human being growing larger and reaching out his limbs to grasp the rim of the circle by virtue of this power. Emerson then described the human being as the receiver and depository of the powers that flowed through Reason, perpetual forces such as Imagination and Memory that make possible Poetry and Science. These powers were the causal forces that allowed the human being to expand and grasp the circle of Nature, in which he now appeared as the Colossus. Emerson pictured these powers as forming the human being into the "receptacle of celestial thoughts" and bringing him into the "august circles of eternal Law," and by the perception of the eternal Law, the human being learned how to bring these powers to manifestation in the world through action. The circle of Nature that the Colossus grasped became the circle of the cosmos. Emerson closed this lecture with the thought that the moral imperative of the cosmos in the present was the eradication of slavery in America, a twisted aberration that had arisen because of a failure in the past to follow the Divine Law.

Emerson gave "Perpetual Forces" twice more in November and eight times in December. When he took the lecture to Albany, his reputation as a firm abolitionist preceded him, and he was greeted by an apprehensive audience that, according to the newspaper report of the lecture, "hoped to hear a discourse with Abolition left out." For Emerson there could be no question that emancipation *was* his theme, and he would attempt to garner the support of his audience for the war to end slavery. A few in the audience applauded him when he advocated forcible emancipation, but they sat in stony silence when he suggested "an equal chance in society with the white man" for the Negro. The lecture at Albany was on December twenty-sixth; when he returned, he settled in to wait for the New Year and the promised official Emancipation Proclamation. It had been the strategy of the abolitionist supporters of the Proclamation to publicize it so widely that Lincoln could not possibly retract it, but they were still fearful. On the night of December thirty-first, abolitionists gathered in Boston anxiously awaited the news. Lincoln had no intention of retreating. On January first he announced that the Proclamation was in effect. That day, Emerson joined with the jubilant abolitionists at Music Hall in Boston, where he read a poem, "Boston Hymn," that he had written especially to celebrate the event. The poem sealed his dedication, made over forty years before in "The Wide World No. 7," to act courageously on behalf of the Spirit of America.

Emerson was firmly convinced not only that the blazing eye of the Intellect would consume the disease of slavery, but that the great conflagration of the war would burn up the veil that shadowed the eyes of his countrymen from perceiving spiritual and moral truth. He had pursued his entire career as a lecturer believing that every person was convertible to an earnest and active life in pursuit of noble ideals, that a god slumbered in every breast, waiting to be awakened. In the Civil War, Emerson saw an event that would rouse his countrymen from lives of complacency and dissipation, that would open wide their eyes to the reality of the spiritual world so that the ideals of self-reliance, self-development, and moral improvement would blaze in the zenith of their heaven and become their guide. "We can see that the Constitution & law in America must be written on ethical principles," he wrote in a war journal, "so that the entire power of the spiritual world can be enlisted to hold the loyalty of the citizen, & to repel the enemy as by force of Nature."[13] In the "Boston Hymn," he called this force an angel named Freedom, who had come to this country and taken the name of Columbia. Whitman, too, heralded Columbia as the guiding spirit of the Union, protectress of the Republic, as she had been in the War for Independence. This spirit was the same that had acted as Emerson's inspiration ever since the Spirit of Idealism had lifted, the spirit that had continually inspired him to dedicate his work to the cause of freedom for a race in chains, the spirit with whom he had struggled as he sought the solitude of the mountaintop. It was the Spirit that the Founders knew to inhabit the Temple of Liberty, the edifice of freedom framed by the Constitution and built upon the foundation of the citizenry. While it is true that Emerson was never directly involved in some of the dramatic actions that had distinguished his friends in the cause of emancipation and Union, Emerson had his own essential role to fill in service to Columbia. The war, as Emerson once noted, appointed its own generals. It appointed its orators as well. Emerson's lectures were the deeds of a hero.

The Window of Opportunity

Shortly after reading "Boston Hymn" at Music Hall, Emerson received a letter from Whitman requesting letters of introduction to Sumner, Seward, and Chase. Weeks earlier, on December sixteenth, while Emerson was giving "Perpetual Forces" at New Bedford, news had come to the Whitman household that Walt's brother, George, had been wounded at Fredericksburg. Walt immediately took a train to the battlefield to look for his brother. Over twelve hundred Union soldiers had been killed in Burnside's great disaster, and some nine thousand six hundred were wounded. Rows of bodies, their uniforms and shoes stolen in the night by Confederate scavengers, lined the battleground, and a string of officer's graves marked the bank of the river; outside the hospital tents, piles of amputated feet, arms, and legs sat under trees. Walt found his brother, but the experience of being in the camp and visiting with the soldiers, Federal and Confederate alike, prompted him to travel to Washington, D.C., to help tend to the wounded soldiers in the overcrowded hospitals there. He needed employment to support himself and thought of his friend in Concord. The last documented time Whitman and Emerson had met was in Boston in 1860 when Whitman was preparing the third edition of *Leaves of Grass*, but they probably had contact sometime in 1862 since Whitman knew about Emerson's connections with Seward and Chase. Whitman was hoping for a government position, and Emerson gladly fulfilled the request for letters of introduction. On January tenth, while he was on tour in Buffalo, Emerson wrote letters to both Seward and Chase introducing "a man of strong original genius, combining, with marked eccentricities, great powers & valuable traits of character: a self-relying large-hearted man, much beloved by his friends; entirely patriotic & benevolent in his theory, tastes, & practice." As for Whitman's writings, which still drew heat from the newspapers and educated circles, Emerson described them as "more deeply American, democratic, & in the interest of political liberty, than those of any other poet." He enclosed all three letters in the self-addressed envelope the conscientious Whitman had provided, along with a note wishing him "best hope," and sent them on their way.[14]

On March twentieth, the lecture season not quite over, Emerson, at the request of Governor Andrew, gave a speech at a fundraiser for the Massachusetts 54th, the all-black regiment later led by Robert Gould Shaw. Frederick Douglass had helped establish the 54th and was recruiting for it at about the same time. Six weeks later, appointed by Secretary of War Stanton to a "committee of visitation," Emerson traveled to the military academy at West Point, where he inspected the cadets and the grounds and was favorably impressed with everything he saw. He was riding a wave of optimism and affirmation, when, on May 1, 1863, Mary Moody Emerson passed away. As the end was approaching, her friends reminisced about how she had always carried her shroud with her since it would be a pity to let it lie unused, and she had worn out many that were put into use as a night gown or day-gown. Not long before her passing Emerson had remarked that her epitaph should read "Here lies the Angel of Death;" in the same stroke he named her muse as Destitution. Now that the release of her spirit was at hand, the event seemed almost comical, and many of her friends were afraid they would laugh at the funeral. Yet after her burial on the hill at Sleepy Hollow, Emerson grew pensive. Three days after the funeral, under the heading of "*Ennui,*" he wrote, "the pursuit of planting a garden or raising a nation occupies the mind, but, at bottom of the heart remains a void which we do not like to feel or complain of." Despite the great positive change the war had brought about in his soul life, something, at bottom, still was not right: "One bustles, & is illuded by the hope of doing good & stifles this gnawing discontent for higher objects in the spiritual world."[15] Emerson knew, as he had known for many years, that he had a mission that was laid up for him by the beings of the spiritual world, who waited for him to accomplish it. Often in the past he had tended to intellectualize these feelings of having a greater task and had concluded he should remove himself to poetic isolation for unhindered communion with the spiritual world. Now, having dedicated himself to the eradication of slavery and the forging of a new nation, though he knew with intuitive certainty it was the only right and proper action, he sighted the old yearning, hidden away in the depths of his soul, stronger than ever before. His service to Columbia's cause was important, but some greater task awaited him.

Emerson buried the feeling quickly, for the war was still omnipresent. July fourth brought the great Union victories at Vicksburg and Gettysburg, and the Confederacy seemed to have been dealt a mortal blow, but nine days later massive riots erupted in New York City when the first names of the new Federal draft were drawn. The angry mob burned and looted, making blacks in the city the special object of their rage. The riots, which touched off smaller insurrections in Boston and other cities, seethed for five days. Damage reports varied, but it was estimated that in New York alone over a thousand people were killed and wounded, and property damage approached $1,500,000. Tension in the North was high. For all of the Union successes, the population was wearying of the war and blaming the seemingly endless days of fighting and waiting on the new stated aim of the war, to press on until the slaves were freed. Emerson could only look on and lament that the streets were swarming with young men, when they were really needed at the front. It must have been especially distressing to him when he heard, the day after the riots ended, of the death of Robert Gould Shaw and almost half of the young black men of the Massachusetts 54th, men whom he had exhorted to take the field for the cause of their own freedom. Though the flames of the New York riots died down, the tension in the North only grew as summer turned to fall and fall to winter. The Federals had not pursued Lee's whipped army after Gettysburg, had not crushed it when they had the chance. The two great armies maneuvered back and forth in Virginia but did not engage in any significant action. The war, it was clear, was going to last into another year.

Just as Meade withdrew the Army of the Potomac across the Rapidan River to wait out the winter, Emerson delivered his lecture on the "Fortune of the Republic" for the first time. The complement of his main lecture of the year before, "Perpetual Forces," this new lecture took the war as its theme and was intended to cheer and fortify his countrymen and advocate perseverance. He illustrated the great fortune of the country with its geography, history, and inherent possibility, a fortune unappreciated by its people. Emerson pointed out that the great experiment of democracy represented the sentiment and future of mankind; the eyes of all Europe turned to her, only to find her in the throes of a crisis. Raising the war above domestic dispute to universal import, Emerson suggested that the way in which the country settled the questions of the war would "make the peace and prosperity, or the calamity of the next ages." As the young country grew, it had often looked to England, to the sophisticated society of London, for a model, but England, who had vacillated since the beginning of the war between recognizing the South as a nation and remaining neutral, who outfitted Confederate ships and sold supplies to the Confederacy, stood aloof and watched "like her old war-wolf for plunder. Never a lofty sentiment, never a duty to civilization, never a generosity, a moral self-restraint is suffered to stand in the way of a commercial advantage. In sight of a commodity, her religion, her morals are forgotten." England receded, weak, and America advanced to the front of the world stage. Throughout history the wars that were most remembered, Emerson illustrated, were those that were not in the interest of feudalism, but society; those that were not dynastic wars, but wars for a principle: "When the cannon is aimed by ideas, then gods join in the combat, then poets are born." The chief among all of these wars for a principle, the very culmination of all the triumphs of humanity, he surmised, was the founding of America. Now, in the present calamity, he told his audience, a principle was being fought for that would prove as much a benefit to the society of nations as the Revolution of 1775. "The slavery is broken, and, if we use our advantage, irretrievably. For such a gain,—to end once for all the pest of all free institutions,—one generation might well be sacrificed...that this continent be purged, and a new era of equal rights dawn on the universe." For such a cause, "who would not consent to die?"[16] He gave the lecture fourteen times that winter.

The opening months of 1864 had their share of events for Emerson: a dinner for General Ambrose Burnside, a benefit for black orphans, and the three hundredth anniversary of Shakespeare's birth in April, for which the Saturday Club hosted a huge celebration. The spring was punctuated, however, by another death in Concord. On May twenty-third the townspeople gathered at Sleepy Hollow to bury Nathaniel Hawthorne, not far from Henry's grave. The tormented writer could not have asked for a more noble carriage to his final resting place; among his pall bearers were Longfellow, Lowell, Oliver Wendell Holmes, Louis Agassiz, Bronson Alcott, and Hawthorne's neighbor of many years, Waldo Emerson. The day was "so bright and quiet that pain or mourning was hardly suggested," and Emerson noted that Hawthorne had borne his "painful solitude" till it "could no longer be endured, & he died of it." That summer Atlanta, the jewel of the South, fell, and General Grant besieged Petersburg. In November, after a heated Presidential campaign marked by political backstabbing, switching allegiances, and violent rhetoric from both the political parties and the newspapers, Lincoln was elected to a second term in office by a landslide. Emerson took little notice of these military and political events in his Journal.

That winter, at the age of sixty-one, Emerson resumed his western lecture tours, which the war had made impossible up to this point. He gave an astonishing fifty-seven lectures from November through April in Massachusetts, Vermont, Connecticut, New York, Ohio, Wisconsin, Illinois, and Pennsylvania. Though he felt himself becoming an old man, he was able to joke of old age that "'tis proposed to call an indignation meeting" to protest it. He cheerfully reported that "within I do not find wrinkles & used heart, but unspent youth." When he returned home from Chicago in February he complained of the "obstructions & squalor of travel," but summed up the economic necessity of "dragging a decorous old gentleman out of home" for this "juvenile career" as a bet of "fifty dollars a day for three weeks, that you will not leave your library & wade & freeze rivers, ride & run, & suffer all manner of indignities, & stand up for an hour each night reading in a hall.'" Emerson's answer: "'I'll bet I will,' I do it, & win the $900."[17]

On Tuesday, April eleventh, Emerson gave the penultimate lecture of the season after hearing word of General Lee's surrender to Grant at Appomattox Courthouse. The war had ended. Three days later a shot rang out in Ford's Theater, and John Wilkes Booth vaulted out of the President's box onto the stage. Lincoln died the next day. Emerson was supposed to have concluded his spring lectures with a final address on Tuesday the eighteenth, but instead the last lecture of the season was a eulogy for the fallen President, which he delivered Wednesday at the memorial service in Concord. "We meet under the gloom of a calamity which darkens down over the minds of good men in all civil society," he opened the address, "as the fearful tidings travel over sea, over land, from country to country, like the shadow of an uncalculated eclipse over the planet. Old as history is, and manifold as are its tragedies, I doubt if any death has caused so much pain to mankind as this has caused, or will cause, on its announcement." Despite this great loss, Emerson's optimism at the end of the war was undiminished. The Union triumph, with unconditional victory over the Slave Power, meant to Emerson "the dawn of a new era, worth to mankind all the treasure & all the lives it has cost, yes, worth to the world the lives of all this generation of American men, if they had been demanded." Emerson, in his excitement, began to see what he had predicted throughout the war, that victory would establish a conviction in many minds that right could triumph, that chronic hope could supplant chronic despair. As maps of America were unrolled in houses and shops across the nation, the unifying and enlarging nature of the war, he affirmed, had made every citizen "a skilled student of the condition, means, & future, of this continent."[18] The victory of the North was the sign to Emerson of the progressive, ameliorative force of the Intellect and the probity of the spiritual world. Emerson was certain that the spiritual forces that had brought about victory over the evil stain of slavery would magnetize the citizens of the country to bring their daily action into alignment with the high ideals of the spirit. The close of the great War gave promise of the dawn of the spiritual development of a whole people.

The summer after the war ended, Emerson stood poised to observe this epoch-making event. The "Natural History of the Intellect" project stirred to life once again in anticipation. He started a new notebook entitled "Moral Law;" at about this time or soon after, he was also working in two other journals dedicated to the project, entitled "Notes on Intellect" and "To Intellect the Guardian." Lincoln's death, however, had deprived the country of a leader capable of unifying and leading a factional people through the difficult task of reconstruction. Instead of malice towards none and charity for all, as Lincoln had urged, the country fell into squabbling and meanness.

The Radical Republicans wished to treat the South as conquered territory; jealous of the political dominance they had gained during the war, they locked the doors of Congress against the Democrats until they could push through their own plan for Reconstruction. The North adopted a policy of military occupation of the seceded States—a marked departure from Lincoln's own view that the South had never left the Union and needed to be healed rather than bludgeoned—and President Johnson proved incapable of formulating a policy that would make anyone happy. When Emerson saw that everything was as it had been before, that the "energy of the nation seems to have expended itself in the war, and every interest is found as sectional & timorous as before;" that even though the war had eradicated slavery it had not prompted a single one of his fellow citizens to turn his or her gaze inward and root out the imperfections within, he became depressed and disillusioned. [19] The window of opportunity for a profound change in the American character had closed. The light of the new era had fallen on blind eyes.

Emerson accepted an invitation, in the midst of the dark winter of 1866, to give a series of lectures at Chickering Hall in Boston and take up the "Natural History of Intellect" project for a third time. Despite his profound disappointment at the missed opportunity, the war had shown Emerson something. It had shown him the Intellect descending into the world and becoming active in it through the lives of human beings, revealing the higher purposes that stood behind and worked through worldly events. Here was the third aspect of the Natural History project on which he had been working and reshaping for almost thirty years: the Intellect becomes active in history through the men and women who take up its high ideals and make them a part of their daily lives, and those who develop the powers of the mind can perceive and describe the facts of its activity. He finally discovered his true mission, the one task that could satisfy the gaping emptiness of the deep void that he had endured for so many years. The war had not shown his fellow citizens the way to the spiritual world, but *he could*. He saw that his task was to lay out a path of self-development that would enable his countrymen to develop the moral virtues and attain the higher faculties of perception that would lead to their discovery of the spiritual world. When he gave the series in late April and early May, 1866, he had expanded his series of four lectures to six. The first four described the aspects of Intellect and the powers of the human being associated with its action: "Seven Metres of Intellect;" "Instinct, Perception, and Memory;" "Genius, Imagination, and Taste;" and "Common Sense." The last two lectures in the series directly took up the themes of right action revealed to him by his experience of the Civil War: "Conduct of the Intellect" and "Relation of Intellect to Morals." The title for the series as a whole revealed Emerson's new insight into what the purpose of these lectures actually was: "Philosophy of the People."

IX.

THE MASTERWORK

Return to Harvard

By the time he delivered "Philosophy of the People," Emerson's fame had risen to such a level that Harvard forgave him the decades-old heresy of the Divinity School "Address." In July of 1866, the college awarded him an honorary Doctor of Laws, though Emerson did not learn of it until someone congratulated him the evening after the ceremony. The next year he was invited to give the Phi Beta Kappa oration. It would be the first time he had spoken at Harvard since his address to the graduating class of the Divinity School almost thirty years earlier. The day before the oration, the college appointed him as an overseer of the corporation. Emerson served two terms from 1867 to 1879 and took his duties seriously, attending meetings regularly and serving on, as well as chairing, numerous committees. Of immediate concern to the overseers was the dire financial situation of the college, which Emerson described as "poverty." Harvard benefited handsomely from the fame of its once-estranged alumnus. At the request of the college in the spring of 1869, Emerson threw himself into fundraising and started writing letters to his class of 1821. He raised some $10,000, more than he made from lectures and royalties in an entire year.[1]

The leading educational issue during Emerson's first term as overseer arose from a growing doubt about the integrity of the school's program and the fear that the credibility of its degree was steadily eroding. The overseers wished, as Emerson phrased it, that Harvard should become a "university for men" rather than a "college for boys." In order to accomplish this transformation, Charles Eliot, the new college president, proposed that Harvard organize courses of "University Lectures," complete with examinations, to be given for a fee in the spring of 1870. These lectures were part of Harvard's attempt to establish a graduate school for the liberal arts. Emerson, who was himself invited to give lectures in the philosophy department, met with Eliot in the summer of 1869 and set the project in motion. In the fall Emerson attended planning sessions, assisted in recruiting speakers, and helped negotiate contracts for the lecturers. In all, seven lecturers on philosophy, including Emerson, were hired to give the courses that would form the various components of the philosophy department. Their subjects ranged from Positivism to Stoicism. Emerson announced his topic as "The Natural History of the Intellect." On November 30, Emerson wrote to a friend that he took "some pleasure in the prospect" of preparing the lectures, and his daughter reported that he was excited by the opportunity of giving his personal project of so many years a final form. "Our living gradually bends," Emerson had written in 1837, "in long years, to our idea." After thirty-three years, the parallel lines of his personal project to develop the ideas of the Natural History of the Intellect and his public career as lecturer and essayist had bent to meet each other.

Emerson was scheduled to give eighteen lectures over a period of six weeks. To date, his most ambitious attempt to present the Natural History of the Intellect, the "Philosophy of the People" series, had been only six lectures in length. The enormity of the task struck him in the summer of 1869,—he was also preparing revisions for a new edition of his works and writing essays for his new book, *Society and Solitude*,—and he began sending apologetic letters to friends and acquaintances canceling all unnecessary commitments and engagements. Emerson was by vocation, first and foremost, a circuit lecturer who gave a lecture or a series of lectures again and again, traveling from place to place, town to town, honing and refining his delivery with every new hall, every new audience. Generally, Emerson drew on Journal materials from the past two or three years to write lectures that he would develop through several deliveries and revisions over the course of weeks or months. When a lecture had outlived its useful life on the circuit, it in turn became the raw material for the finished essays. Emerson's preparation for the "Natural History of the Intellect" course was typical of this cycle of development, though magnified to the scale of an entire career rather than weeks or months. Emerson hoped that after delivering this new series of lectures he would finally be able to shape the "Natural History of the Intellect" project into essays. In the fall of 1869 he started a new notebook, "*PH*—Philosophy," to help him organize his material. The sum total of the resources that he brought to bear on the project were the three lecture series from 1848, 1858, and 1866; five topical notebooks dedicated to the subject; and ten-thousand days worth of Journal entries, indexed and cross-referenced.

As Emerson tried to give the project its final form he struggled with how to coordinate the three overarching themes that he had sketched out in his previous versions of the lecture cycle. The idea at the heart of the 1848 version was still active: that the laws of the mind, discernable as fit objects for study through their correspondence with the laws of nature, form the basis for right action by men of conscience. This theme was Emerson's pillar of strength, the activity of the Intellect through self-trust. To this theme he added a second from the 1858 "Natural Method of Mental Philosophy" series: that the virtue of self-trust, or instinct, leads to the development of higher faculties of perception, powers of the mind that allow the student not only to become a conduit for the activity of the Intellect, but to describe its activity in pictorial words or artistic gestures. This theme became Emerson's pillar of beauty, a realm of art in which poets who develop the lost art of writing rule over culture and reveal the beauty of the Intellect to their fellow man, holding before their gaze the symbols of the Intellect until they are able to perceive it unaided. Emerson drew his third theme from the Civil War lectures and the 1866 "Philosophy of the People" series: the burning eye of the Intellect is observable in the events of human history, and the student who develops a new power of vision becomes capable of comprehending the activity of higher laws in daily events, of observing the activity of higher beings in the signs of the times and describing them precisely. This theme was Emerson's pillar of wisdom, and it completed the triad that Emerson had once called, in his essay "The Poet," the three children of the universe: the Doer (Strength), the Sayer (Beauty), and the Knower (Wisdom).

The powers of the mind, the higher stages of knowledge, gave Emerson particular difficulty. In all of his previous attempts he "never could get beyond five steps in my enumeration of intellectual powers; say, Instinct, Perception, Memory, Imagination (including Fancy as a subaltern), Reasoning or Understanding. Some of the lower divisions, as Genius, Talent, Logic, Wit, and Humour, Pathos, can be dealt with more easily." The problem of enumerating the powers of the mind was indicative of the struggle that Emerson was experiencing in applying his usual methods to building a lecture cycle on such a grand scale. His habit had always been to collect passages from his Journal that ran along a given theme and place the thoughts next to each other in order to observe them and allow them to fall into their natural order. To Emerson "the synthesis, the architecture, gives the value to all the stones. A thought contents me, but has little value to any other to whom I speak it. But, as soon as greater mental activity, or more scope, places that thought with its right foregoers and followers, and we have a right Discourse, we have somewhat impressive and powerful, and the worth of the solitary thought vastly enhanced."[2] Throughout his career Emerson had set himself the goal, in every lecture that he had given, of creating a temple into which a muse or inspiring spirit could descend in the moment of delivery; the building blocks for each lecture, the thoughts that would construct the temple, were typically drawn from Journals of recent months and years. Now, from an entire lifetime worth of material, he sought to build a temple for the Intellect itself. To sift through such a mass of building material, to draw out the themes, lay the foundation, and raise the frame for a dwelling crafted for the Intellect itself to inhabit was indeed something of a challenge.

The enrollment for Emerson's course started at thirty, but only four persevered to the end of the series, primarily because of the high cost Harvard charged per lecture. Two of the students who attended the whole cycle were Annie Fields, the wife of Emerson's publisher, and Francis Peabody, who had recently earned a degree in business from Harvard and was attending lectures in all seven philosophy courses that spring. The notes that both students made revealed that Emerson's approach to his "course on Philosophy," as he called it in his introductory lecture, was markedly different from what one might expect in an academic course. Fields reported that Emerson was unsettled by the sight of anyone taking notes and disliked having notebooks in the hall while he spoke, so after each lecture she wrote out as much as she could remember in long narratives that attempted to paraphrase Emerson's language. The lectures often tended to be short, she reported, sometimes only twenty or thirty minutes and at their longest no more than an hour.[3] Emerson gave no titles for the lectures—he simply rose at the lectern and began speaking, leaving the students to discern the topic as they listened. The ultimate indication that "The Natural History of the Intellect" did not adhere to the academic model followed by the other lecturers came at the end of the course. Emerson gave no final exam.

Whereas Fields wished to capture the flavor and impression of Emerson's words, Peabody's goal was to outline the logical structure of the lectures. Apparently able to sneak in his notebook, Peabody attempted to create outlines of each topic as Emerson spoke, naturally assuming that he would be able to distill the thought construct of Emerson's lectures much as he was doing in the other philosophy courses. Certainly Francis Bowen, whose subject that spring was seventeenth-century philosophy, would have conveyed a comprehensive grasp of elaborate metaphysical systems, but Emerson, as he indicated to his class in the introductory lecture, did not find value in such "jejune outlines," nor did he presume such wholeness of system. Emerson did not have, nor had he ever tried to develop, the disciplined logic that philosophical thought demanded. He was content "with only a sketch of the whole," with the "two termini" rather than the entire structure of "arches and abutments of reason." He coordinated thoughts in the manner of an essayist, but did not seek to build them into a logical system. Unable to capture Emerson's organic structure with his outline, Peabody recorded Emerson's more striking aphorisms and provocative insights, which he described as poetry and compared to the music of the spheres.

Despite the unmatched beauty of Emerson's eloquence and his captivating presence at the lectern, Peabody could not help but conclude that Emerson's attempt to organize his thought along the model of a college course severely hampered his success in delivering the lectures. The academic setting, Peabody observed, seemed to be a harness placed on one who, like Pegasus, was not meant to be reined.[4] Emerson himself was so doubtful of his performance after his first lecture that he questioned the value of continuing. The students could not help but notice in several subsequent lectures that Emerson had collected such a large volume of material that he sometimes lost his place or could not decide what to read next. The lecturer was no less aware of the problem; in conversation with Annie Fields after the seventh lecture, he explained that he had had plenty of time to prepare but had spent most of it collecting material, and promised that next year's lectures would be better.[5] The difficulties mounted to the point that in the eleventh lecture, on "Identity," he lost his line of thought and walked out of the lecture hall in mid-sentence. Emerson was also clearly hampered by the strain of preparing three lectures a week and the tiring sixteen-mile journey from Concord to Cambridge and back again. Unable to get the fifteenth lecture ready in time, Emerson simply failed to appear. When the course was finally completed, Emerson had to view them as a proving ground rather than a real accomplishment. In a letter sent to Carlyle on June seventeenth, two weeks after the course ended—a course cut short by two lectures— Emerson wrote that preparing the readings "made me a prisoner, took away all rights of friendship, honor, & justice, & held me to such frantic devotion to my work as must spoil *that* also;" the only "shining side" to the experience was that "materials are collected & a possibility shown me how a repetition of the course next year,—which is appointed,—will enable me partly out of these materials, & partly by large rejection of these, & by large addition to them, to construct a fair report of what I have read & thought on the Subject."

The Constitution of Man

Despite his misgivings about the 1870 cycle, Emerson, at sixty-seven years of age, had succeeded in giving the longest lecture cycle of his entire career, which at sixteen lectures was six longer than any he had given even at the height of his career. The 1871 cycle of the following spring, with seventeen lectures, would be the greatest undertaking of his entire life. As he had expressed to Carlyle, Emerson arrived at the insight that the course for the next spring could be no mere re-reading of the '70 course. A large-scale revision was needed before he could give the lectures again, and that revision would involve throwing out a good portion of what he had done in 1870. On July nineteenth he met with Alcott and told his friend that he would not be able to participate in a joint western lecture tour because he had to prepare the next iteration of the Harvard lectures. By mid-August he plunged into reading and collecting materials on Plutarch for an introduction to William Goodwin's translation of Plutarch's *Morals*. After a short vacation at the beginning of September, Emerson finally had time to begin preparing the new lecture series.

Although the lectures would be given at Harvard again and would technically still be within the philosophy department, Emerson abandoned the attempt to approach his subject "philosophically." Two lectures, "Introductory" and "Common Sense," he set aside completely and started over from the beginning. The 1870 versions of these lectures still survive, and a comparison of their content with that of the 1871 versions shows how Emerson abandoned philosophical argument and criticism for a tone of writing that he called "calm affirming," which he had once characterized by saying, "write nothing that will not help somebody." The key to creating this mood, as he had described it on another occasion, was to "omit all negative propositions."[6] The mood of calm affirming, which pervaded the 1871 lectures, showed a move away from the academic disputation that had given him such difficulty during the first course. The revision of the 1870 course continued before and during the 1871 cycle. The more relaxed pace of the '71 lectures—only two a week instead of three—gave him more time between lectures to prepare. He combined the third and fourth lectures from the first course, "Instinct" and "Perception," into a single lecture, throwing out much material that had been extraneous and adding some new thoughts. In an effort to pare down all of the lectures, to streamline and focus the thoughts, he pulled out lengthy anecdotes and tangential passages, added new writing, and selected passages of poetry from Tennyson, Byron, and others to better illustrate his ideas. He threw out most of the lecture on "Identity," which had given him such trouble in 1870, salvaging some of the pages to combine with "Laws of Mind." He added four new lectures: "Wit and Humor," "Demonology," "Transcendency of Poetry," and "Will." Finally, in an effort to restructure the first third of the cycle, he moved "Imagination" up one lecture, placing it between the two lectures on "Memory."[7]

Emerson's daughter Ellen attended the first lecture in 1871 and wrote that "ever so many people came. It was a large audience and a beautiful lecture." Ellen also pointed out that her father's lectures were again much shorter than those he used to give—"only half an hour sometimes."[8] As the new cycle progressed, it became clear that, in this final effort, Emerson wished to convey what the undertaking itself represented, what it meant that he had nurtured his subject for thirty-three years. "My belief," he told his students, "is that each soul represents a certain fact in nature . . . whose demonstrator or orator he is and should be, that justice may be done to that particular fact among men." The fact of the Intellect was, as it were, the fact most genial to Emerson's soul, the loadstone that determined the bias of his soul and pointed him to his true North. For Emerson, the power of the individual to speak his fact, to be its orator, corresponded directly to his ability to follow that compass unerringly. What he said of the painter was equally true of the lecturer: "But the real difference between picture and picture is the age of thought in the painter's mind." Emerson tried to convey to his audience that he was giving them the best thoughts of a lifetime, collected and ordered; that he was offering them the results of a patient labor that showed "the difference between the force of a single day and that of 10,000 days, between the force of a single soldier, and a column of the army." His audience was witness to something more than his usual lecture. As the answer and complement to his "Intellectual Declaration of Independence," embodied in "The American Scholar" in 1837, he had set forth his best thoughts defining the character and spiritual dimensions of the Constitution of Man.

Its Most Illustrious Halo

Shortly before the end of the course, Emerson received an invitation to join a group of friends on a trip to California by Pullman car, a unique opportunity and a chance for much-needed rest. His family convinced him that he should go. The arrangements for the trip had already been made, but the departure date of April tenth conflicted with the last two lectures of the course, scheduled for April eleventh and fourteenth. Emerson hastily rearranged the final lectures, moving "Relation of Intellect and Morals" up a week—so that he gave three lectures Easter week rather than the usual two—and eliminating "Platonists" from the cycle. On April ninth, just two days after finishing the course and the day before he departed, Emerson wrote Carlyle once again, telling him of the "eighteen lectures [actually only seventeen], each to be read sixteen miles away from my home, to go & come,—& the same work & journey twice in each week, & I have just got through the doleful ordeal." He hoped "the ruin of no young man's soul will here or hereafter be charged to me as having wasted his time or confounded his reason." What Emerson was conveying to Carlyle was what he had described just a week and a half before, in "Metres of Mind," as the natural feeling of the orator after a performance. The orator should "value his talent as a door into nature," he had said; "Let him see his performances only as limitations." The experience of his performances as limitations was common for Emerson; he was so disgusted with the progress of the first series of *Essays* in 1840, with their failure to convey the grandeur of his thought and his aspiration for the spirit, that he wrote in his Journal he wished never to see them again. Several of the essays in that collection, including "Self-Reliance" and "The Over-Soul," are considered to be among his greatest achievements as a writer.

Emerson himself provided no further reflections upon the 1871 performance, but James Thayer, who accompanied Emerson to California and recorded the trip in *A Westward Journey with Mr. Emerson*, made observations on the journey that indicate the powerful effect this final shaping of his life's work had on Emerson's health and character:

> "How can Mr. Emerson," said one of the younger members of the party to me that day, "be so agreeable, all the time, without getting tired!" It was the naïve expression of what we all had felt. There was never a more agreeable traveling-companion; he was always accessible, cheerful, sympathetic, considerate, tolerant; and there was always that same respectful interest in those with whom he talked, even the humblest, which raised them in their own estimation. One thing particularly impressed me,— the sense that he seemed to have of a certain great amplitude of time and leisure. It was the behavior of one who really believed in an immortal life, and had adjusted his conduct accordingly, so that, beautiful and grand as the natural objects were, among which our journey lay, they were matched by the sweet elevation of character and the spiritual charm of our gracious friend.[9]

Thayer's observation pointed to the deep significance of the meeting of the parallel lines of Emerson's life and his thought in the 1871 lecture cycle. Such a meeting of outer duties and inner calling was as much about Emerson's own self-development as it was about arranging a lecture cycle. In the vast and wild beauty of the untamed West, Thayer's greatest discovery was a human being, a true teacher of the spirit. The weariness that had dogged Emerson for the last year evaporated. The yearning that had gnawed at him year in and year out, that had driven him half-crazed to the mountaintop in an effort to assuage it, that had not abated even during the great Civil War, was gone. Content with having achieved his life task, Emerson attained a deep and magnificent peace and beauty of character that his friends, relatives, and visitors would marvel at to the end of his days.

Emerson had many projects after he returned from California, including the final preparation and revision of essays for a new book, which would later become *Letters and Social Aims.* In November and December of 1871 he made a lecture tour as far as Iowa and kept up a heavy schedule of lecturing through the following spring. Then, on July 24, 1872, disaster struck. A fire started in the early morning, touching off a blaze that began to consume the Emerson house. The town awoke to Emerson's cries for help and rushed to his aid. A brigade of young men bravely covered their faces and dragged Emerson's books and manuscripts from the smoke-filled study. A fine rain started, and Emerson stood outside, half-clothed, directing the removal of furniture and the household goods. The fire destroyed much of the house, rendering it unlivable. The shock of witnessing the fire, the exposure he suffered that night, and the hardship of not being able to live in his familiar home for months afterwards led to a long illness. After the great disaster, Emerson's friends donated over $18,000 in an outpouring of support that left him speechless and humbled.[10] Emerson, the old proponent of self-reliance, was at first reluctant to accept the gift, but when he saw the long list of the names of the people who had contributed these tokens of love, he could not but accept them with amazement and gratitude. The money was intended to send him on a trip to England and Egypt and to ensure that he would not have to earn his keep by lecturing ever again. When he returned from this trip, he discovered that his friends had rebuilt his house as well.

The fire signaled the beginning of the closing chapter of Emerson's life journey. His memory began to fail, and he soon found himself incapable of the effort required to select and arrange materials for lectures, nor could he summon the far greater concentration that writing essays demanded. Concerned that his journals and manuscripts might fall into the hands of people who might not do them justice, Emerson suggested to his daughter, Ellen, that James Eliot Cabot might be trusted with them. Cabot, a scholar and philosopher, had known Emerson since the days of Transcendentalism and had given a parallel course in philosophy at Harvard in 1870. She complied with his wishes, and, in 1874, Cabot accepted the task. The last published volume to appear under Emerson's name, as well as numerous individual essays published in the late 1870s, was largely or entirely Cabot's work. Though, as Cabot later explained, he never published a word Emerson did not write, it was Cabot himself who pieced together the sentences and paragraphs, created the structure of the essays, and performed the editing and proofing.

On the evening of Thursday, April 27, 1882, after saying parting words to his closest friends and the members of his family, Waldo Emerson passed away. The news of his death spread throughout Massachusetts almost instantly, and soon obituaries and memorials appeared in newspapers throughout the country. On Friday and Saturday, carpenters worked in the basement of the First Church in Concord to shore up the floor so that it would be able to accommodate the weight of the large number of people expected for the funeral services. Special trains were chartered in Boston to bring mourners to Concord; one of these carried a special delegation from Harvard, led by Charles Eliot. People arrived by carriage and on foot, and it seemed as if residents from the whole countryside had roused themselves to come and pay tribute to the man who had so often traveled to speak to them. On Sunday, dark rain clouds gathered over the town. The old bell in the tower of the First Church called the people together for the funeral service. Over one thousand people answered the clear-ringing sound. Henry James described this final gathering as "the most striking I have ever seen provoked by the death of a man of letters." James Thayer, recalling his trip West with Emerson a decade earlier, remembered a line from Emerson's essay "Immortality" that reoccurred to him throughout the day: "Meantime the true disciple saw through the letter of the doctrine of eternity, which dissolved the poor corpse and Nature also, and gave grandeur to the passing hour." Over Emerson's resting place on the ridge in Sleepy Hollow Cemetery, the family erected a great boulder of unshaped rose quartz, fixed with a simple plaque that bore the epitaph:

> This passive master lent his hand
> To the vast soul that o'er him planned.

Shortly after Emerson's death in 1882, James Elliot Cabot wrote in his *Memoir of Ralph Waldo Emerson* that Emerson appeared to have regarded the Natural History of the Intellect as the "chief task of his life." Cabot was in a unique position to make such a statement. Not only was he a close friend of Emerson, but the family had selected him as Emerson's literary executor, editor and biographer. Cabot had at his disposal thousands of pages of journals, notes, letters and lectures dating back to Emerson's youth. It was the evidence provided by this large paper record, along with supporting statements from Emerson's family and his own personal knowledge as one of Emerson's oldest friends, that led Cabot to describe the Natural History of the Intellect in such terms. However, as editor, Cabot chose not to publish the capstone of Emerson's life: the 1871 cycle of lectures given at Harvard College. When Cabot prepared the 1883 edition of Emerson's *Complete Works*, Emerson's last great lecture cycle had no place in it.

Cabot eventually changed his mind about withholding Emerson's chief task from the public, and in 1893 he published a new, twelfth volume of the *Complete Works* that bore the title of the 1871 lectures. Cabot's representation of Emerson's 1871 cycle was, however, a strange patchwork, a heavily edited compilation of Emerson's several attempts to give the "Natural History of the Intellect" over the years, interspersed with passages from the Journals and from other lectures. Cabot was not trying to cannibalize Emerson's work; he was primarily concerned with bolstering Emerson's high public image, and he tried to do so by giving the most complete sample of the thirty-three-year project that he could. In the end Cabot only drew on a small fraction of the 1871 lectures for the essays, which he entitled "The Natural History of Intellect" and "Memory." Despite his failure to properly portray Emerson's last, best effort on the subject most dear to his heart, Cabot lived up to the faith that his friend had placed in him. Emerson had suggested Cabot for a reason: his integrity. Emerson knew that whatever else happened, Cabot would treat his manuscripts with respect and approach them with methodical patience out of an unflagging sense of duty toward the responsibility entrusted in him. Cabot firmly believed that he was the executor of a legal trust meant for future generations, and he treated the papers accordingly.

Another friend stood by Emerson's grave and saw not papers to be guarded and a life fulfilled, but a continuing presence and active inspiration for the future. Walt Whitman, at the beginning of his career, had recognized Emerson as the discoverer of the moral continent of America, the explorer who had rendered the first report of her spiritual shores and had indicated the way for all who would follow after him. Thirty-six years later, Whitman anticipated that Emerson's role as "the original true Captain" would somehow continue. He remembered those final days he had spent in the essayist's home and felt that something new was beginning, something not tinged by the sadness of death, something that stirred words to rise in his soul as the most fitting eulogy for his friend. It seemed to Whitman that here was a man "beyond the warriors of the world" in the great deeds he had accomplished in life, a "just man, poised on himself, all-loving, all-inclosing, and sane and clear as the sun." Here was a man, Whitman perceived, who, though he had charged in no battle nor stood in the thick of any dramatic danger, had died the death of a hero. Emerson's laurels were not to be made up of the sum of his accomplishments—his lectures, essays, and poems—but were composed of something far greater:

> Perhaps the life now rounded and completed in its mortal development, and which nothing can change or harm more, has its most illustrious halo, not in its splendid intellectual or esthetic products, but as forming in its entirety one of the few, (alas! How few!) perfect and flawless excuses for being, of the entire literary class.

The path of self-development, signaled by Emerson's "siege of the hencoop" and culminating in his startling insights into the Constitution of Man, could now become a real possibility for every American who sought help from this spirit guide. Whitman saw Emerson, through the example of his character, the most illustrious halo of his life, become the guide who, despite having passed over the threshold of death, would yet assist his countrymen. In contemplating this new role of Emerson, Whitman was moved to think of Lincoln's address at Gettysburg honoring the men who had fallen for their country. Borrowing the words of the President on that occasion, Whitman tried to describe this new thing that was now possible in the wake of the hero's earthly passing:

> It is not we who come to consecrate the dead—we reverently come to receive, if so it may be, some consecration to ourselves and daily work from him.

GENEALOGY

CHRONOLOGY

SELECTED BIBLIOGRAPHY

NOTES

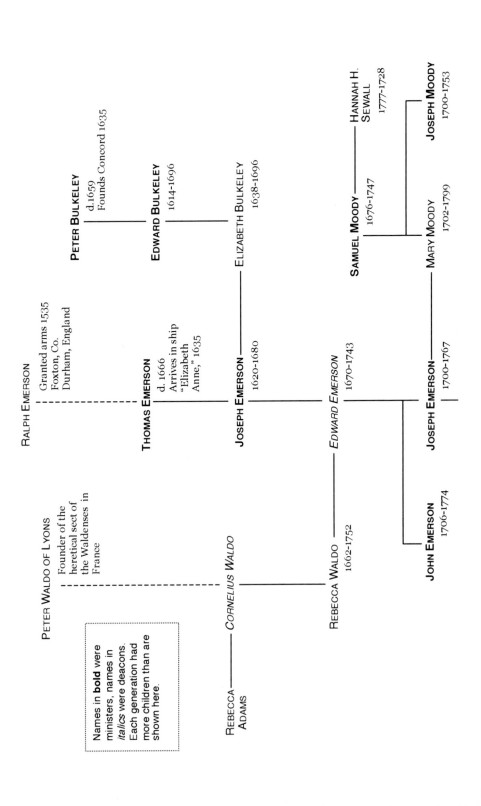

RALPH EMERSON

Granted arms 1535
Foxton, Co.
Durham, England

PETER WALDO OF LYONS

Founder of the
heretical sect of
the Waldenses in
France

THOMAS EMERSON
d. 1666
Arrives in ship
"Elizabeth
Anne," 1635

PETER BULKELEY
d.1659
Founds Concord 1635

EDWARD BULKELEY
1614-1696

JOSEPH EMERSON
1620-1680

ELIZABETH BULKELEY
1638-1696

Names in **bold** were
ministers, names in
italics were deacons.
Each generation had
more children than are
shown here.

REBECCA ——— *CORNELIUS WALDO*
ADAMS

REBECCA WALDO
1662-1752

EDWARD EMERSON
1670-1743

SAMUEL MOODY
1676-1747

HANNAH H.
SEWALL
1777-1728

JOHN EMERSON
1706-1774

JOSEPH EMERSON
1700-1767

MARY MOODY
1702-1799

JOSEPH MOODY
1700-1753

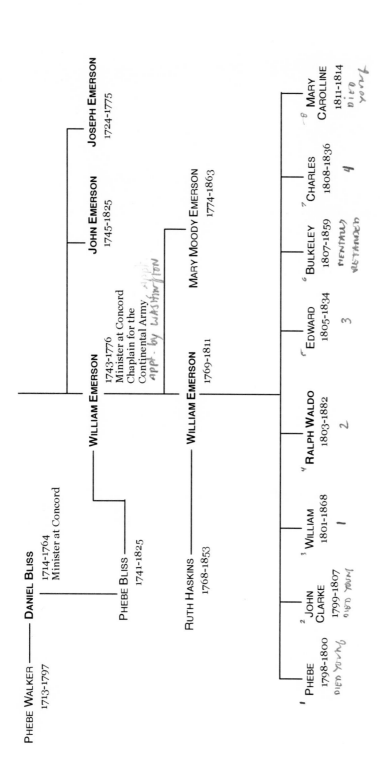

EMERSON GENEALOGY

CHRONOLOGY

1803   May 25th—Born in Boston

1811   Father, Rev. William Emerson, dies

1817   September 17th—Enters Harvard

1820   January—Starts Journal and asks to be called "Waldo"

        October—Experiences hollowness at Harvard

1821   August—Graduates from Harvard

        November?—Begins teaching a girls' finishing school with William

1822   May—Experiences coldness at girls' school

        July 11th—Journal dedication to the Spirit of America

1823   September—Disillusionment with poetic dream, turns towards Milton as ideal

1824   April 18th—Dedicates self to the ministry

        December—Experiences mechanical thought in studies and Journal

1825   January—Closes girls' school

        February—Enters Harvard Divinity School

        April—First illness (blindness, stricture in chest, lameness). Retires to Uncle Ladd's farm for the summer. Stops writing in Journal. Overcome by fear of death.

1826   June—Ordained as minister

        December 1826 to April 1827—Second illness and voyage south. Meets Achille Murat.

1827   May—Returns to Old Manse. Begins recovery and hiatus from Journal.

1828   June—Brother Edward's mental collapse

December—Engaged to Ellen Tucker

1829 January—Accepts call to be Junior Pastor at 2nd Church in Boston. Edward recovers sanity.

September—Marries Ellen Tucker

1830 February to March—Journey south for Ellen's health

Experiences lack of freedom to write as he will

1831 February—Ellen dies

1832 June—Takes trip to White Mountains after announcing controversial views on communion to his congregation

September—Resigns position as pastor

October—Writes poem "Self-Reliance"

December—Departs for Europe

1833 January—Experiences vision on the Atlantic

February to June—Travels in Italy

June to July—Travels in France. Visits Jardins des Plantes in Paris.

July to August—Travels in London and Scotland. Meets Wordsworth and Coleridge. Meets Thomas Carlyle.

September—Voyage home. Sees new mission written in "pencil of fire."

October to December—Lectures on topics of Natural History

1834 April—Cry to god sleeping within to awake

August—Sets task of becoming a popular lecturer

October—Brother Edward dies in Puerto Rico

November—Return to Concord and vow at the Old Manse to utter only his own unique thoughts

Winter—Lectures on Biography

1835 September—Marries Lidian and buys house in Concord

Winter—Lectures on English Literature

1836 February—Reading journals of Bronson Alcott, whom he met the previous fall

May—Brother Charles dies

July—Meets Margaret Fuller

September—Helps to found Transcendental Club on the 8th. Publishes first book, *Nature*, on the 9th.

October—First child, Waldo, born

Winter—Lectures on "The Philosophy of History"

1837   Spring—Assists Henry Thoreau in graduating from Harvard

August—Delivers the Phi Beta Kappa address on "The American Scholar" at Harvard

Fall—Gives himself the imperative to "write the natural history of Reason." Begins friendship with Thoreau.

Winter—Lectures on "Human Culture"

1838   July—Delivers the "Divinity School Address" at Harvard

September—Attacks from Unitarian establishment increasing because of the "Address." Renews vow of independence at the Old Manse.

Winter—Lectures on "Human Life"

1839   Winter—Lectures on "The Present Age"

1840   February—Experiences loss of inspiration in lectures

July—First issue of Dial appears under editorship of Margaret Fuller

May to September—Emerson's "Summer of Friendships"

October—Ripley, Alcott, and Fuller visit to talk about plan for Brook Farm community

1841   Spring—Publishes first book of *Essays*

March—Thoreau moves in to Emerson household as gardener

April—Brook Farm becomes operational

Winter—Lectures on "The Present Age"

1842   January—Thoreau ill with lockjaw. Son Waldo dies.

March—Delivers lecture "The Poet" in Brooklyn. Reporter Walter Whitman is present.

April—Takes over editorship of the *Dial*

September to October—Discussions and walks with Nathaniel Hawthorne

Winter—Pays costs of *Dial* out of pocket

1843   May—Thoreau moves to New York

1844   January—Alcott's "Fruitlands" experiment fails

April—Publishes last issue of the *Dial*

August—Delivers address "Emancipation in the British West Indies"

September—Buys land at Walden Pond

October—Publishes *Essays: Second Series*

1845   July—Thoreau moves into cabin on Walden Pond

August—Second address on emancipation in the British West Indies

September—Indignation meeting on annexation of Texas with Garrison, Phillips, et al.

November—Declines to speak at New Bedford because of racist vote in the Lyceum

Winter—Lectures on "Representative Men"

1846   May—War declared on Mexico

July—Thoreau spends night in jail for not paying tax

August—Fuller leaves for Europe

December—Publishes Poems

Winter—Second delivery of "Representative Men" lectures

1847   Experiences absence of inspiration

October—Sails for England

November to May 1848—Travels and lectures in England

1848   May—Visits Paris and witnesses Revolution

June—Lectures on "Mind and Manners in the 19th Century"

July—Return voyage to America

1849   January to March—Delivers "Mind and Manners in the 19th Century" lectures

March—Town & Country Club founded

Fall—Walks with Ellery Channing

December—Publishes *Representative Men*

1850   March—Webster supports Fugitive Slave Bill in Congress

May to June—First lecture tour West in response to letter signed by 1000 Cincinnatians

July—Margaret Fuller dies in shipwreck off Fire Island

August—Begins work on memorial volume for Fuller

September—Fugitive Slave Law enacted

1851   March—Denounces Fugitive Slave Law. Delivers "Conduct of Life" lectures.

May—Campaigns for John Gorham Palfrey using address on the Fugitive Slave Law

Winter—Delivers "Conduct of Life" lectures

1852   February—Publishes Fuller memoir

April—Begins work on *English Traits*

October—Delegate to Women's Rights convention in Worcester

1853   Working on *English Traits*. Withdraws from Abolition movement.

November—Mother, Ruth Emerson, dies at age 85

1854   March—Delivers second address on Fugitive Slave Law

May—Alcott and others attempt rescue of Anthony Burns, fugitive slave, from Boston Courthouse. Kansas-Nebraska Act passed.

December—Saturday Club founded

1855   January—Lectures on "American Slavery"

July—Receives *Leaves of Grass* in the mail and writes letter to Whitman

September—Addresses Women's Rights convention in Boston

December—Meets Walt Whitman in Brooklyn

1856   May—Charles Sumner assaulted in the senate by Preston Brooks

June—Speaks at Kansas aid meeting in Concord

August—*English Traits* published

September—Addresses Kansas relief meetings in Concord

1857   March—Meets John Brown for first time, hears him speak in Concord

May—Helps found *Atlantic Monthly* and starts publishing in it through the rest of the year

1858   March—Delivers "The Natural Method of Mental Philosophy" lectures in Boston

April 1858 to April 1859—Ceases to write in Journal

June—Begins correspondence with Herman Grimm, writes to Gisela von Arnim

November—Repeats "Natural Method of Mental Philosophy" lectures

1859   May—Hears John Brown speak in Concord for the second time. Spends summer raising money for him.

October—Brown captured after raid on Harper's Ferry. F.B. Sanborn flees to Quebec. Emerson speaks and writes in support of Brown's cause.

December—John Brown executed

1860   January—Delivers lecture on "John Brown"

March—Spends day with Whitman in Boston

November—Hears of Lincoln's election

December—Publishes *Conduct of Life* essays. First printing of 2500 sells out in two days.

1861   April—Fort Sumter attacked. War declared between the States.

Winter—Cancels usual lecture tour West because of the war

1862   January to February—Thoreau falls mortally ill

February—Trip to Washington, D.C. Meets Lincoln and visits with his cabinet.

May—Thoreau dies. Lectures on Thoreau in June, publishes essay in August.

October—Delivers lecture "The Emancipation Proclamation"

November to February 1863—Delivers lecture "Perpetual

Forces" to many audiences in support of the war as a means to eradicate slavery

1863   January—Reads "Boston Hymn" to celebrate Emancipation Proclamation. Writes letters of recommendation for Whitman to William H. Seward and Salmon P. Chase.

March—Speaks at fundraiser for Massachusetts 54th

May—Aunt, Mary Moody Emerson, dies at age 89

December to February 1864—Delivers lecture "Fortune of the Republic," supporting the Northern cause, fourteen times

1864   May—Pallbearer for funeral of Nathaniel Hawthorne in Concord

July—Begins collecting material on Thoreau in a new notebook

November—Lincoln re-elected

1865   April—Lincoln assassinated. Emerson speaks at Concord memorial service.

July—Atlantic Monthly declines to print essay "Character" on the grounds that it is blasphemous and will ruin the magazine.

December—Henry James lectures in Concord and stays with Emerson

1866   April to May—Delivers "Philosophy of the People" lectures

July—Awarded honorary LL.D. at Harvard Commencement

1867   April—Publishes new volume of poetry, *May Day and Other Pieces*

July—Appointed overseer of Harvard. Serves until 1879.

1869   Spring—Raises $10,000 in funds for Harvard

Summer—Works with President of Harvard, Charles Eliot, on project to start Harvard's graduate school of the arts. Helps plan lectures to make up the "department" of philosophy in spring of 1870.

1870   Publishes *Society and Solitude* essays

April to June—Delivers 16 lectures on "The Natural History of the Intellect" at Harvard

July—Declines western lecture tour with Alcott so that he can rework Harvard lectures

August—Writes introduction for Plutarch's Morals

Fall—Works on rearrangement of Harvard lectures to be delivered next spring

1871   February to April—Delivers second version of "The Natural History of the Intellect," 17 lectures, at Harvard

April—Leaves for trip by rail to California

1872   July—House burns

1873   Third trip to Europe, including trip to Egypt. Emerson travels the Nile, meets Herman Grimm.

1874   Appoints James Eliot Cabot editor and executor of his papers

1881   September—Whitman visits Concord for the first time

1882   April—Dies in Concord

Selected Bibliography

In addition to the standard print sources, a wealth of Emerson's writings and other primary material has become available online in the last few years. RWE.org hosts the full text of the 1903 Centenary edition of the *Complete Works*, in addition to a wealth of other resources. The Google Book Search project (http://books.google.com) will eventually include not only available full-text of all works by and related to Emerson published before 1923, but also allows free searching of most of the major critical and biographical works published after 1923, with at least limited previews available for majority of them (including this book). Both of these projects provide an unprecedented level of access to Emerson's life and work. Books currently available to search and preview in Google Book Search are marked with a †. Those available to search and view in full text in Google Book Search are marked with a ††. In some cases the Google Book Search edition may be different from the one listed below. GBS is constantly updated—most titles listed below will probably be added eventually.

Ahlstrom, Sydney E., and David D. Hall. *A Religious History of the American People.* New Haven: Yale University Press, 2004. †

Allen, Gay Wilson. *Waldo Emerson: A Biography.* New York: Viking Press, 1981.

Allen, Joseph Henry, and Richard Eddy. *A History of the Unitarians and the Universalists in the United States.* Christian Literature, New York, 1894.

Baker, Carlos. *Emerson among the Eccentrics: A Group Portrait.* New York: Viking, 1996.

Barfield, Owen. *Romanticism Comes of Age.* 1st American ed. Middletown, Conn.: Wesleyan University Press, 1967.

Borst, Raymond R., and Henry David Thoreau. *The Thoreau Log: A Documentary Life of Henry David Thoreau, 1817-1862.* American Authors Log Series. New York: G.K. Hall, 1992.

Bosco, Ronald A. "His Lectures Were Poetry, His Teaching the Music of the Spheres." Harvard Library Bulletin 8.2 (1997).

Cabot, James Elliot. *A Memoir of Ralph Waldo Emerson.* 2 v. Houghton Mifflin, Boston, 1888. ††

Cameron, Kenneth Walter. *American Great Ones: Hawthorne, Emerson, Thoreau.* Hartford: Transcendental Books, 1997.

———. *Thoreau Discovers Emerson; a College Reading Record.* New York: New York Public Library, 1953.

Coleridge, Samuel Taylor. *Biographia Literaria.* London: Oxford University Press, 1967. ††

Cremin, Lawrence Arthur. *American Education, the National Experience, 1783-1876.* New York: Harper and Row, 1980.

———. *American Education; the Colonial Experience, 1607-1783.* 1st ed. New York: Harper & Row, 1970.

Emerson, Edward Waldo. *The Selected Writings of Ralph Waldo Emerson.* Modern Library. Ed. Brooks Atkinson. New York: Random House, Inc., 1992.

Emerson, Mary Moody. *The Selected Letters of Mary Moody Emerson.* Ed. Nancy Craig Simmons. Athens: University of Georgia Press, 1993.†

Emerson, Ralph Waldo. *The Complete Works of Ralph Waldo Emerson.* Ed. Edward Waldo Emerson. Centenary ed. Boston: Houghton Mifflin and Company, 1903. ††

———. *Early Lectures of Ralph Waldo Emerson.* Ed. Stephen E. Whicher and Robert E. Spiller. Cambridge: Harvard University Press, 1959.

———. *Emerson's Antislavery Writings.* New Haven: Yale University Press, 1995. †

———. *The Heart of Emerson's Journals.* Ed. Bliss Perry. Boston, New York: Houghton Mifflin Company, 1926. †

———. *Journals and Miscellaneous Notebooks.* Ed. William H. Gilman. Cambridge: Belknap Press of Harvard University Press, 1960.

_____. *Journals of Ralph Waldo Emerson, with Annotations*. Eds. Edward Waldo Emerson and Waldo Emerson Forbes. Boston: Houghton Mifflin, 1909. ††

_____. *The Later Lectures of Ralph Waldo Emerson, 1843-1871*. Eds. Ronald A. Bosco and Joel Myerson. 2 vols. Athens: University of Georgia Press, 2001.

_____. *The Letters of Ralph Waldo Emerson*. Eds. Ralph Leslie Rusk and Eleanor M. Tilton. New York: Columbia University Press, 1939. †

_____. *The Portable Emerson*. Ed. Carl Bode. New York: The Viking Press, 1981.

Emerson, Ralph Waldo, and Thomas Carlyle. *The Correspondence of Emerson and Carlyle*. Ed. Joseph Slater. New York: Columbia University Press, 1964. ††

Emerson, Ralph Waldo, and Herman Friedrich Grimm. *Correspondence between Ralph Waldo Emerson and Herman Grimm*. Ed. Frederick William Holls. Port Washington: Kennikat Press, 1971. ††

Epstein, Daniel Mark. *Lincoln and Whitman: Parallel Lives in Civil War Washington*. 1st ed. New York: Ballantine Books, 2004.

Gardener, John Fentris. *American Heralds of the Spirit: Emerson, Whitman, and Melville*. Hudson: Lindisfarne Press, 1992.

Geldard, Richard. *The Esoteric Emerson*. Hudson: Lindisfarne Press, 1993.

Gougeon, Len. *Virtue's Hero: Emerson, Antislavery, and Reform*. Athens: University of Georgia Press, 1990.

Grant, Ulysses S. *Memoirs and Selected Letters: Personal Memoirs of U.S. Grant, Selected Letters 1839-1865*. Library of America. New York: Literary Classics of the United States, 1990. †

Hall, Thomas Cuming. *The Religious Background of American Culture*. American Classics. New York: Ungar, 1959.

Hofstadter, Richard, and Walter P. Metzger. *The Development of Academic Freedom in the United States*. New York: Columbia University Press, 1955.

Holmes, Oliver Wendell. *Ralph Waldo Emerson*. Boston, New York: Houghton Mifflin, 1890. ††

Loving, Jerome. *Walt Whitman: The Song of Himself*. Berkeley, Calif.: University of California Press, 1999. †

Matthiessen, F. O. *American Renaissance; Art and Expression in the Age of Emerson and Whitman*. London, New York etc.: Oxford U.P., 1968.

Miller, Perry. *The Transcendentalists, an Anthology*. Cambridge: Harvard University Press, 1950.

Richardson, Robert D. *Emerson: The Mind on Fire*. Berkeley: University of California Press, 1995. †

Rosenwald, Lawrence Alan. *Emerson and the Art of the Diary*. New York: Oxford University Press, 1988.

Rusk, Ralph Leslie. *The Life of Ralph Waldo Emerson*. New York: Charles Scribner Sons, 1949.

Shepard, Odell. *Pedlar's Progress; the Life of Bronson Alcott*. Boston: Little Brown and Company, 1937.

Thayer, James Bradley. *A Western Journey with Mr. Emerson*. Boston: Little Brown and Company, 1884. ††

Thayer, V. T. *Formative Ideas in American Education, from the Colonial Period to the Present*. New York: Dodd Mead, 1965.

Thoreau, Henry David. *Walden*. Boston: Beacon Press, 1997. †

Von Frank, Albert J. *An Emerson Chronology*. New York: G.K. Hall, 1994.

Whitman, Walt. *Complete Poetry and Collected Prose*. Library of America. Ed. Justin Kaplan. New York: Literary Classics of the United States, Inc., 1982. †

———. *Leaves of Grass*. Library of America. New York: Literary Classics of the United States, 1992. †

NOTES

THESE NOTES SERVE A DUAL PURPOSE OF CONVERSATIONAL BACK STORY TO the biography and as record of the trail through the principle sources that support it. It is common practice to use *The Journals and Miscellaneous Notebooks of Ralph Waldo Emerson* (*JMN*) as the standard edition when citing passages from Emerson's Journal. In these notes, I break somewhat with that practice and cite from two other sources for the Journal in addition to *JMN*: *The Journals of Ralph Waldo Emerson* (1909), edited by Emerson's son Edward Waldo Emerson, and *The Heart of Emerson's Journals* (1926), edited by Bliss Perry. My own discovery of Emerson over the last decade started with Perry's excellent selection, graduated to the more complete 1909 edition, and finally grew into the authoritative *JMN*. Rather than go back and standardize the passages drawn from the earlier sources—which I believe have their own unique value quite apart from *JMN*—I have chosen to retain the story of that journey by leaving the citations as the record of where I originally found the passage. The principal sources are listed in the "Selected Bibliography," though I owe a debt to many others besides. The main abbreviations used in the "Notes" follow; complete bibliographic information for these other references may be found in the "Selected Bibliography."

EL	Whicher and Spiller, ed. *Early Lectures of Ralph Waldo Emerson*, 1959.
HEJ	Bliss Perry, ed. *The Heart of Emerson's Journals*, 1926.
LL	Bosco and Myerson, eds. *The Later Lectures of Ralph Waldo Emerson, 1843-1871*, 2001.
Journals	Edward Waldo Emerson, and Waldo Emerson Forbes, eds. *Journals of Ralph Waldo Emerson, with annotations*, 1909.
JMN	Gilman, Orth et al., eds. *The Journals and Miscellaneous Notebooks of Ralph Waldo Emerson*, 1960.
MME	Simmons, ed. *The Selected Letters of Mary Moody Emerson*, 1993.
Letters	Rusk and Tilton, eds. *The Letters of Ralph Waldo Emerson*, 1939.
Works	Edward Waldo Emerson, ed. *The Complete Works of Ralph Waldo Emerson*, 1903.

I. Ancestral Voice

1. 10/19/32, *Journals*, II.525.
2. 5/7/37, *Journals*, IV.230.
3. 3/11/20, *MME*, 136.
4. 2/22/13, *MME*, 70.
5. February 1832, *MME*, 314.

II. Ordeals of Soul

1. The themes for disputation were divided into two categories: the philological, which included grammar, rhetoric, and logic; and the philosophical, which included physics, ethics, and metaphysics. By 1652 a fourth year was added to the curriculum and arrangements were made for the awarding of the M.A. degree. The system of teaching at Harvard was accomplished by tutors, who would have a single class assigned to them that they would stay with throughout its four years. The tutors would instruct the class in the broad range of studies, with supplemental lectures by the college president, who had the freedom to teach on all subjects or to confine himself to his own area of expertise as he saw fit. Eventually Harvard, along with several other colleges established in the colonies, began to move towards specialized professorships and established the Hollis professorship of Divinity in 1721, the Hol-

lis professorship of Mathematics and Natural Science in 1727, and the Hancock professorship of Hebrew and other Oriental languages in 1764. All of these areas had previously been covered by the tutors alone, who in 1766 were reorganized to specialize in specific topics, with all of the students studying under each of the tutors at different times.

2. This short history of Harvard is based on the excellent survey of American collegiate education given by Cremin in *American Education: the Colonial Experience, 1607-1783*. For a detailed look at how Locke influenced the philosophy and development of education, see Thayer, *Formative Ideas in American Education*. For an extensive look at the history of Harvard in particular and other colleges in general, see Hofstadter, *The Development of Academic Freedom in the United States*.

3. He later observed that "the regular course of studies, the years of academical and professional education have not yielded me better facts than some idle books under the bench at the Latin School."

4. 10/25/20, *Journals*, I.70.

5. 12/15/20, *HEJ*, 8. It should not be surprising that certain contemporary and later passages reveal that Emerson did not want to leave Harvard and in fact had some sentimental fondness for it, despite the difficulty he had with his education there. Such a feeling did not arise out of any particular love for the place, though on a very real and human level he formed attachments to the people he had lived with and the grounds he had wandered through for four years. Rather, he saw these as the "last best years of his life," for he knew that once he left he would have to go to work for the family, as had his brother William. Lacking William's ability to be a workhorse, to simply do the duty, he feared or despised what would come after, and so sometimes wished to remain with the demon he knew.

6. 4/23/23, *MME*, 170.

7. 3/25/21, *Journals*, I.78-9.

8. The bulk of this paragraph is distilled from Laurence Rosenwald's excellent description of the early development of Emerson's journals in *Emerson and the Art of the Diary* detailed on pp. 30-53.

9. 5/7/22, *Journals*, I.137-9.

10. 5/13/22, *Journals*, I.140.

11. 5/13/22, *Journals*, I.141. Some critics have suggested that his depression and isolation were exaggerated, citing his close relationship to his brothers and mother as evidence of the warmth in his character; certainly Emerson was no misanthropic exile, no desperate isolatoe that knew no human touch. The outer signs of depression are, however, indicative of a very deep spiritual crisis, one character-

ized in the journals by a penetrating coldness, for which these relationships cannot account.

12.   *Journals*, I.174.

13.   6/26/22, *MME*, 155.

14.   7/11/22, *Journals*, I.160. In this entry, Emerson first identifies the Spirit of America as a he, but in later entries describes her as a female. In his thoughts on the Spirit of America, Emerson was probably heavily influenced by the broad culture of Columbia that permeated the country in the latter part of the eighteenth century and throughout the nineteenth. The national anthem of the country was the song "Hail! Columbia," written in 1798, and songs and poems to and about Columbia, the goddess of the nation and its guiding spirit, proliferated by the hundreds. The earliest poem addressed to Columbia seems to have been the one that the slave-poetess Phillis Wheatley wrote in 1775, "To His Excellency George Washington." Wheatley, writing to honor Washington as he took command of the Continental army, began the poem,

> Celestial choir! enthron'd in realms of light,
> Columbia's scenes of glorious toils I write.
> While freedom's cause her anxious breast alarms,
> She flashes dreadful in refulgent arms.
> See mother earth her offspring's fate bemoan,
> And nations gaze at scenes before unknown!
> See the bright beams of heaven's revolving light
> Involved in sorrows and the veil of night!
>
> The goddess comes, she moves divinely fair,
> Olive and laurel binds her golden hair:
> Wherever shines this native of the skies,
> Unnumber'd charms and recent graces rise.

Many poems praising Columbia in her aspects of both peace and war appeared regularly over the next decades. In 1825, three years after Emerson wrote this dedication, Joel Barlow published his vast patriotic poem, *The Columbiad*, which totaled over three hundred and sixty pages. Two years later, Richard Emmonds published his even more ambitious *Fredoniad*, a three-volume epic that detailed the struggle between Columbia and her counterpart, the Spirit of England known as Britannia. Emmonds launched his epic with the lines:

Of loud, impetuous War, whose brazen tongue
Hath round the borders of Columbia rung,
Wag'd to maintain the freedom of the sea,
And Independence,—righteous Liberty,—
I venturous sing,—which made Britannia feel
A blow, that caus'ed her stubborn joints to kneel.

Images and invocations of Columbia reached their height during the civil war, and remained pervasive through the latter part of the nineteenth century. She found her way into sculpture and art as well as poem and song; three of the most famous representations of her are a golden statue created for the Columbia World's Fair, which still stands in Chicago's Jackson Park; the statue that stands atop the Capitol building in Washington, D.C.; and the Statue of Liberty.

15. 12/21/22, *Journals*, I.201-202.

16. 3/12/23, *Journals*, I.228-30. In these beliefs Emerson was still very much within the Christian tradition, as his rhetoric indicates. In a passage from March, 1823, he expressed his great disappointment in the leading Thinkers of the time, that they had discarded religion and cast a malign light upon the earth, turning the sweet waters to bitter; within the ranks of these he included the Enlightenment thinkers in America, especially Franklin. Their names were nothing next to Bacon, Newton, and Milton, those that he felt clung to the Divine Name.

17. *Journals*, I.343-344.

18. 3/18/23, *Journals*, I.236-7 and I.344. The full passage reads, "I have often found cause to complain that my thoughts have an ebb and flow. Whether any laws fix them, and what the laws are, I cannot ascertain. I have quoted the memory of Milton and tried to bind my thinking season to one part of the year, or to one sort of weather; to the sweet influence of the Pleiades, or to the summer reign of Lyra." Emerson's flaw as described by Aunt Mary, that he was too much the "Nursling of surrounding circumstances," took a sinister turn. The notion that an inspiration could be bound at all, much less to a time of year or type of weather, probably would have enraged her.

19. 2/20/24, *HEJ*, 16.

20. 3/21/24, *HEJ*, 17.

III. Triumph of the God of Fire

1. English Unitarianism began in the first half of the 18th century with a Dissenting movement that, in argument of Locke's "Reasonableness," defended a

religion of miraculous revelation. Attempts by the Church of England to have Dissenters agree to adhere to the 35 doctrinal articles of the Church, but not the remaining four that asserted the absolute authority of the Church, were unsuccessful, and the first Unitarian chapel was founded in 1774 in Essex Street, London, by Theophilus Lindsey, who espoused the gladness of all sentient things and the goodness and justice of God as displayed in Nature, as well of the restoration of all souls in the life to come. The major conflict between the conservatives and the liberals began with Jonathan Edwards and the revivals of the Great Awakening in the 1730's. Edwards openly attacked what was then known as "Arminianism." The Hopskinsians, educated mostly at Yale, were a zealous group of Edwardians, followers of his revivalist theology. For their own part, the liberals strongly denounced the revivalist tendencies of the evangelicals; Mayhew said that "men are converted only out of their own wits," not "in dragoons." He further held that Christianity was not a scheme of salvation defined by dogma, but an "art of living virtuously and piously."

William Ellery Channing's Baltimore discourse is sometimes called the *magna charta* of the American Unitarian movement, for it laid out for the first time in clear language what the Unitarians believed concerning five major points of theology; more importantly, it maintained a bold, public, and positive tone that gave muscle and bone to the liberal argument against the evangelicals, encouraging the congregations in their conviction. This is not to say that Channing made Unitarian doctrine transparent or even dimly perceivable. To do such a thing was not his aim, nor did he pretend that it was; he once characterized the movement by saying, "we are vague because we are faithful." Channing's first point stood at the root of the "Arminianism" of the mid-18th century that eventually developed into Unitarianism: the refutation of the doctrine of the Trinity as a proposition of three gods, which caused confusion as to the object of worship, and the establishment of the doctrine of God's Unity, that there is one God and one only. The second point expanded the first: Jesus Christ is one mind, soul, and being distinct from God, not two beings, human and divine. By this point Channing wished to clarify that there was but one mind that suffered in the dying Jesus, not merely a human mind that suffered while the divine mind experienced infinite happiness at the right hand of God. Christ, therefore, he placed as distinct from and inferior to God.

Channing's third point essentially refuted the doctrine of innate depravity, that all men are born sinful and only a few, "the elect," have hope of salvation through grace that is imputed to them according to their faith and their acceptance of grace. Channing considered this the major point of difference with his conservative opponents, one that could not be overlooked or treated with indifference, for "we consider no part of theology so important as that which treats of God's moral character." The Unitarians held the moral perfection of God as a keystone: God is infinitely benevolent and good in disposition and act to every individual and to the general creation, and his justice is that of "a good being, dwelling in the same mind, and acting in harmony." They would have no more of Jonathan Edward's "Sinners in the Hands of an Angry God," and they shrank from the kind of Edwardian, evangelical revivalism that such rhetoric was used to promote. Accordingly, the Unitarians appealed to the individual conscience, the reason, to effect the means of salvation, and therefore, with the infinite benevolence of God and possession of reason by all men, put forward the doctrine of the salvation of all men. For Channing evil was not present in the world because of any "blighting curse" placed on or inherent to humanity; rather, God, in a benevolent paternal role, employs "aids and obstructions" to train men "by prosperity and adversity" for "union with himself, and for a sublime and ever growing virtue in heaven."

This position led to Channing's fourth point, the redemptive role of Christ and his mission among humanity. Christ was sent by the Father, in essence, to effect a moral or spiritual liberation of men from sin, not by changing the mind of God in punishing them, but by changing the minds of men themselves. Thus followed the fifth point: true Christian holiness and virtue "has its foundation in the moral nature of man, that is, in conscience, or his sense of duty, and in the power of forming his temper and life according to conscience." Chief among the virtues were, first, the love of God, and, beyond that, the love of Jesus Christ. Though Channing's Unitarianism did indeed embrace a kind of warm humanism that was accused of taking away Christ's divinity and lowering an obscuring fog over Christianity as a whole, it yet saw itself as standing firmly within the congregational tradition, a claim secured by its adherence to scripture text and its affirmation of Jesus Christ as the only master of Christians. Though he considered scripture to be the perfect revelation of God, and the words of Christ and his apostles to be perfect divine authority, he also maintained that it was written in the language of men in order to be understood by men and so could only be interpreted by careful subjection to the faculty of reason. Channing sought to raise Christianity out of the realm of the heart and into the realm of the head; yet in doing so, Unitarianism left the heart weakened and dangerously exposed.

2.   Allen, *Unitarians*, 118. Allen has as many as 120 churches in eastern Massachusetts and about 130 overall.

3.   4/18/24, *HEJ*, 17-22.

4.   1/4/25, *Journals*, II.41-2.

5.   His divorce from society and embrace of solitude were not careless or ill-conceived, but rather carefully considered and weighed. Long passages arguing the merits of society versus solitude marked several pages of the Journal. He did not seek a false asceticism and heartily declared that "I commend no absurd sacrifices. I praise no wolfish misanthropy that retreats to thickets from cheerful towns, and scrapes the ground for roots and acorns, either out of a groveling soul, or a hunger for glory that has mistaken grimace for philosophy." His aim was far different: "It is not the solitude of place, but the solitude of soul which is so inestimable to us," he wrote in late January, for the purpose in withdrawing was "to nurse your solitary faculties into a self-existence so that your thoughts and actions shall be in a degree your own."

6.   1/4/25, *Journals*, II.36.

7.   *Journals*, II.20-21.

8.   9/27/25, *MME*, 199.

9.   1/8/26, *Journals*, II.71.

10.   *JMN* III.15.

11.   *JMN* III.13-14.

12.   9/10/26, *Journals*, II.115.

13.   9/23/26, *Journals*, II.117.

14.   1/4/27, *Journals*, II.145.

15.   1828, *HEJ*, 39.

16.   4/30/28, *Letters*, I.233.

17.   The vote by the Church for the official invitation did not take place until January 11, 1829, but Emerson's son, in the notes to the Journals, records that he knew of the invitation before the engagement. Emerson had already begun to supply the pulpit of the second Church as early as July of 1828 because of the ill health of the current pastor, Henry Ware.

18.   *JMN*, II.258-260.

19.   *MME*, 1/28/29, 252-53.

20.   1/17/29, *Journals*, II.262.

21.   7/1/29, *Letters*, 273.

22.   2/8/30, *Journals*, II. 294.

23.   7/20/30, *Journals*, II.301.

24.   2/13/31, *HEJ*, 47.

IV. Hitch your Wagon to a Star

1.   6/20/31, *HEJ*, 49.

2.   1/10/32, *HEJ*, 55.

3.   7/14/32, *Journals*, II.494-5.

4.   6/2/32, *HEJ*, 57.

5.   Of this unusual recovery Allen writes (in *Waldo Emerson*), "It is useless to speculate on exactly what cured him."

6.   1/3/33, *Journals*, III.5-6.

7.   2/10/33, *Journals*, III.28-9.

8.   7/13/33, *Journals*, III.163.

9.   11/3/33, *Journals*, III.226-7. Emerson had been introduced to these ideas through Sampson Reed's short book, *Observations on the Growth of the Mind*, in 1826. Reed based his ideas on the works of Swedenborg, whose books did not appear in English translation until the 1840's. For more on Reed and his influence on Emerson, see Richardson. In 1821 Aunt Mary sent her nephew a letter in which she related two German principles for studying nature: first that the world is made after the model of the human soul; and second that the analogy for every part of the universe is so close that the same idea is reflected from the whole in every part and from every part to the whole (*MME*, 2/24/21). In 1824 Emerson, apparently swayed by more dogmatic arguments in the ongoing theological battles, wrote to his Aunt complaining about those who seek analogies of the divine in natural things and commenting that nature lost its charms when subjected to the scrutiny of science. Mary wrote back, "The longer you live the more you will have to endure the elementary existence of society, and your premature wisdom will dictate quiesence, when the old become gay & the young queer at the portature of a fly & the Gallen dissection of a flower." She went on to tell him not to dislike those who looked at nature in such a way, for "Then you find no nesecery sacredness in the Country. Nor did Milton—" (*MME*, 4/13/24, 182). This was at the time when Milton was rising in Emerson's esteem as the type of the poet. Ultimately Emerson would carry his insights in a very different direction from those who were kin to him in thought, Reed, Swedenborg, Coleridge, Goethe, and Kant.

10.   Coleridge defined "Understanding" as the faculty of thinking that forms judgements from information collected by the senses combined with the function of memory. It is reflective and discursive, breaking things apart into their components. It stands apart from things and refers itself to a higher faculty as the ultimate authority for its judgments. "Reason" is this higher faculty, the "power by which we become

possessed of principles," the fixed ground of substance and truth that refers only to itself for its authority. Rather than reflection, it is contemplation, an inward behold-ing. According to Coleridge, Reason does not manifest *in* human beings and neither does it involve a process of "reasoning about" an object; rather it is something *in which* human beings are manifest and in which the individual mind subsists, so that the exercise of the Reason is not to *reason about that* but to *become that*. For Coleridge Reason is both the organ that perceives and that which is perceived, the universal laws of thought that constitute Truth. In order to rise from Understanding to pure Reason, or Spirit, a certain triumph over the distinction between subject and object must be attained, for the individual mind must be immersed in the world and not merely look on at it; this union of subject and object is accomplished by what Coleridge calls Imagination, which he defines as "the living power and prime Agent of all human perception, and as a repetition in the finite mind of the eternal act of creation in the infinite I AM." Coleridge's aim in addressing these terms was to give them a philosophical definition within the realm of pure ideas, a task which was so daunting when he actually pursued it that he sometimes had to break off his inves-tigation in the very midst before it became too convoluted to be understood even by himself. Coleridge was building on Kant's terms *Verstand* (Locke's "Judgement"), that which analyzes and distinguishes ideas and sense phenomena from one another, and *Vernunft* (Locke's "Wit"), that which again unites them and discovers unity in multiplicity. Goethe's triumph in natural science was to take the latter from literature and art and return it to science, where it had almost died completely, as "esemplas-tic imagination." Goethe's scientific work became integral to Emerson's lectures in the first few years of his career as a lecturer. For excellent examinations of the rela-tion between Goethe and Coleridge, the German Idealists and the English Romantics, and Coleridge's philosophy, see Barfield's essays in *Romanticism Comes of Age.*

11.   8/30/33, *Letters*, I.394.

12.   9/8/33, *Journals*, III.200-201. The passage in context: "A man contains all that is needful to his government within himself. He is made a law unto himself. All real good or evil that can befal [sic] him must be from himself. He only can do himself any good or any harm. Nothing can be given to him or taken from him but always there is a compensation. There is a correspondence between the human soul and everything that exists in the world; more properly, everything that is known to man. Instead of studying things without the principles of them, all may be pene-trated unto within him. Every act puts the agent in a new condition. The purpose of life seems to be to acquaint a man with himself. He is not to live to the future as

described to him, but to live to the real future by living to the real present. The highest revelation is that God is in every man. ... That which I cannot yet declare has been my angel from childhood until now. It has seprated me from men. It has watered my pillow. It has driven sleep from my bed. It has tortured me with guilt. It has inspired me with hope. It cannot be defeated by my defeats. It cannot be questioned, though all the martyrs apostatize. It is always the glory that shall be revealed; it is the 'open secret' of the universe. ... I have to do no more than you with that question of another life. I believe in *this* life. I believe it continues. As long as I am here, I plainly read my duties as writ with pencil of fire. They speak not of death; they are woven of immortal thread."

13.   7/11/33, *HEJ*, 74.

14.   10/24/33, *Journals*, III.225.

15.   2/22/34, *Journals*, III. 262-3.

16.   4/20/34, *Journals*, III.277. Twenty years later, Henry Thoreau would write this about the conscious life and being truly awake:

> Moral reform is the effort to throw off sleep. Why is it that men give so poor an account of their day if they have not been slumbering? They are not such poor calculators. If they had not been overcome with drowsiness, they would have performed something. The millions are awake enough for physical labor; but only one in a million is awake enough for effective intellectual exertion, only one in a hundred millions to a poetic or divine life. To be awake is to be alive. I have never yet met a man who was quite awake. How could I have looked him in the face?
>
> We must learn to reawaken and keep ourselves awake, not by mechanical aids, but by an infinite expectation of the dawn, which does not forsake us in our soundest sleep. I know of no more encouraging fact than the unquestionable ability of man to elevate his life by a conscious endeavor. It is something to be able to paint a particular picture, or to carve a statue, and so to make a few objects beautiful; but it is far more glorious to carve and paint the very atmosphere and medium through which we look, which morally we can do. To affect the quality of the day, that is the highest of arts.

17.   8/30/34, *Journals*, III.334.

18.   12/9/34, *Journals*, III.387.

19.   11/15/34, *Journals*, III.361.

20.   12/8/34, *Journals*, III.386.

21.   *Letters*, 2/1/35, p.435.

22.   5/16/36, *Journals*, III.394.

23.   *Emerson Chronology*, 129.

24.   10/32/37, *Journals*, IV.336.

25.   8/9/37, *Journals*, IV. 271.

26.   *JMN*, IX.112.

27.   8/19/38, *Journals*, V.21.

28.   *EL*, II.49.

29.   For an individual who, at the age of 21, described the path of self-development as one that was long, arduous, and labor intensive, offering little or no reward until after death itself, the approach to the task of lecturing that he had given himself as part of that development could be nothing less than precise and structured. The general character of the lecture Emerson had gained in his years as a minister. It was a character that had behind it a tradition as old as the colonies. The lecture topic was presented from a single point of view in order to maintain focus and interest; it was written in the Plain Style, a direct and unadorned style of speaking and writing that treated the superlative degree as the death of language and drew on images and metaphors of common life in order to carry the message to the listener in the most direct and unassuming manner; and the ideas were constructed and arranged in a logical order that flowed from one point to the next with such predictable regularity that the different points were often numbered and lettered, as an outline would be. Emerson's adoption of the first practice has led to charges of both narrowness, as he would not acknowledge other viewpoints within the same lecture, and contradiction and inconsistency, as he had a habit of presenting the same subject from a different point of view in a later lecture or essay. His complete mastery of the Plain Style led one contemporary to comment that Emerson threw out glittering coins to his audience in his sentences, but in the end all they were left with was these coins, and nothing of larger worth or substance. Generations of readers since have had to stop short at the remarkable craft of Emerson's prose, considering these flashes of captured insight to be his real achievement. It is in his transformation of the last aspect of the lecture, however, that of the flow and "logic" of the various ideas, that Emerson departed so far from tradition that he created an entirely new medium in which to deliver his thoughts.

30.   9/28/38, *Journals*, V.63-64.

31.   *JMN*, IX.280.

32.   4/20/34, *Journals*, III.278. This organizing principle also gave the lectures a type of built-in safety feature that could protect the listener from ideas he was not yet ready for and protect the ideas themselves from perversion or exploitation by others. The listener could only understand as much as he himself was prepared for according to his own self-development. If he was not prepared to enter into the ideas themselves, the lecture would simply seem incomprehensible, and the listener would leave wondering what had just been said. For the success of Emerson in his lectures, he could ask for no better advocate than Bliss Perry, who says of those who find problems with Emerson's philosophy that "if a man believes there are no stars in the sky, he will naturally conclude that fine talk about hitching your wagon to a star is eccentric nonsense." Perry records that though the audience did not always understand him, no one ever left the hall. He also notes the friend of Emerson's who said that the glittering coins of the polished sentences made it hard to grasp the lecture as a whole. In his Memoir, Oliver Wendell Holmes recounts how the crowd who attended the Phi Beta Kappa oration left the hall afterwards in perfect silence, apparently stunned by what they had just heard. As for the degree to which Emerson could shape and disguise his material, Edward Emerson records this anecdote given by Mrs. D. Cheney:

"After hearing the lecture on Memory, a smart young lawyer approached a lady the next evening, who was talking of it to a friend. 'O, it was all very pretty and pleasant,' he said, 'but no real thought in it! I can't remember anything he said; can you?' 'Yes,' replied the lady, 'he said "Shallow brains have short memories."'" (*Works*, XII, 446).

33.   *JMN*, X.427.

34.   7/6/37, *Journals*, IV.189.

V. The Transcendentalist

1.   Miller, *The Transcendentalists*, 68.

2.   Ibid., 86.

3.   I take this sequence of events from Miller's chronology in his anthology. For a more complete picture of how the "new school" unfolded, and the other minor players who were involved in it, see his anthology. The elder Unitarians always maintianed the importance of the historicity of miracles to reveal the divine existence to human beings—if the miracles were true, then God existed. The younger Unitarians maintained that since nature was the language of the divine mind, the

"universal Man" could discover the Divine for himself by directly confronting nature. As was the case when the Unitarians split with the Congregationalists, the question of miracles was simply the surface issue that arose out of a much deeper agitation

4.   While the groundwork of the rebellion against Harvard and the Unitarians was laid by others, it was Emerson's book that gave the movement a central cohesiveness and direction. *Nature* is the founding work of American Transcendentalism because of its power and comprehensiveness and in spite of the fact that the first five hundred copies took thirteen years to sell out. There was simply no other work that could fill its place among the young Unitarian ministers of Boston who were beginning to feel the confining limits of their religion, nor among those such as Alcott and Margaret Fuller who knew that there was much more in society, in the human being, than had yet been imagined. That Transcendentalism emerged among a group of individuals who had been brought up as Unitarians is of significance only to the point of historical accuracy. The voice of Transcendentalism carried far beyond the parish squabble in Eastern Massachusetts. As the editors of the Western Messenger properly observed, "there is a large and increasing number of clergy and laity, of thinking men and educated women, especially of the youth in our different colleges, who are dissatisfied with the present state of religion, philosophy, and literature." The people who begged Emerson on his lecture tours to tell them about the "new philosophy" were certainly not all Unitarians. There was a hunger that was spreading throughout the country, a hunger for spirit, a hunger for social reform, a hunger for culture. Emerson had felt it before he left for Europe; he sought to fill it upon his return.

5.   4/19/38, *Journals*, IV.431.

6.   3/5/38, *Journals*, IV.406.

7.   3/18/38, *Journals*, IV.413.

8.   7/8/38, *Journals*, V.7.

9.   9/29/38, *Journals*, V.69.

10.   12/22/34, *HEJ*, 89. This passage in a slightly altered form is one of the most famous statements in the essay "Self-Reliance."

11.   Emerson was, obviously, no stranger to controversy and the strange allegiances and antipathies it brings in its wake. Certainly he had faithful defenders among the congregation at the Second Church. In April of 1837 he had been reintroduced to controversy on a much wider public scale when the papers began to persecute Bronson Alcott for his *Conversations*. On that occasion Emerson had written, "I have never more regretted my inefficiency in practical ends. I was born a

seeing eye, not a helping hand. I can only comfort my friends by thought, not by love or aid. But they naturally look for this also, and thereby vitiate our relationship throughout" (4/16/37, *Journals*, III.205). He did, however, send letters in defense of Alcott to two papers, one of which acquiesced to publish the one sent to it. In light of the events of a year and a half later, it seems that Emerson felt that his friends damaged their relationship to him not only by looking for help, but by giving it as well.

12.   7/1/38, *Journals*, V.4.

13.   Shepard, *Pedlar's Progress*, 199.

14.   One year after Emerson's address, Andrews Norton had delivered an address to the graduating class at the Divinity School graduation entitled "The Latest Form of Infidelity," an attack on the heresy of the "Transcendental Movement."

15.   10/18/39, *HEJ*, 147.

16.   2/9/40, *Journals*, V.374.

17.   10/1/40, *Letters*, II.340.

18.   9/12/40, *Letters*, II.330.

19.   5/27?/40 and 5/29?/40, *Letters*, II.299; 6/7/40 and 8/40, *Letters*, II.304.

20.   *Letters*, II.324, 8/16?/40.

21.   *Letters*, II.337.

22.   9/29/40, *Letters*, II.341n.

23.   10/17/40, *HEJ*, 156-157.

24.   9/28/36, *Journals*, IV.106.

25.   As he entered the final stages of writing in the fall and winter of 1840, several passages appeared in the Journal defending the necessarily sedentary lifestyle that he had to accept in order to finish the essays. "What you call my indolence," he wrote, "Nature does not accuse; the twinkling leaves, the sailing fleets of waterflies, the deep sky, like me well enough and know me for their own" (10/7/40, *Journals*, V.470). The entreaties of his friends to participate in outright social reform caused him, in his effort to finish his essays, to attempt to redefine for himself what action really was; action, he decided, did not necessarily have to contain the forthright components of "good action," time and the use of his hands, but could be "that which I have put my time into, namely, my letter, or my poem, the expression of my opinion, or better yet an act which in solitude I have learned to do" (10/7/40, *Journals*, V.470). Later that winter he went so far as to admit that "I should unsay all my fine things, I fear, concerning the manual labor of literary men. They ought to be released from every species of public and private responsibility"(2/4/41, *Journals*, V.517).

Whereas the friendships of the summer had redressed the problem with *delivering* the lectures the previous winter, Emerson's entire devotion to the literary task of the essays was no less than what was required of him in order to overcome the problem he had faced in *preparing* the lectures. He was consistently unhappy with the essays, even after their publication in May. The following September his disappointment turned him back towards lecturing, for, he wrote William, "I hope I shall one day write something better than those poor, cramp, arid 'Essays' which I almost hate the sight of'"(*Letters*, II.444). Despite his complaints about the *Essays*, many of the pieces included in that first collection stand as his most powerful and widely known compositions, including "Self-Reliance," "The Over-Soul," and "Spiritual Laws."

26.　1/1/41, *Journals*, V.506.

27.　1/30/42, *Journals*, VI.157.

28.　Quoted in the notes to the *Works*, IX.453.

29.　1/30/42, *Journals*, VI.152.

30.　Thoreau seemed the attendant and guide to another world as they boarded the boat and "left all time, all science, all history, behind us, and entered into Nature with one stroke of a paddle." *JMN*, VII.455.

31.　HEJ, 165.

32.　*Journals*, VI.154-5n.

33.　1/30/42, *HEJ*, 173.

34.　2/4/42, *Letters*, III.9.

35.　*EL*, III.363.

36.　1/30/44, *Journals*, VI.488.

37.　3/20/42, *HEJ*, 174.

38.　*JMN*, 8.229.

39.　3/21/42, *Letters*, III.36.

40.　3/21/42, *Journals*, VI.170n.

41.　The day after the great socialist meeting he had "the feeling, to a degree not experienced by me before, that discussions, like that of yesterday . . . invade and injure me. I often have felt emptiness and restlessness to a sort of hatred of the human race after such prating by me and my fellows" (11/11/42, *Journals*, VI.299). Alcott grated especially, mostly because he had become indistinguishable and inseparable from his new friends. When a week later he came to Emerson suggesting that, in order to carry out the great plan, "there should be found a farm of a hundred acres in excellent condition, with good buildings, a good orchard, and grounds which admitted of being laid out with great beauty; and this should be purchased and given them in the first place," he raised his friend's ire. Emerson challenged him that he asked too much, that "there are hundreds of innocent young persons, whom, if you will thus stablish and endow and protect, will find it no hard matter to keep their innocency." Emerson suggested it were far more to build such "unaided, in the midst of poverty, toil, and traffic." Alcott asked, "how is this to be done? How can I do it who have a wife and family to maintain?" Emerson shot back that Alcott "was not the person to do it, or he would not ask the question" (11/19/42, *Journals*, VI.306-7).

42.   11/21/42, *Letters*, III.98.

43.   Holmes, *Memoir*, 108. Emerson had earlier framed the same sentiment with his own characteristic style: "A man should stand among his fellow men as one coal lies in the fire it has kindled, radiating heat, but lost in the general flame" (3/5/36, *Journals*, IV.18).

44.   This statement would later become the famous passage in *Walden*:

> I went to the woods because I wished to live deliberately, to front only the essential facts of life, and see if I could not learn what it had to teach, and not, when I came to die, discover that I had not lived. I did not wish to live what was not life, living is so dear; nor did I wish to practise resignation, unless it was quite necessary. I wanted to live deep and suck out all the marrow of life, to live so sturdily and Spartan-like as to put to rout all that was not life, to cut a broad swath and shave close, to drive life into a corner, and reduce it to its lowest terms, and, if it proved to be mean, why then to get the whole and genuine meanness of it, and publish its meanness to the world; or if it were sublime, to know it by experience, and be able to give a true account of it in my next excursion.

VI. To the Mountaintop

1.   *JMN*, IX.71.

2.   *JMN*, IX.85.

3.   The account, entitled "The First of August in Concord," appeared in the *Liberator* for August 23, 1844.

> After the singing, the President, Dr. Farnsworth, introduced the orator of the occasion. He rose, and we soon felt that the spirit of liberty had possession of him. Those who have heard Mr. Emer-

son have, we doubt not, noticed that peculiarly spirited appearance, which he sometimes presents, and at times for moments makes us feel as if a pure spirit was speaking. This day it seemed as if the spirit of liberty had left the British Isles, where she has so long been nestling under the wings of monarchy, with a queen for a nursing mother, and revisited once more her old resting place. She was filled with pathos; for all seemed as though they must weep when she began to speak in her finest tones. She told of British wrongs and British redress. She told of the noble few, who commenced the redress. She told of the great ones—great as to station, but greater as to soul—who devoted themselves to the slaves' emancipation—and gave a running history of the cause, until its completion. She then returned to Massachusetts, and in tones of indignation, related the wrongs of some of our free-born citizens, who were sold into perpetual slavery in the southern part of our boasted republic; and we so weak, so pusillanimous, so much slaves ourselves, that we uttered no stern rebukes of such enormities. We hoped she would have spoken in equally strong tones of rebuke, of injuries done daily to thousands of free-born Americans in other States, whose rights are as dear to the heart in which justice dwells, as the rights of the citizens of Massachusetts; but perhaps she found no words—perhaps a feeling of sickening despair seized her, and she feared longer to stay, lest her pure garments should be stained, were she to lead us through the awful chambers of iniquity and wrong which she must unfold. So back she fled, and left her poor devotees to open and cleanse these Aegean stables, if perchance they may be able, and once more make this polluted land a residence for her who has so long been banished hence.

4.   *JMN*, IX.123-126.
5.   *Emerson's Antislavery Writings*, 33.
6.   *JMN*, IX.126.
7.   *JMN*, IX.163.
8.   *JMN*, IX.102.
9.   *JMN*, IX.195.
10. *JMN*, IX.238.

11.   *Emerson's Antislavery Writings*, 43-44.

12.   *JMN*, X.29-30.

13.   *JMN*, X.244.

14.   *Letters*, IV.51.

15.   *JMN*, X.340.

16.   *JMN*, XI.15.

17.   *JMN*, XI.52.

18.   *JMN*, XI.250.

19.   *JMN*, XI.345.

20.   *JMN*, XI.434.

VII. Something Less than My Best Task

1.   *JMN*, XIII.80.

2.   *JMN*, XIII.229-232.

3.   *JMN*, XIII.282. Though his views on slavery had continually evolved over the years, he had always been a natural proponent of moral suasion over political agitation, for it was one of the deepest tenets of his philosophy as a lecturer that true reform of Humanity—which would signify a recovery of a spiritual view of Nature and the true divinity of human beings, and which would comprehend all reform and not just a single issue like slavery—could only be accomplished by the perfection of individual character. Whatever his reservations about the cantankerous and difficult Garrison as a man, this belief placed him squarely in Garrison's camp, as far as he could ever have been said to be in the Abolitionist camp. Though he was clearly a gentle and non-violent man himself, it dos not appear that he ever subscribed to Garrison's doctrine of strict nonviolence. The idea of Garrison's that did influence Emerson very strongly was that of disunion. The great split in the Abolition movement had come in 1855 when the self-styled leader of the movement dug in his heels and declared, "No union with slaveholders, socially or religiously, and up with the flag of Disunion."

4.   *JMN*, XIII.283.

5.   *JMN*, XIII.405.

6.   *Leaves of Grass* (Library of America), 5-7.

7.   This line is from his famous 1844 essay *The Poet*. This essay, in fact, provides an excellent example of the process that Emerson went through in transforming lectures into essays. When laid side by side with the 1842 lecture "The Poet," which was the crucible for the essay, it is clear that both share the same fun-

damental core of ideas, but it soon becomes apparent that the essay is entirely unique from its forebear. For Emerson the process of writing an essay was not merely translating what he had spoken into written form. It required completely tearing down the architecture he had built for the idea, for the inspiring spirit, and building a new architecture appropriate for the print medium, a medium that lacked the connection of immediacy between the audience and the orator that formed a habitable temple into which the inspiration could descend. It was a laborious and intensive process in which he used the lecture as only one resource; indeed, the lecture was no longer a lecture, but simply raw material, just the same as the journals and other lectures he had at hand. Paragraphs, sentences, clauses could be endlessly extracted and recombined in service to the new governing idea and structure.

8.   *EL*, III.356

9.   *Leaves of Grass* (Library of America), 8.

10.   Emily Dickinson worked with this idea in poetic form in 1862:

> I died for Beauty—but was scarce
> Adjusted in the Tomb
> When One who died for Truth, was lain
> In an adjoining Room—
>
> He questioned softly "Why I failed"?
> "For Beauty", I replied—
> "And I—for Truth—Themselves are One—
> We Brethren, are", He said—
>
> And so, as Kinsmen, met a Night—
> We talked between the Rooms—
> Until the Moss had reached our lips—
> An covered up—our names—

11.   Loving, 209.

12.   Whitman, *Poetry and Prose*, 1326.

13.   Ibid., 1327.

14.   Ibid., 1336-1337.

15.   The idea of the Slave Power conspiracy, the concerted effort by the Southern slave holders to expand slavery beyond the boundaries set on it by the Constitution, first came into being at the time of the Mexican War. Lincoln devel-

oped the idea in detail in his famous "Spot" speech in the House of Representatives. Grant, as a soldier in the army that was sent to start a war with Mexico in order to gain territory that the South could expand slavery into, lived through the military results of the political machinations of President Polk and his Southern allies, which he described in detail in his *Memoirs*. From this distance in time, the conspiracy power that Sumner was attacking is not merely theory, but fact. The South was indeed working to spread slavery into the territories by any means necessary.

16. *JMN*, XIV.93-4.

17. *JMN*, XIV.298.

18. $25 in 1857 was equivalent to approximately $525 in 2002 dollars.

19. *JMN*, XIV.146.

20. *JMN*, XIV.167.

VIII. A New Power of Vision

1. *JMN*, XIV.248.

2. *JMN*, XIV.308-9.

3. *JMN*, XIV.330, 335, 332.

4. *JMN*, XIV.335. The draft of this letter is in the Journal, but there is some doubt as to whether it was ever sent; Alcott may have convinced Emerson, by the time that he finished it, that Brown's case was too hopeless for the letter to make a difference.

5. *JMN*, XIV.336.

6. *JMN*, XIV.361.

7. *JMN*, XV.11.

8. *JMN* XV.28.

9. The entire series of entries recording Emerson's experiences of the capital take up some eighty pages of the journal. They can be found in *JMN*, XV.186-200.

10. The story of Lincoln's discovery of *Leaves of Grass* is told in greater detail by Epstein, *Lincoln and Whitman*, pp.3-13.

11. *JMN*, XV.291.

12. *JMN*, XV.380.

13. *JMN*, XV.221.

14. *Letters*, IX.91-94.

15. *JMN*, XV.347.

16. *LL*, II.322, 323, 325, 334.

17. 2/13/1865, *JMN*, XV.457.

18. *JMN*, XV.64.

19. *JMN*, XV.98.

IX. The Life Task

1. $10,000 in 1869 was roughly the equivalent of $210,000 in 2002 dollars.

2. Fall 1867, *JMN*, XVI.219.

3. Cameron, 266, and Bosco, pp. 27, 29. The complete accounts of the 1870 lectures from the perspective of Fields and Peabody are in Bosco, "His Lectures Were Poetry, His Teaching the Music of the Spheres."

4. Bosco, 11. Bosco describes this observation of Peabody's as the attempt of an admiring student to shift blame away from Emerson for being ill-prepared and no longer capable of organizing and delivering his material with the success that he once could.

5. Bosco, 35.

6. *Works*, XII.440. This passage is quoted by Edward Waldo Emerson in his notes to the volume. In the third lecture of the 1848 series, "Tendencies and Duties of Men of Thought," Emerson had given a longer definition of calm affirming: "And the practical rules of literature ought to follow from these views, namely, that all writing is by the grace of God; that none but a writer should write; that he should write affirmatively, not polemically, or should write nothing that will not help somebody,—as I knew of a good man who held conversations, and wrote on the wall, 'that every person might speak to the subject, but no opinion should be made to the opinions of other speakers,'—that we must affirm and affirm, but neither you nor I know the value of what we say; that we must be openers of doors and not a blind alley; that we must hope and strive, for despair is no muse, and vigor always liberates." (*LL*, I.183).

7. Our appraisal of the change between the 1870 and the 1871 cycles owes much to Bosco's work. By working from the presumption that the manuscript copy of "The Natural History of the Intellect" lectures at Harvard's Houghton Library are, for the most part, the 1871 lectures as Emerson intended to give them, rather than the chaotic leftover leaves of the 1870 lectures, it becomes possible to make a detailed comparison between the students' 1870 notes and the text of the 1871 lectures. Such a comparison, when combined with evidence from Emerson's journals, gradually reveals an alternative story to the one that generally has been told about these lectures since Cabot's first effort to edit them in the 1890s. We make the case

for such an alternative history in the scholar's edition of *The Natural History of the Intellect: Emerson's unpublished last lectures, delivered at Harvard University in 1871.*

8.   *Emerson Chronology,* 463.

9.   Thayer, *Western Journey,* 97.

10.   The gift of $18,000 in 1872 would be roughly equivalent to $375,000 in 2002 dollars.

Lightning Source UK Ltd.
Milton Keynes UK
UKOW04f2324050116

265850UK00002B/157/P